AF614838

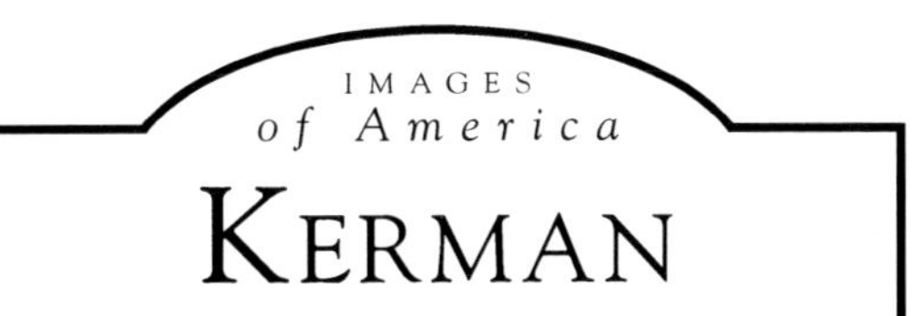
IMAGES
of America
KERMAN

On the Cover: This view of the Kerman Livery Stable offers a glimpse into early life in Kerman. (Courtesy of the Kerman Historical Society.)

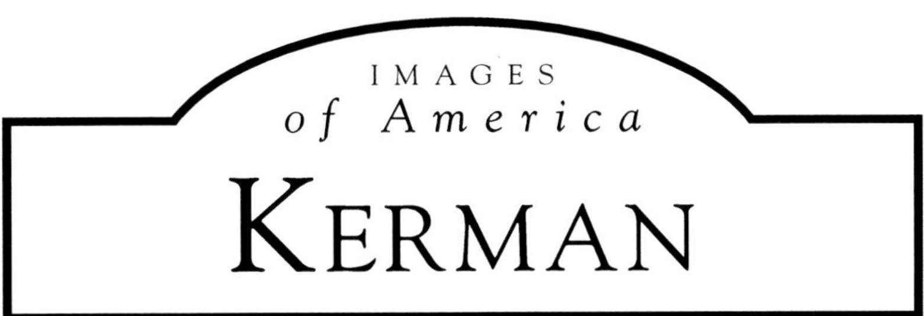

Paul Betancourt

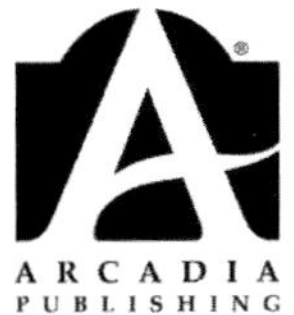

ISBN 978-1-4671-1542-1

Published by Arcadia Publishing
Charleston, South Carolina

Printed in the United States of America

Library of Congress Control Number: 2015955331

For all general information, please contact Arcadia Publishing:
Telephone 843-853-2070
Fax 843-853-0044
E-mail sales@arcadiapublishing.com
For customer service and orders:
Toll-Free 1-888-313-2665

Visit us on the Internet at www.arcadiapublishing.com

This book is dedicated to the people and the spirit of Kerman.

Contents

Acknowledgments

A book like this cannot be created by one person. My thanks go to the Kerman Historical Society, which is dedicated to preserving the memories of our hometown. This book is just a glimpse of what the Kerman Historical Society has gathered. Many other stories and photographs can be found on the historical society's website at www.tostepharmd.net/kermanhistoricalsociety/. Unless otherwise noted, all images are courtesy of the Kerman Historical Society.

I want to thank Olen White and Scott Toste for the use of their photographic archives. Thanks also to the countless others who took the time to reminisce about their early years in Kerman.

INTRODUCTION

The city of Kerman began as a train stop in the heart of California's great San Joaquin Valley. The town was originally named Collis Station after Collis Huntington, one of the Big Four railroad men of the 19th century that included Leyland Stanford, Mark Hopkins, and Charles Crocker. The town was incorporated in 1906 and renamed Kerman after two real estate developers, William G. Kerckhoff and Jacob Mansar. Kerckhoff and Mansar purchased 3,027 acres of land in the area, which included the original city limits. The city of Kerman blossomed quickly. The Kerman Inn was built in 1906, and the *Kerman News*, which is still in business, was also established in 1906. Churches and schools followed. Bethany Lutheran Church was built in 1909, and the first class of Kerman High School graduated in 1913.

Farming has long been the mainstay of Kerman's economy. The San Joaquin Valley is one of only five Mediterranean growing areas in the world. The warm summers and mild winters allow for a wide variety of agricultural production. In fact, over 400 different crops are grown in the valley, with many of them in Kerman.

In the early years, farming was dominated by dairies, and alfalfa hay was grown to feed the dairy cows. Farmers could often get five to six cuttings of hay per year. Row crops such as cotton, tomatoes, and cantaloupes were grown in rotation with the alfalfa. Cotton from Kerman and the rest of the valley has commanded a premium price in the global market because of its quality.

Permanent crops such as grapes and peaches were also grown in the area. Thompson seedless grapes can be grown for table grapes, wine, juice, and raisins. For decades, growing Thompsons for raisins was dominant. Other varieties of grapes are also grown for table grapes, such as Flame seedless. In the early years, Kerman grape growers produced bulk wines. With recent innovations in vineyard management, Kerman has begun growing world-class wines such as Cabernet, Pinot Grigio, and Muscat dessert wines. In recent years, vineyards have been replaced with almond orchards, as almond demand around the world has grown.

Kerman's churches and schools have been at the heart of the community. The first tent meeting was led by Henry Lohr in 1907. Bethany Lutheran Church was built in 1909, quickly followed by First Methodist Church in 1901, which was the first permanent religious structure inside the city limits. Other churches followed over the years.

The Kerman Grammar School was built in town in 1909. Other elementary schools were built out in the various farm colonies, mostly north of the city limits. Sunset, Dakota, Vinland, Empire, and Floyd are familiar school names even today. Sunset and Empire were combined in the middle of the last century to form Sun Empire Elementary School. The Kerman Grammar School in town and Floyd Elementary School outside of town were combined to form Kerman Floyd Elementary School.

Kerman High School began with 12 students in the basement of Bethany Church in 1910. Land for the high school building was purchased at the corner of Madera and Clinton Avenues in 1913. In 1920, the historic Kerman High School was built. It was utilized until 1967.

Another feature of Kerman's cultural life was the presence of music, drama, and book clubs in the years before radio, television, and the Internet. The Kerman Music Club was organized as the Kerman Women's Music Club in 1909. The word "Women's" was dropped in 1943. These clubs were at the center of Kerman social life as people came together over shared interests.

Sports have always been popular in Kerman as well. Champions and championship teams have made Kerman proud over the years. These sports have taught young people teamwork and have been part of a well-rounded education.

Outdoor activities have also been part of life in Kerman. Hunting, fishing, horseback riding, motorcycle clubs, water skiing, snow skiing, and just floating down the river on a hot summer day have all been popular pastimes. Trips to the coast or up into the Sierras have also been popular for folks seeking to escape the summer heat.

Over the years, Kerman has continued to grow. The town has stretched from its beginnings near the railroad tracks north to Whitesbridge Road. The Creamery, the bean plant, and even the train station are gone. New businesses have come in to support farming in the area.

Running north from the railroad tracks, Madera Avenue has always been the heart of Kerman's business district. The first commercial buildings were clustered around the north end of Plaza Park. In the photographs in this book, the styles of the cars and even the buildings change, but Madera Avenue has remained the heart of the town for a century now.

With its central location in the valley, Kerman has long been a crossroads. In the early years, the traffic was centered in the south end of town where Madera Avenue crosses the train tracks. Now, the traffic is centered on the north end of town where Madera Avenue crosses State Route 180, also known as Whitesbridge Road.

The people of Kerman come from all over the world. In the early years, European immigrants from Russia and the Basque region of northern Spain, Portugal, and other countries came here. Refugees from Oklahoma and Arkansas came during the Dust Bowl years. More recently, immigrants from Mexico started coming here during the years of the Bracero program in the middle of the 20th century. The Sikh population from the Punjab region in India has grown in recent decades. Other groups have also come to Kerman, drawn by the opportunity to farm good ground with long seasons and lots of sunshine.

The economy of Kerman has always been based on farming. The crops have changed over time, but the fertile ground and abundant sunshine still make this a world-class place to farm. Outside of farming, life in Kerman is centered on family, church, and schools.

Kerman has grown with the times. Walt Von Flue graduated from Kerman High in 1951. His granddaughter, Heidi Betancourt, graduated in 2001, exactly 50 years later. They grew up in the same town but in different eras. For example, Kerman's children today are as connected to the world as their city cousins.

Every place has its story, and this is ours.

One

Historic Kerman

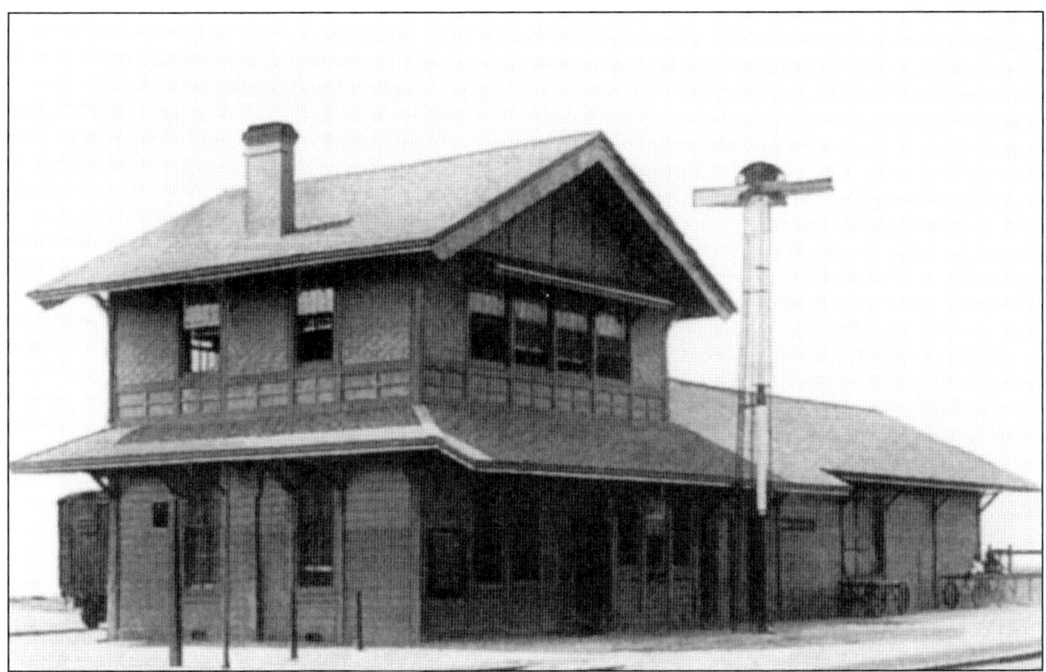

In 1891, Collis Station was built on the site of present-day Kerman. Named after railroad man Collis Huntington, Collis Station was part of the Fresno to Tracy line. In 1920, the *Lark* ran from Kerman to San Francisco. For a fare, one could leave Kerman at 3:00 a.m., go to San Francisco for the day, and return the same evening at 11:00 p.m.

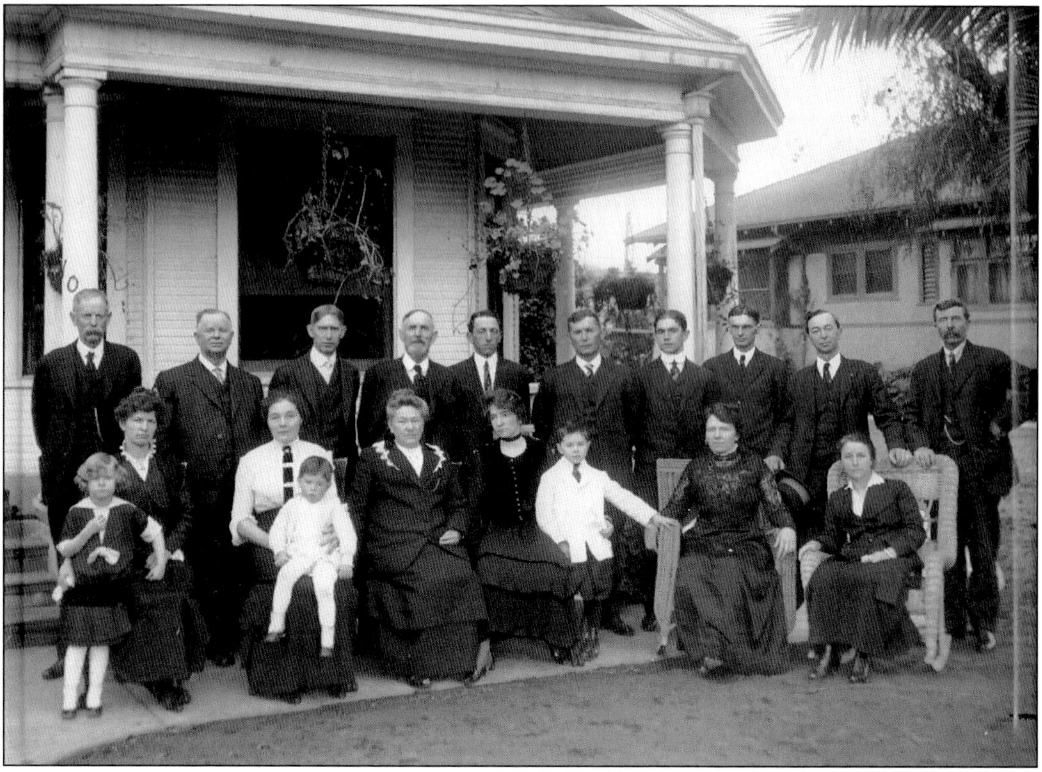

Few people even notice the railroad in Kerman today, until the road is blocked by a passing train, but Kerman's first permanent residents were the railroad men and their families. Trains in the 19th century needed regular coal and water. Kerman began as a stop to service the trains as they rolled up and down California's great Central Valley.

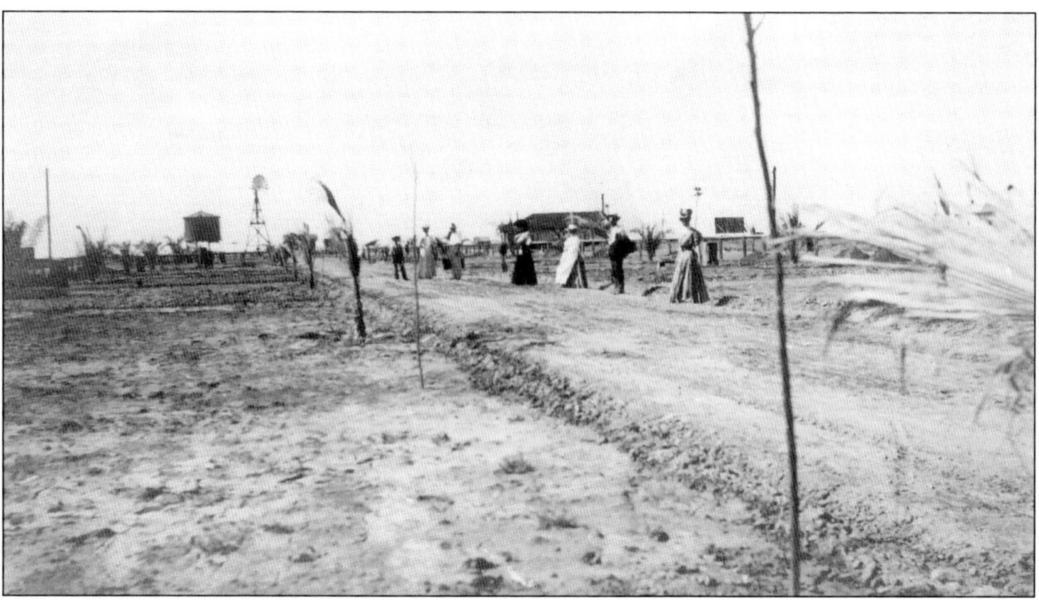

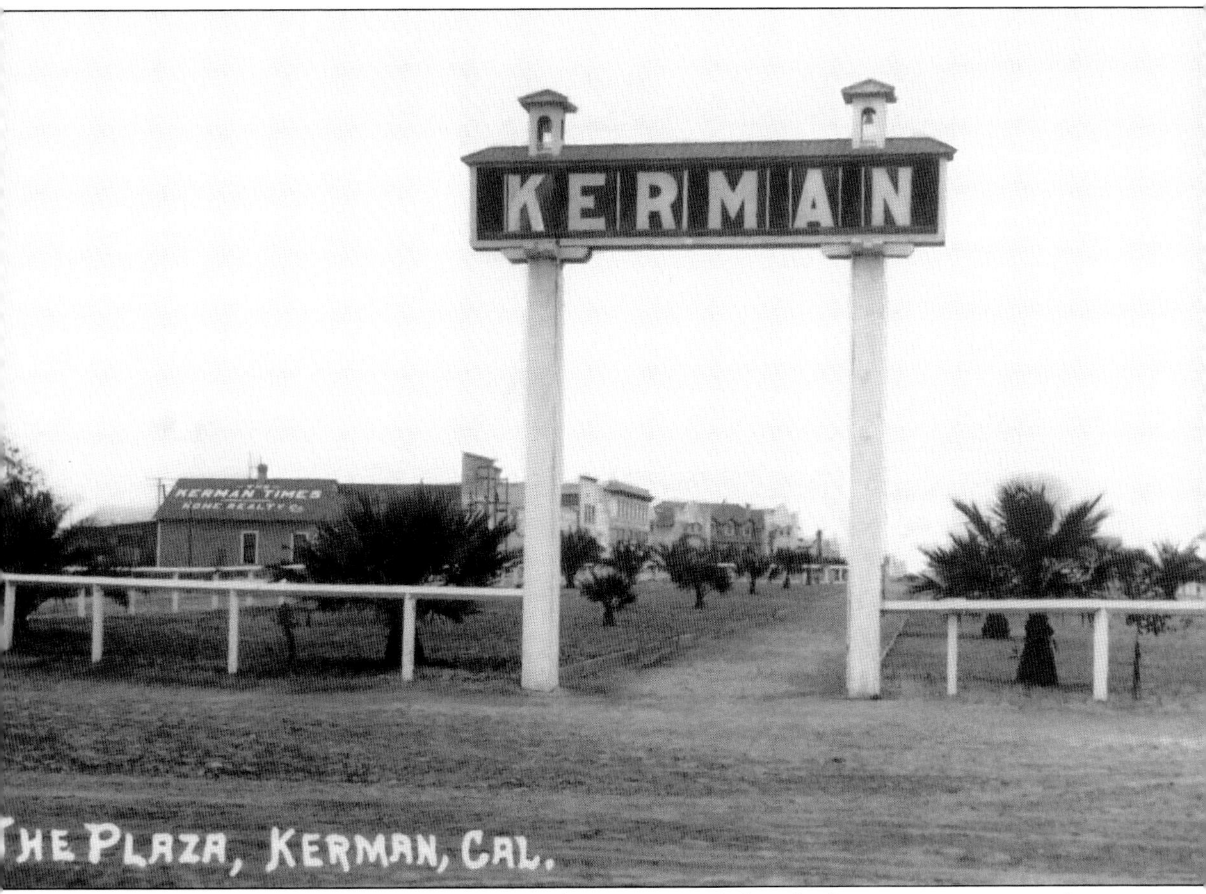

Kerman Plaza Park is at the south end of modern Kerman. A hundred years ago, it was at the center of town. Here, the palm trees that now tower overhead have just been planted.

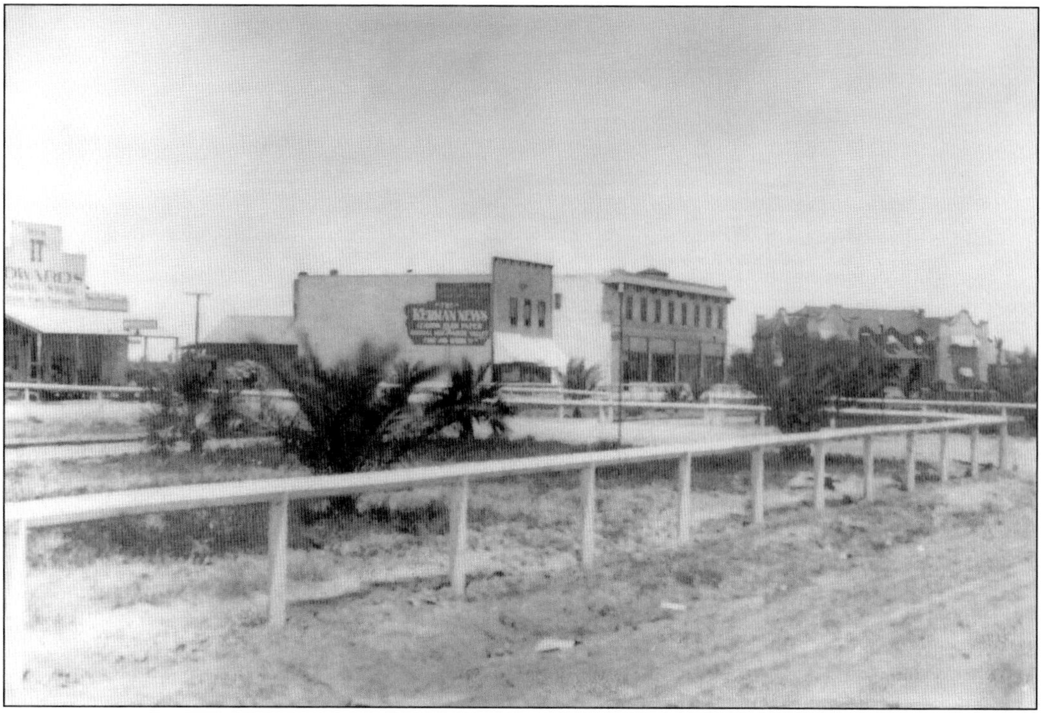

When Plaza Park was the center of town, the train station, the Kerman Inn, the post office, and most of the stores ringed the park. Plaza Park was where people met and enjoyed the fresh air.

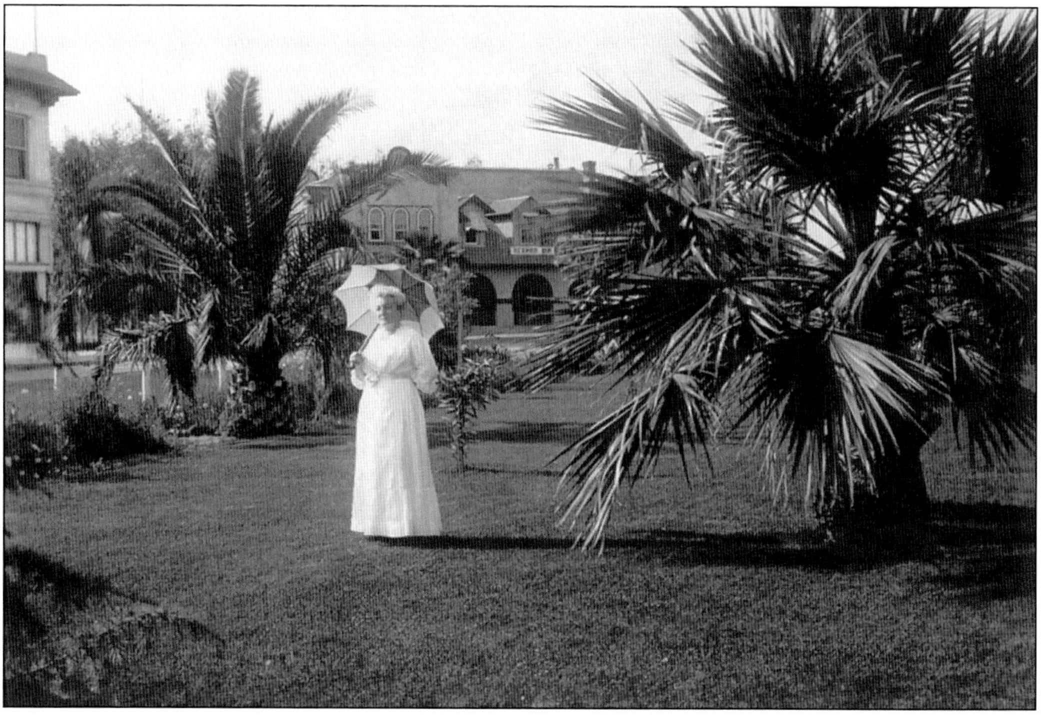

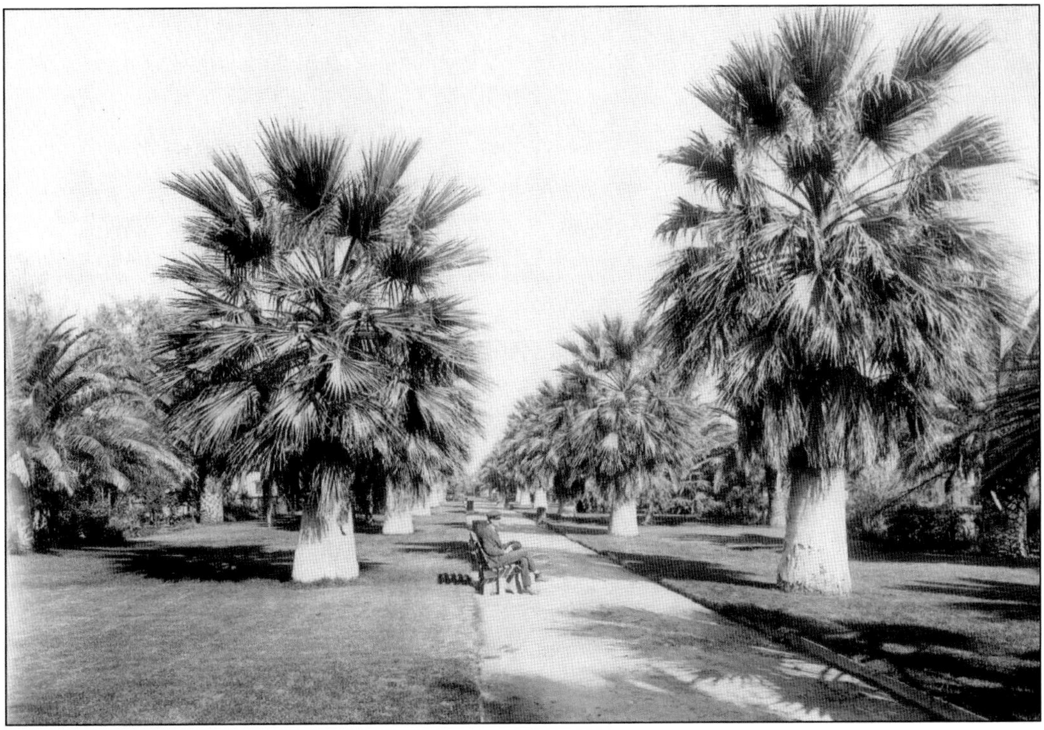

Plaza Park was renamed Veterans Park in 2003. A fence was installed and a new Kerman sign placed on the south side of the park. Flags representing each of the armed services fly in the center of the park, and there are memorials for those who served in the military.

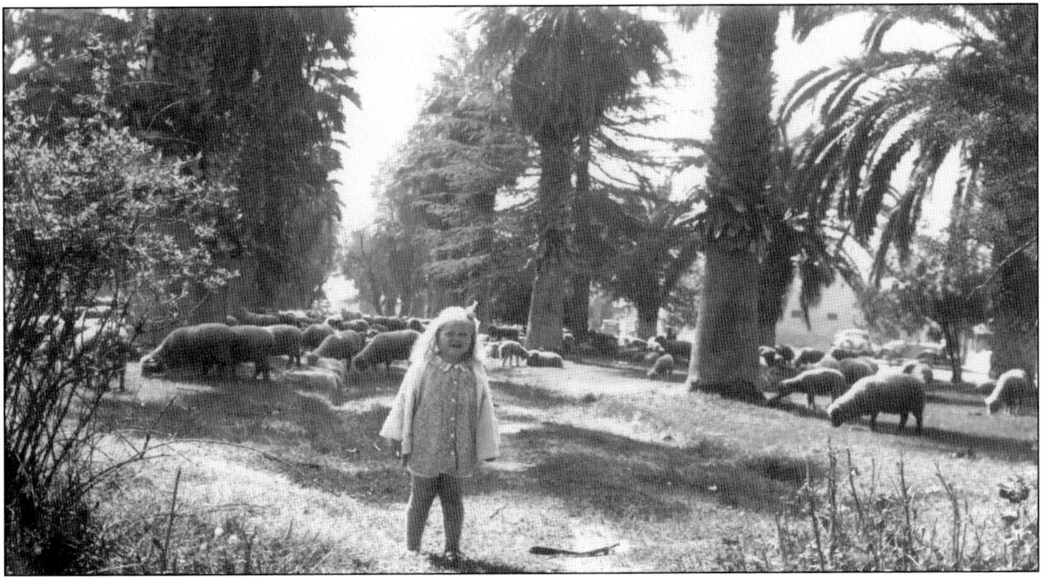

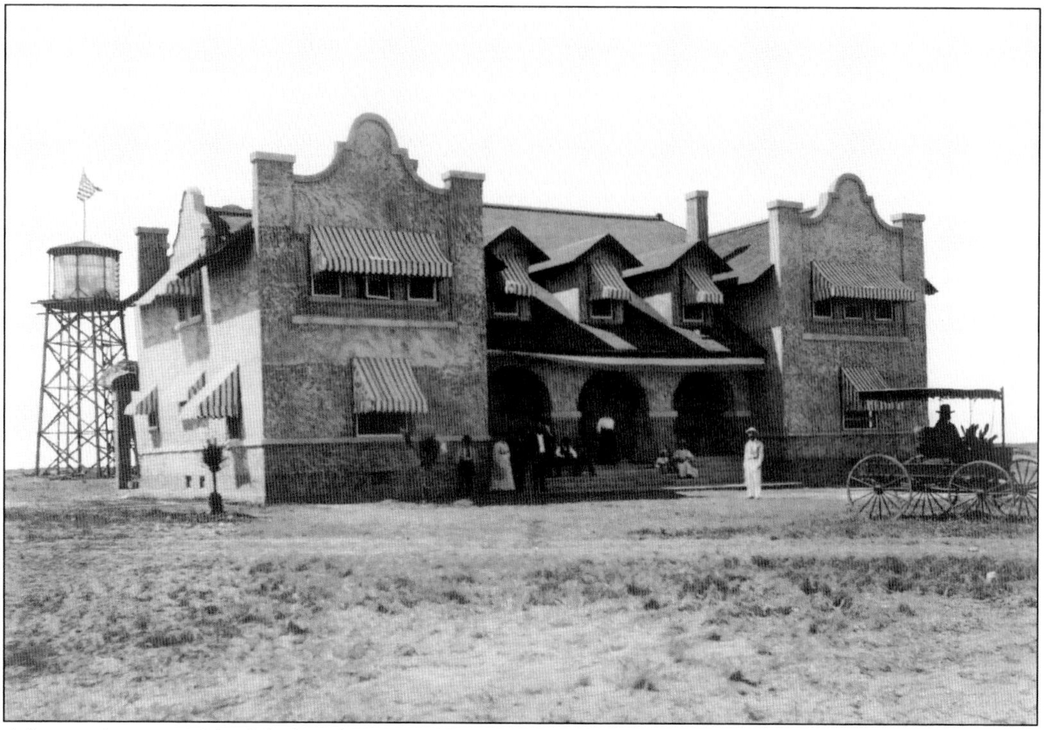

A key architectural highlight of Kerman for almost a century was the Kerman Inn. Built in 1906, it was located at the Northwest corner of Plaza Park, situated near the railroad station and the center of town.

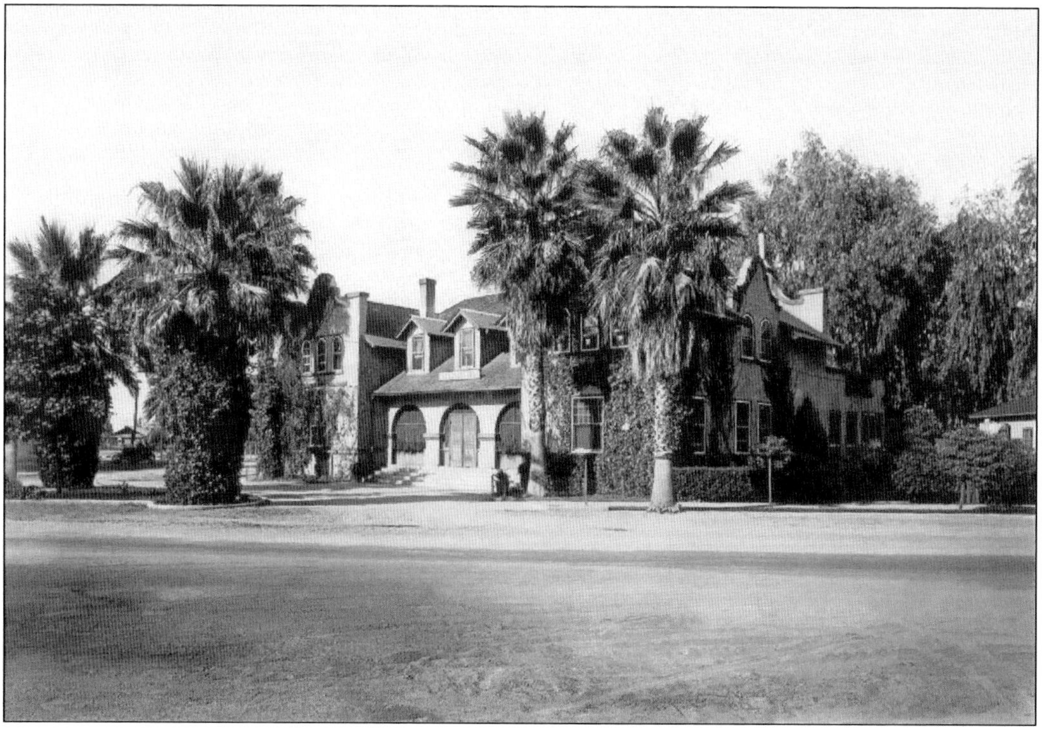

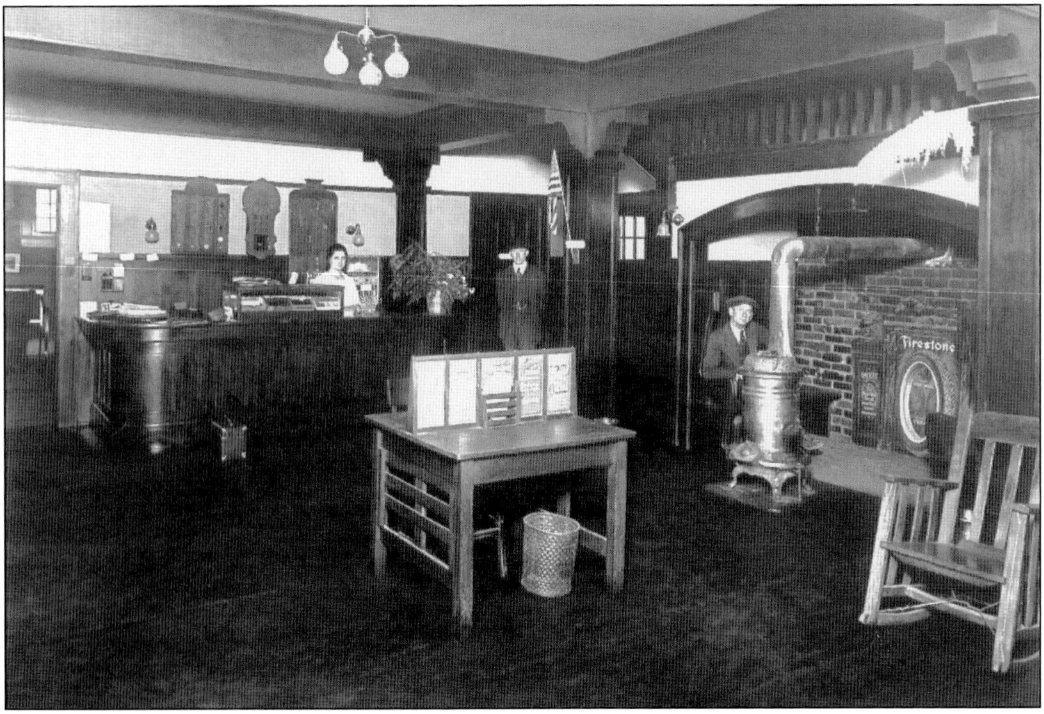

Local tradition holds that guests of the Kerman Inn included Pres. Theodore Roosevelt. Sadly, the inn was demolished in 1993. The site where it was located is now the parking lot between the Kerman Telephone offices and Beijing Gardens Chinese restaurant.

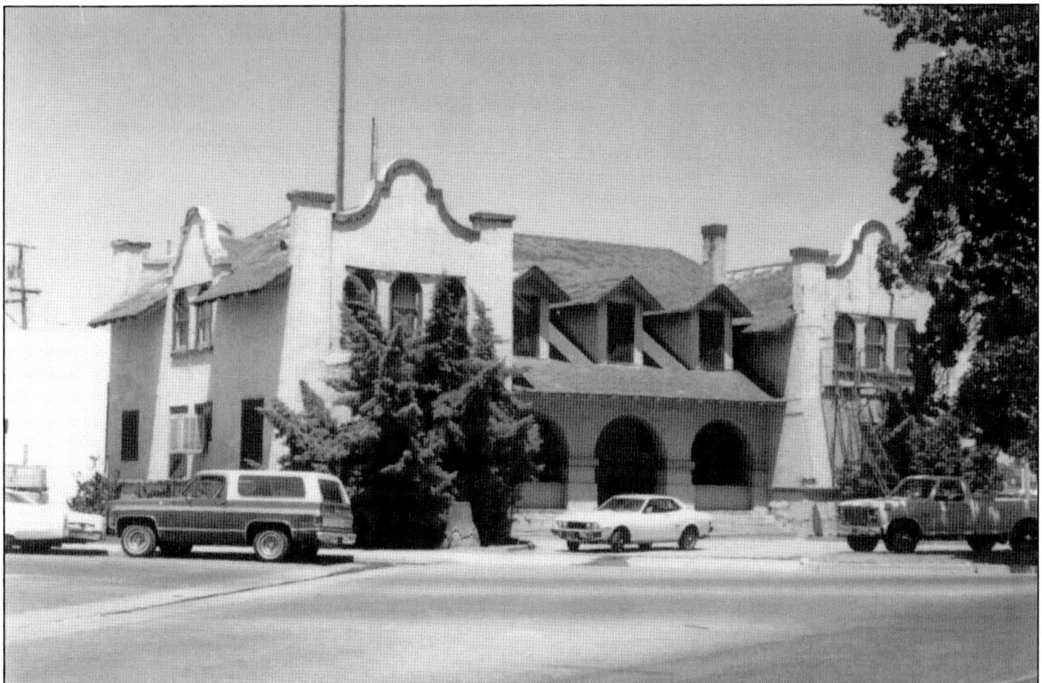

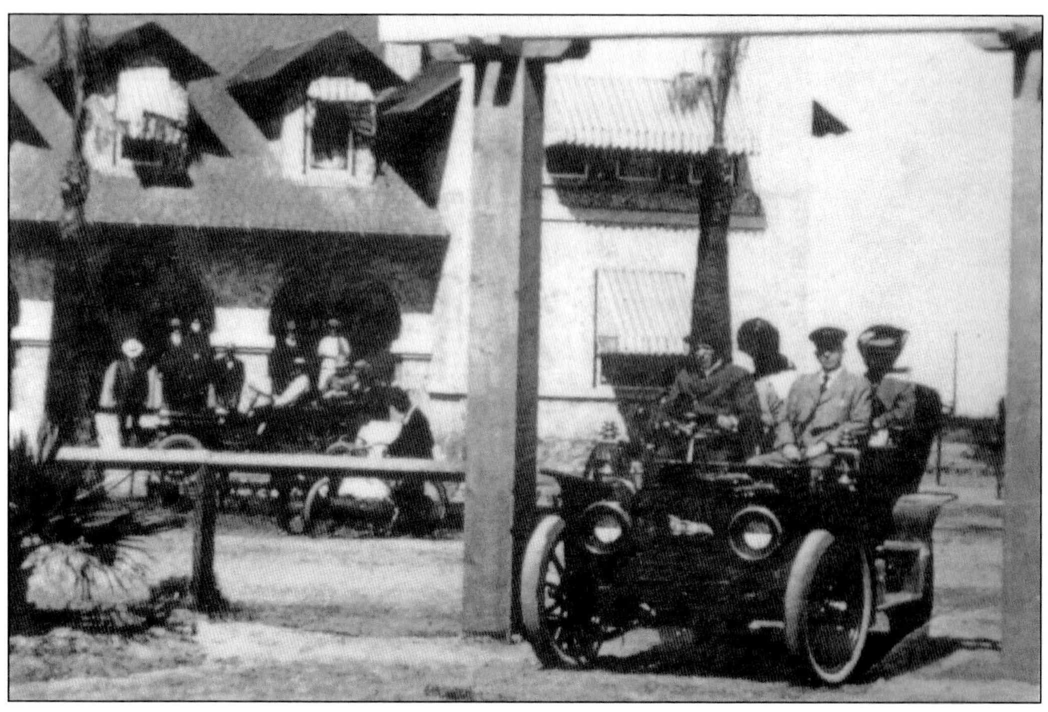

In this photograph, the Kerman Inn is visible behind the old touring car. At the center of Kerman in the early decades, all traffic that went through town also went through Plaza Park. Pictured below is a group of early motorcycles lined up at Plaza Park.

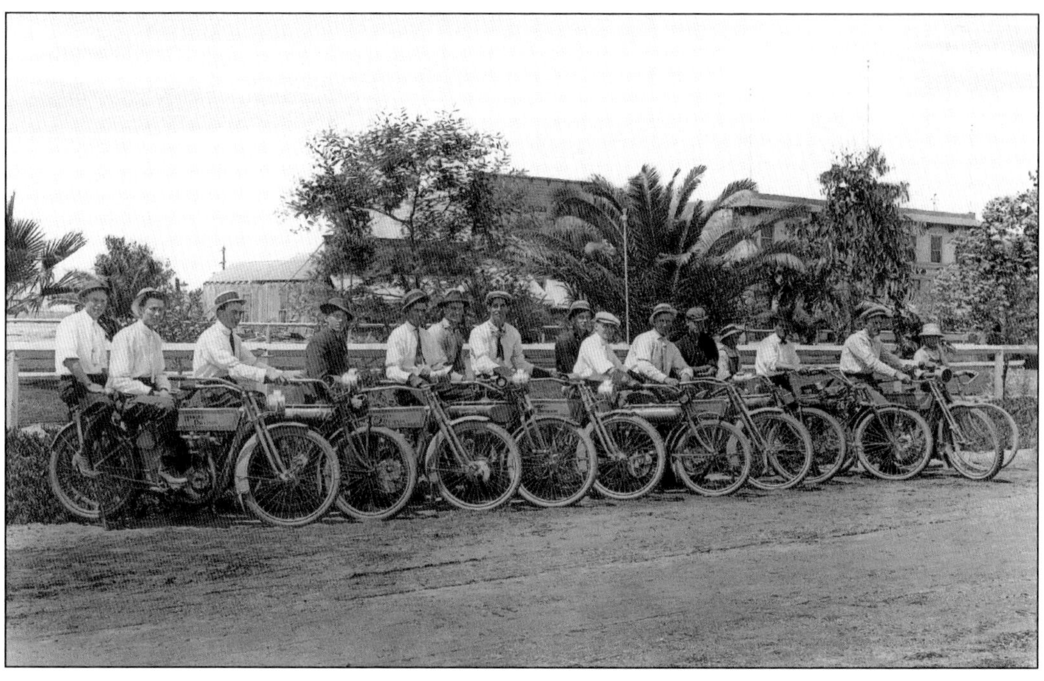

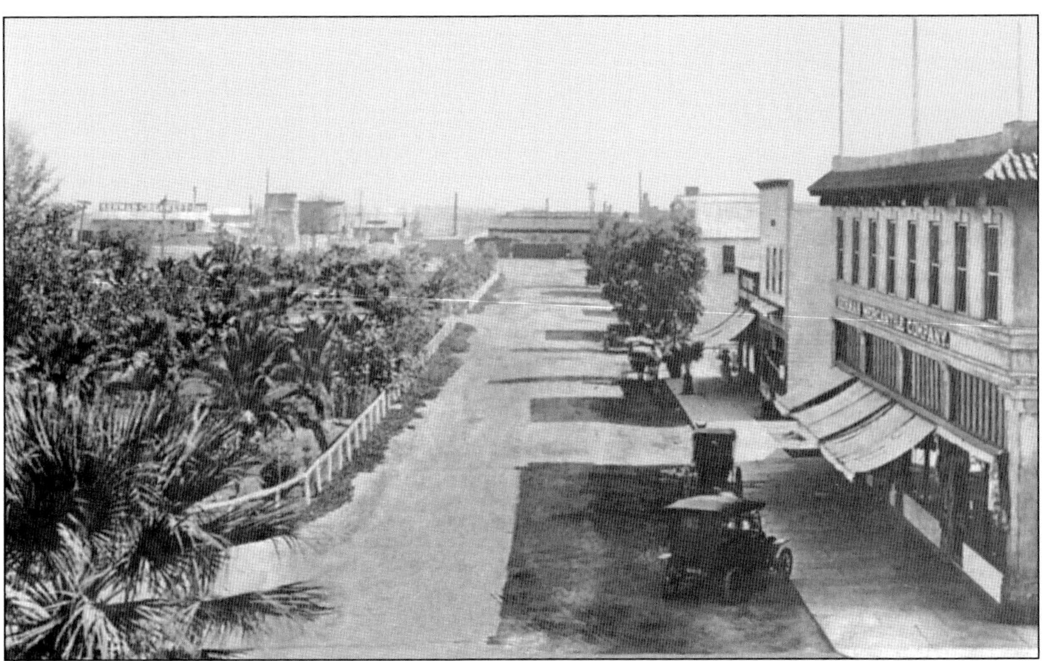

Over the years, Kerman grew north from Plaza Park. The photograph above shows the buildings on the edge of Plaza Park in 1910. Below is the Kerman Mercantile in 1920.

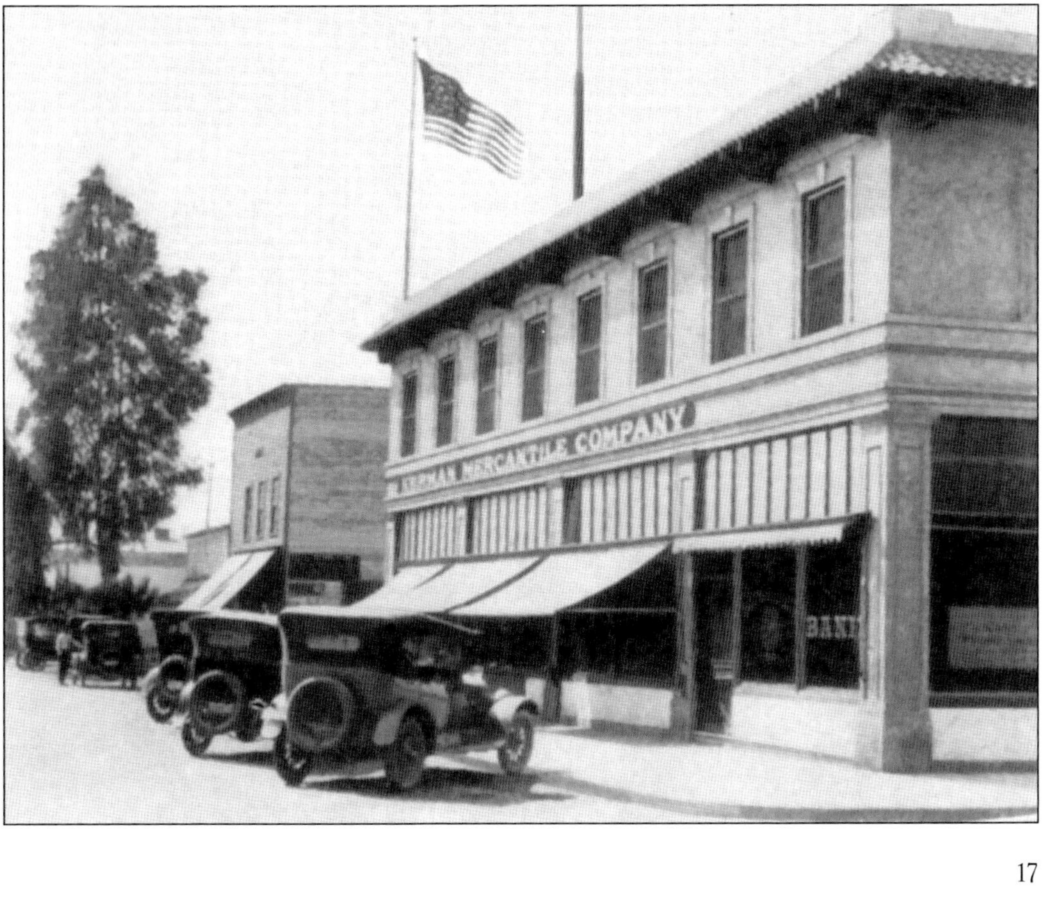

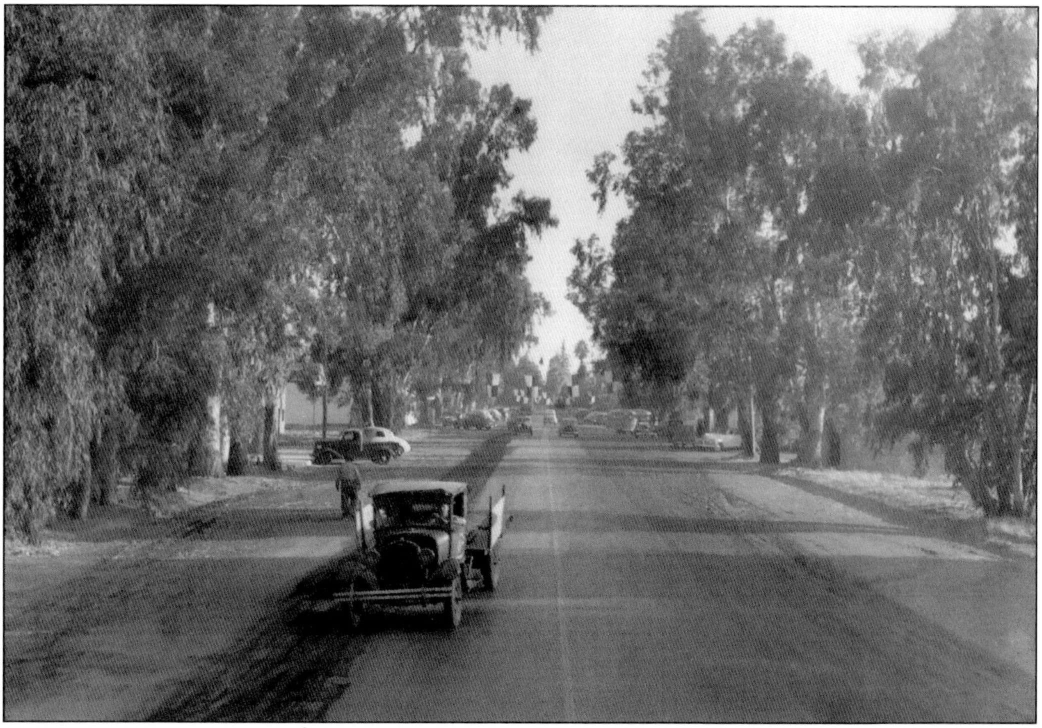

Above, Madera Avenue filled as businesses moved into town. Below, the original tenants for the Bernardi Building were an accountant and a barber.

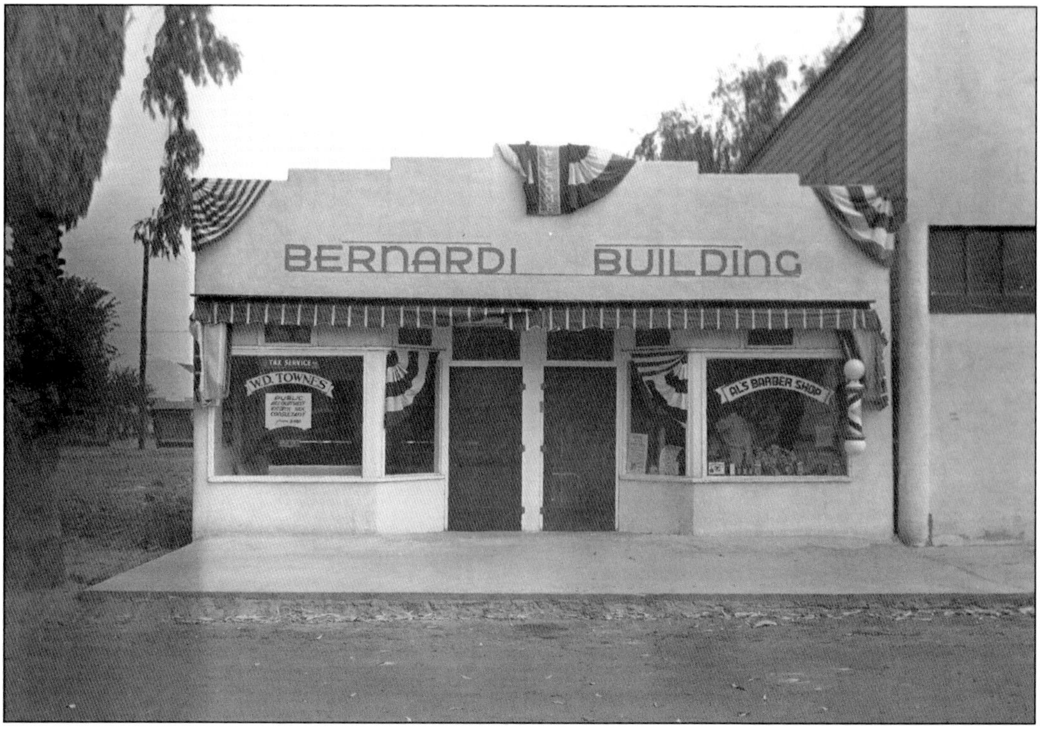

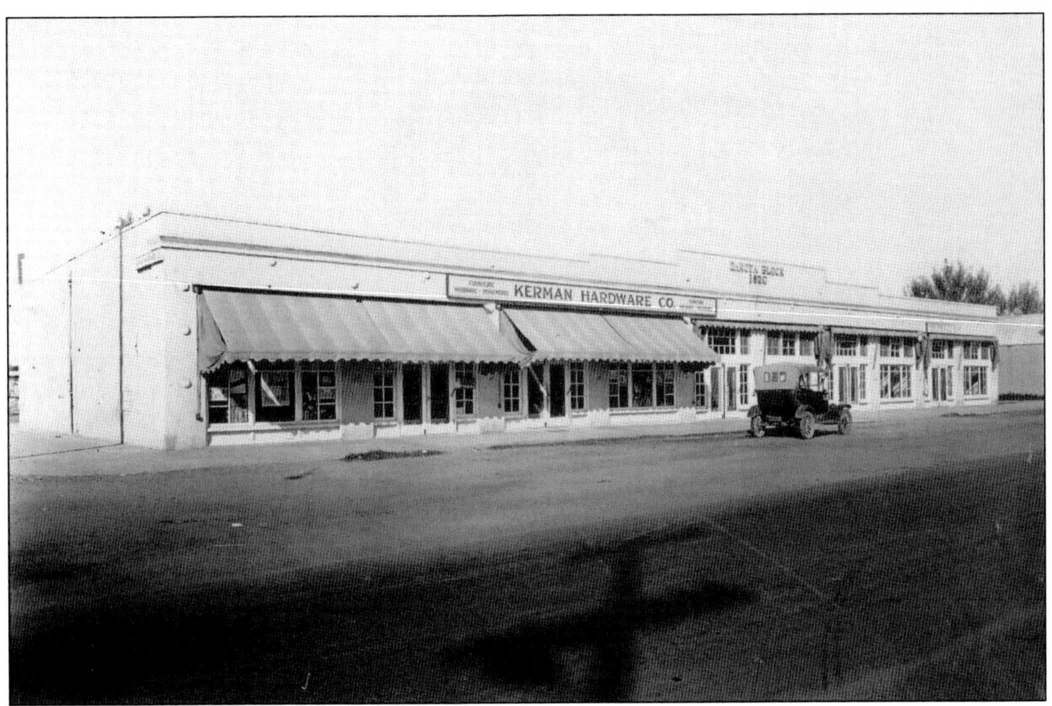

The Dakota Block runs on the west side of Madera Avenue between D and E Streets. A terrible fire on November 29, 1917, gutted the building. Early tenants included Pacific Gas & Electric and Bank of America, which opened in 1937. There was also the Safeway grocery store, a drugstore, barber, and a couple of variety stores.

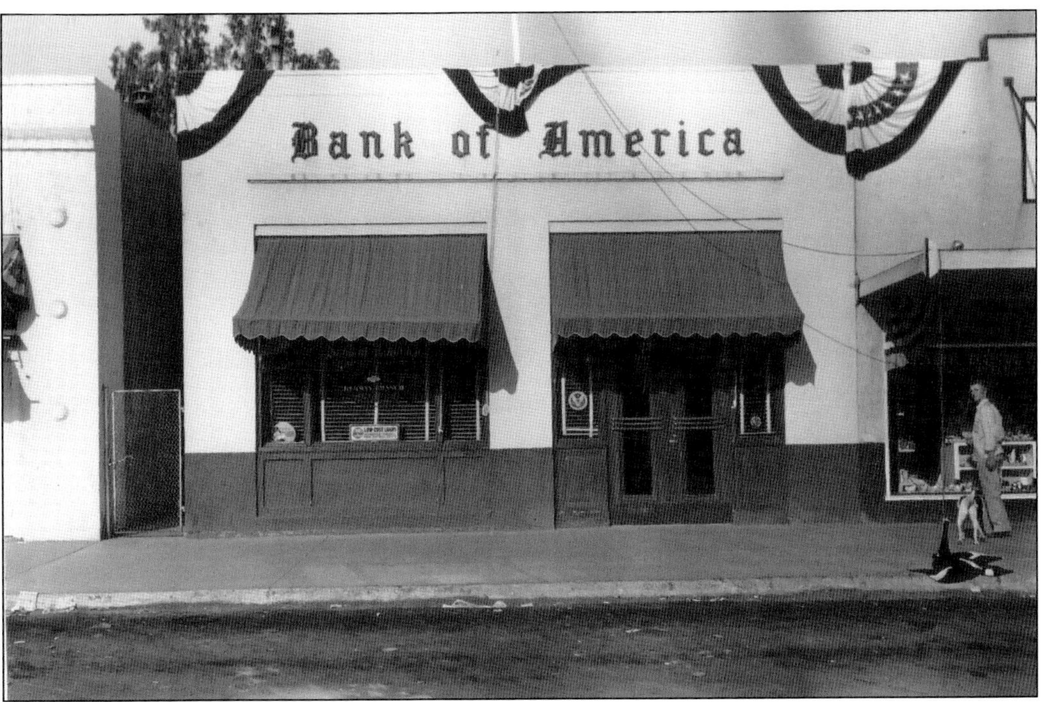

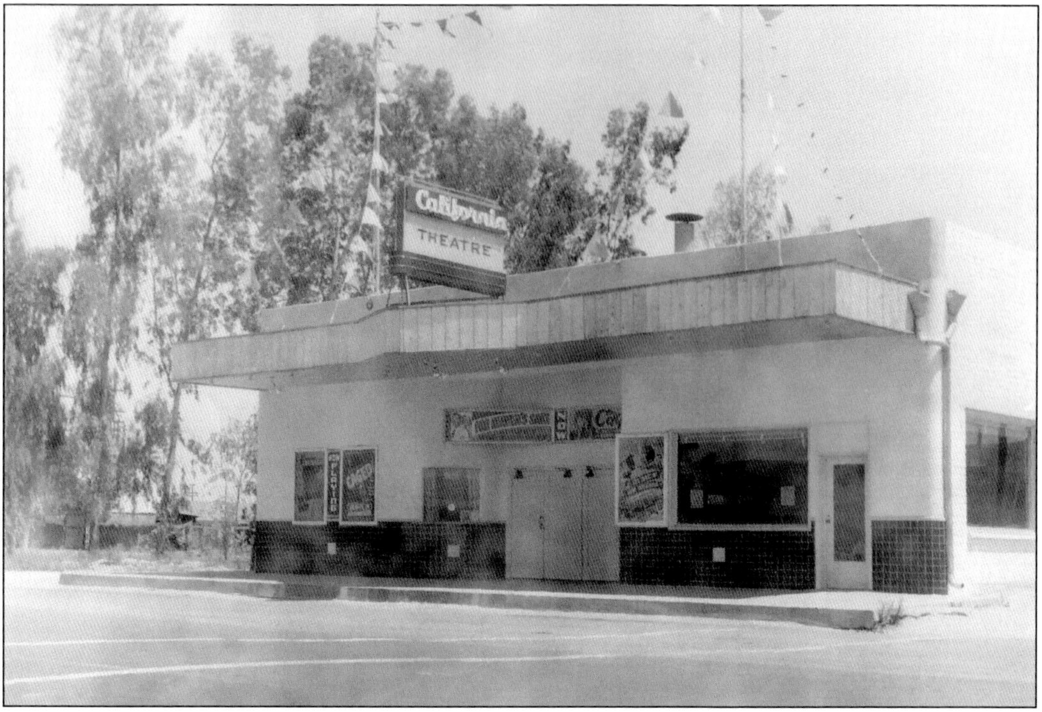

In the days before VCRs and satellite TV, Kerman had its own theater. The California Theatre, owned by Joe Boyd, now houses Las Estrella Market. The theater seating was filled in to make a level floor. The Chat & Chew diner, below, was a popular place for a bite and a chance to get caught up on local news and gossip.

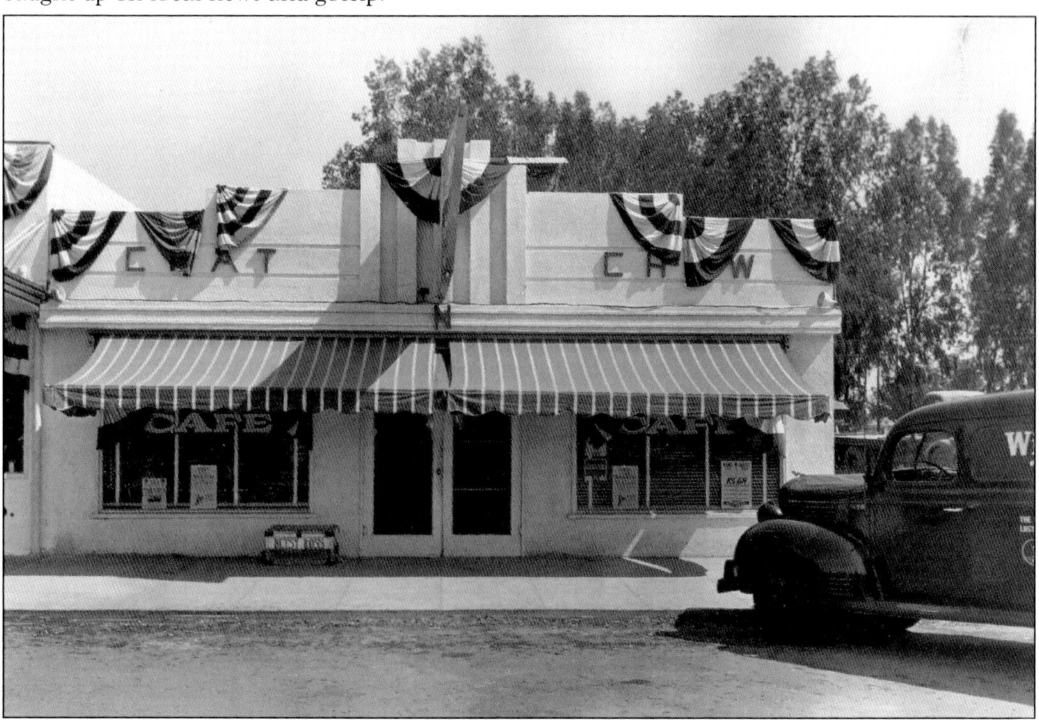

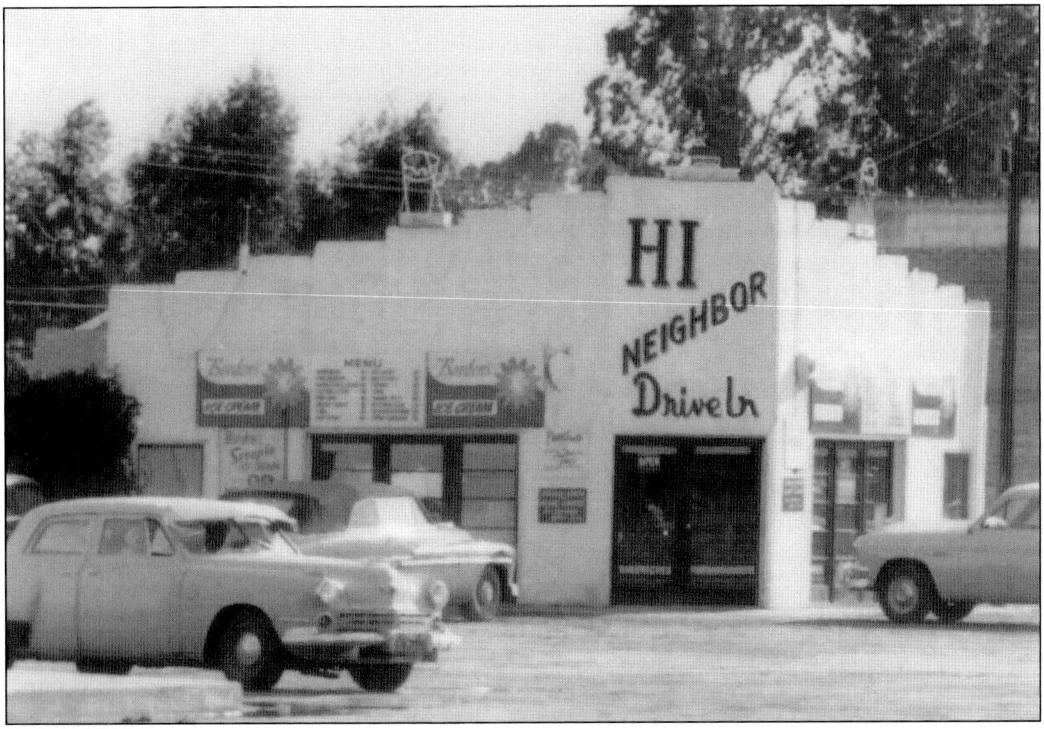

In the days before national chain restaurants, local diners like the Hi Neighbor Drive In and Triangle Café served the community. Many Kermanites have fond memories of meeting their friends at these diners.

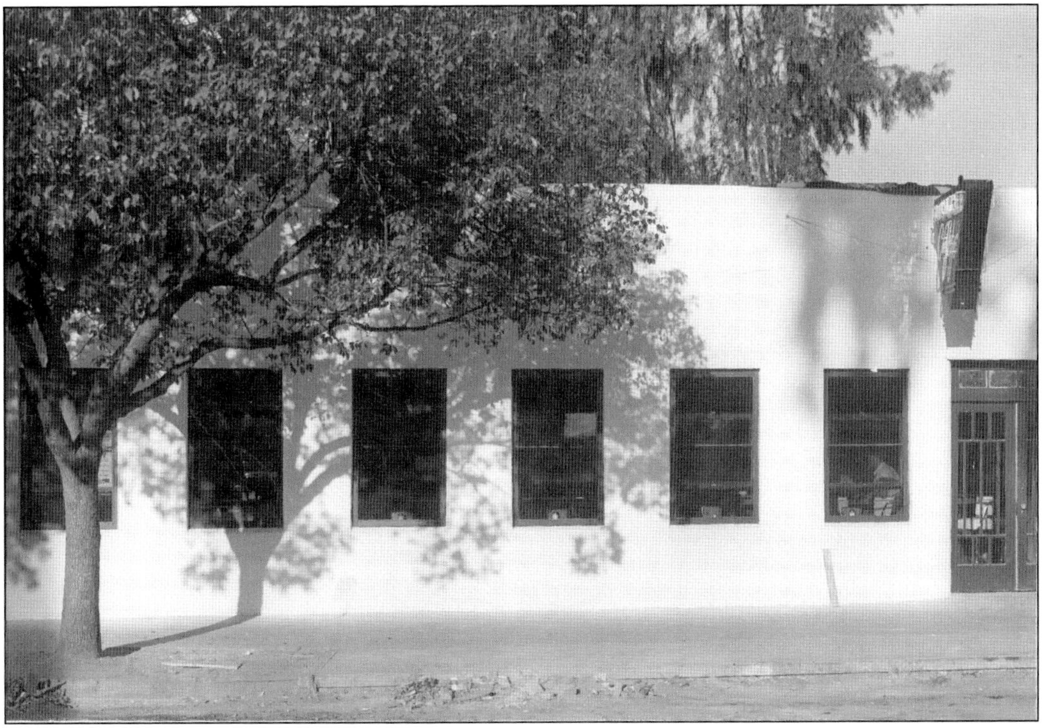

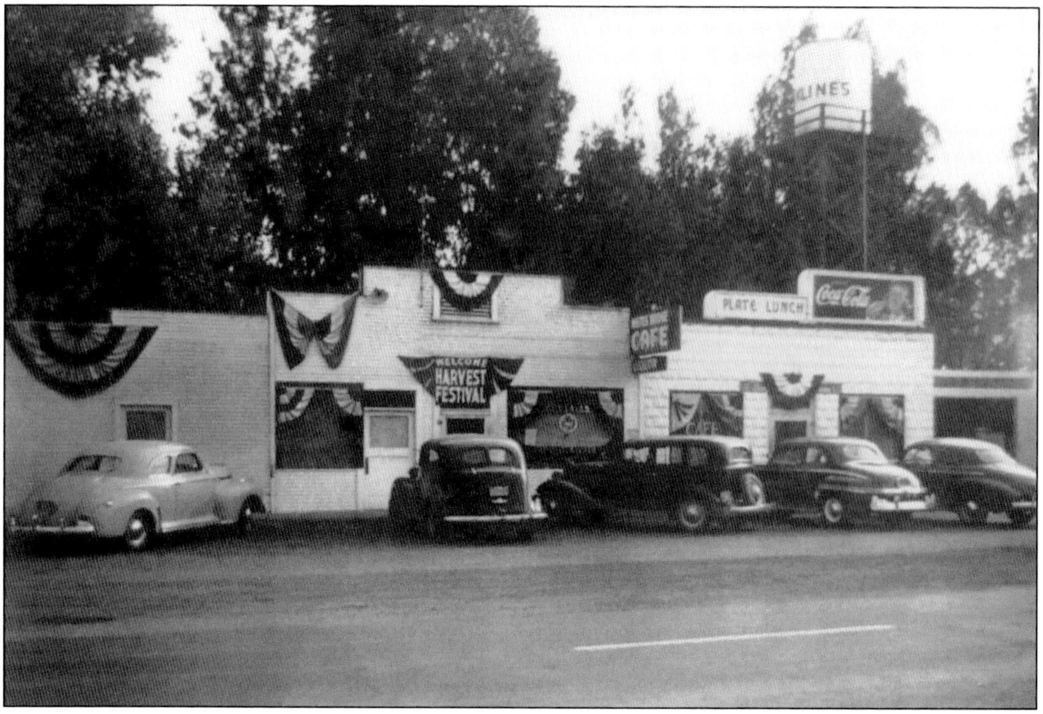

The intersection of Madera Avenue and Whitesbridge Road is also the intersection of two state highways: Route 145 and Route 180. For decades, this intersection was north of downtown Kerman. As the crossroads for two state highways, there was plenty of traffic and a need for good cafés.

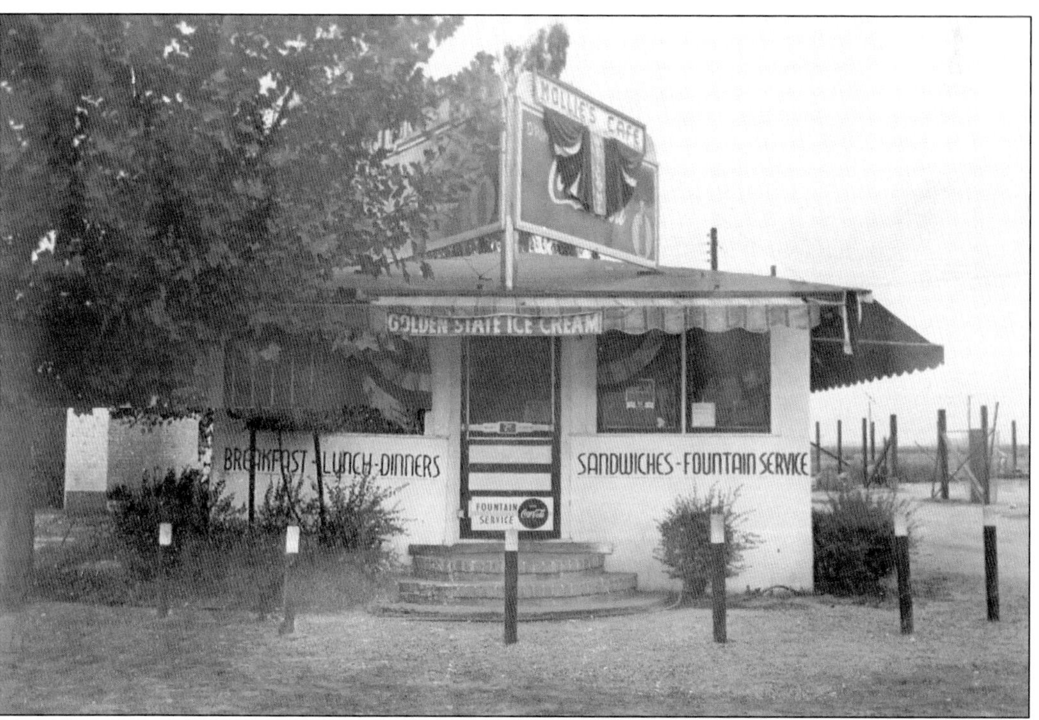

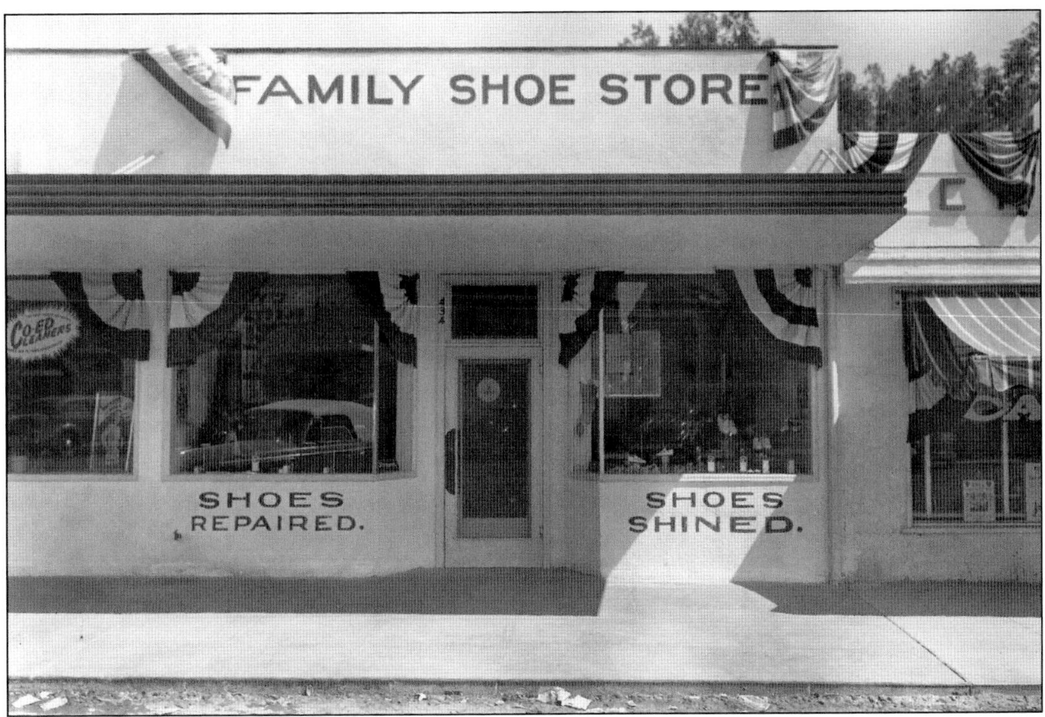

Local merchants took care of customers' needs in the days before online shopping. Personal service was a trademark of small towns. Family Shoe Store, Gordon's Bakery, Wyatt's Variety and Gift Shop, Ideal Variety, the drugstore, and soda shop all lined Madera Avenue.

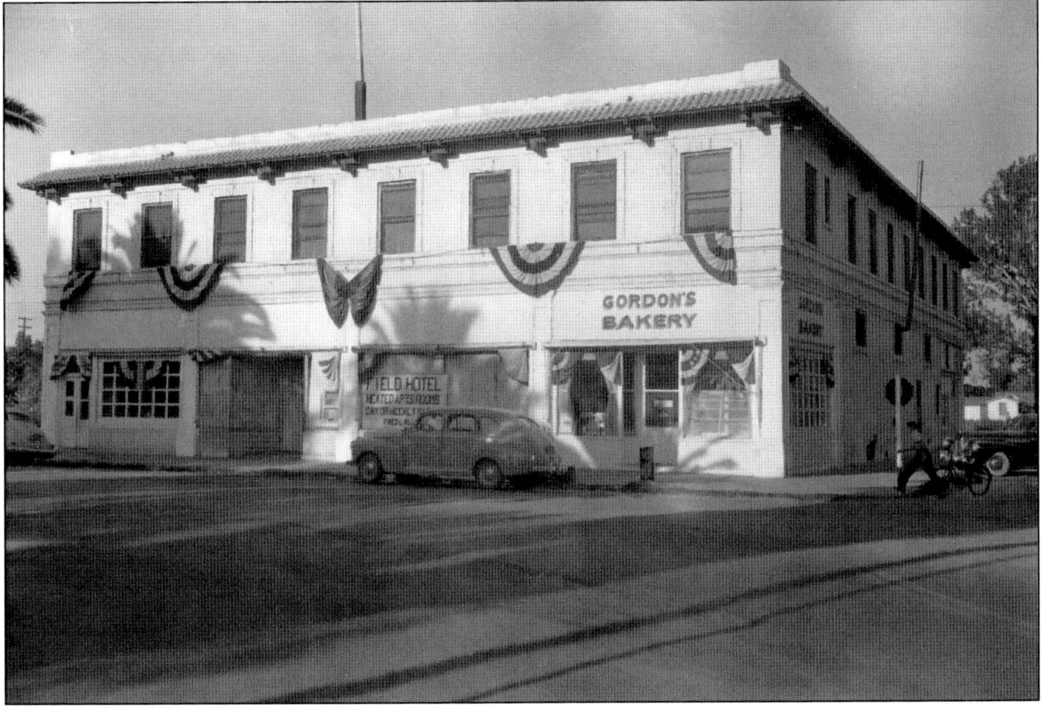

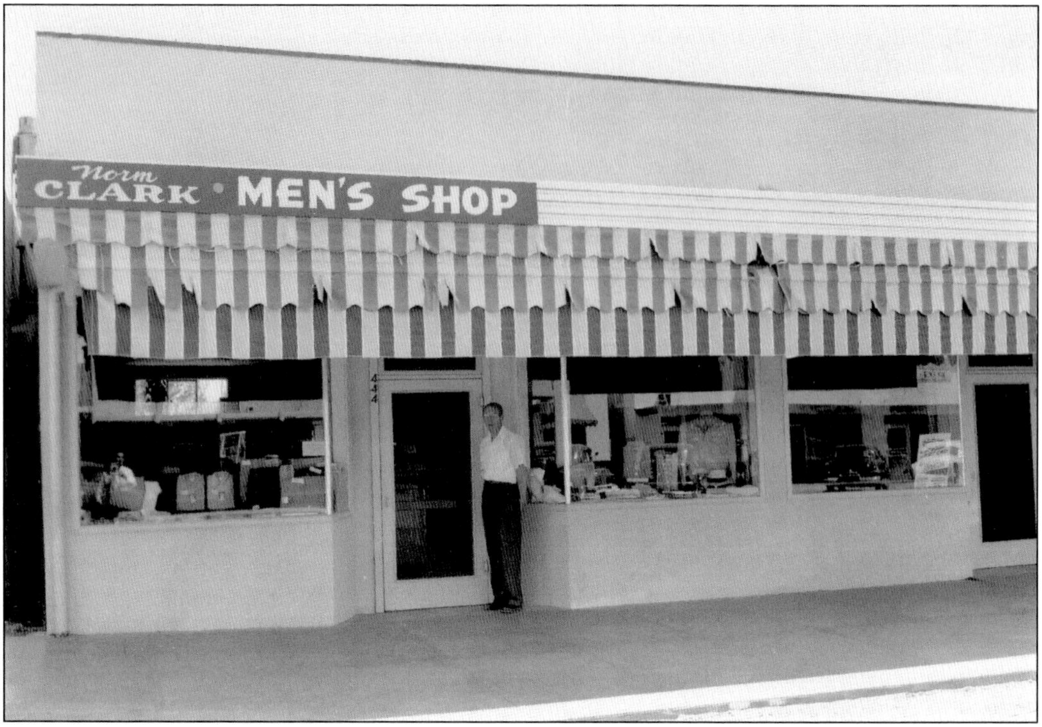

The well-dressed men of Kerman shopped at Norm Clark Men's Shop when dress shirts and hats were everyday wear. Five-and-dime variety stores like Ideal, below, replaced the general stores of the 19th century.

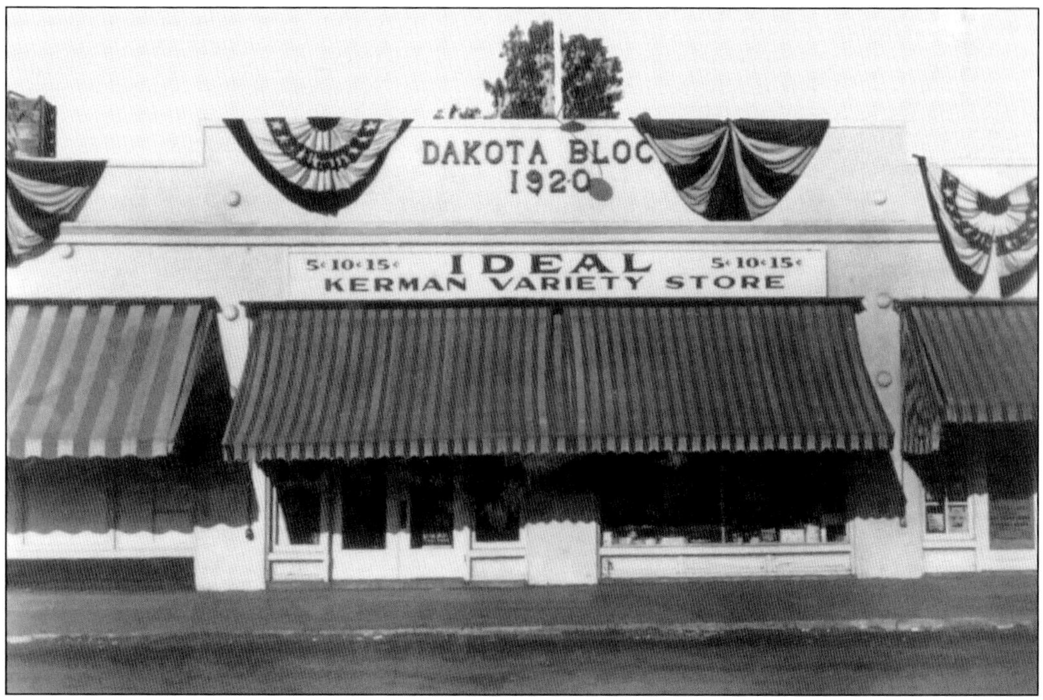

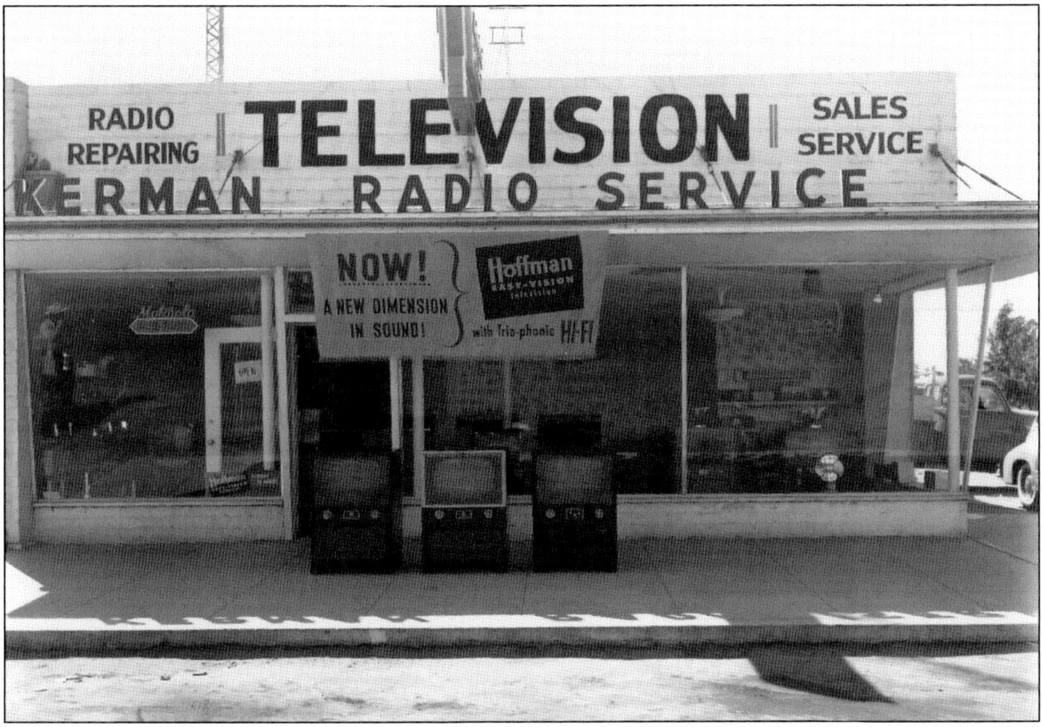

In the days before television, radio was king, and Kerman Radio Service was the place to go for a new tube. Of course, no farm town would be complete without a feed store. The Turner family was there for Kerman's livestock feed needs.

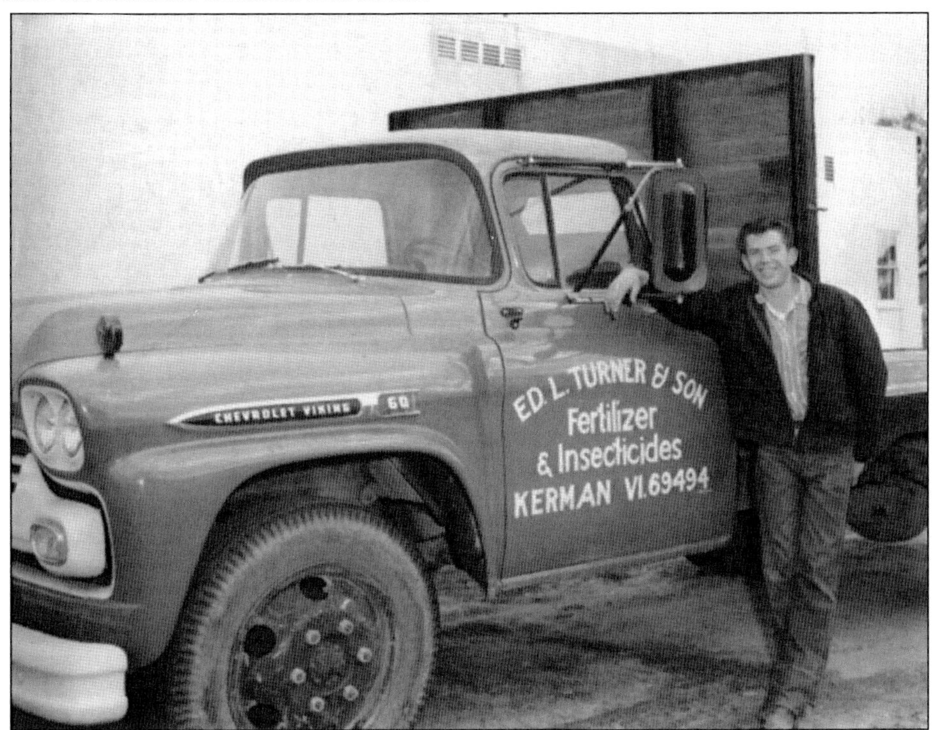

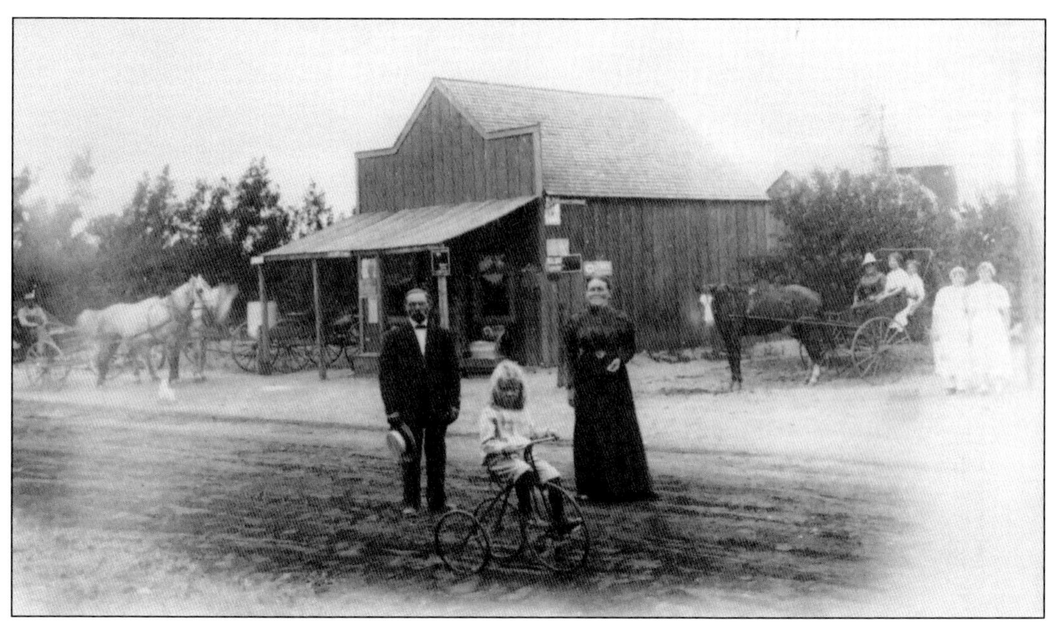

One of the earliest markets in Kerman was the Vinland Store. This was a time of transition; note how some customers came with horse and buggy, above, while others came in cars, below.

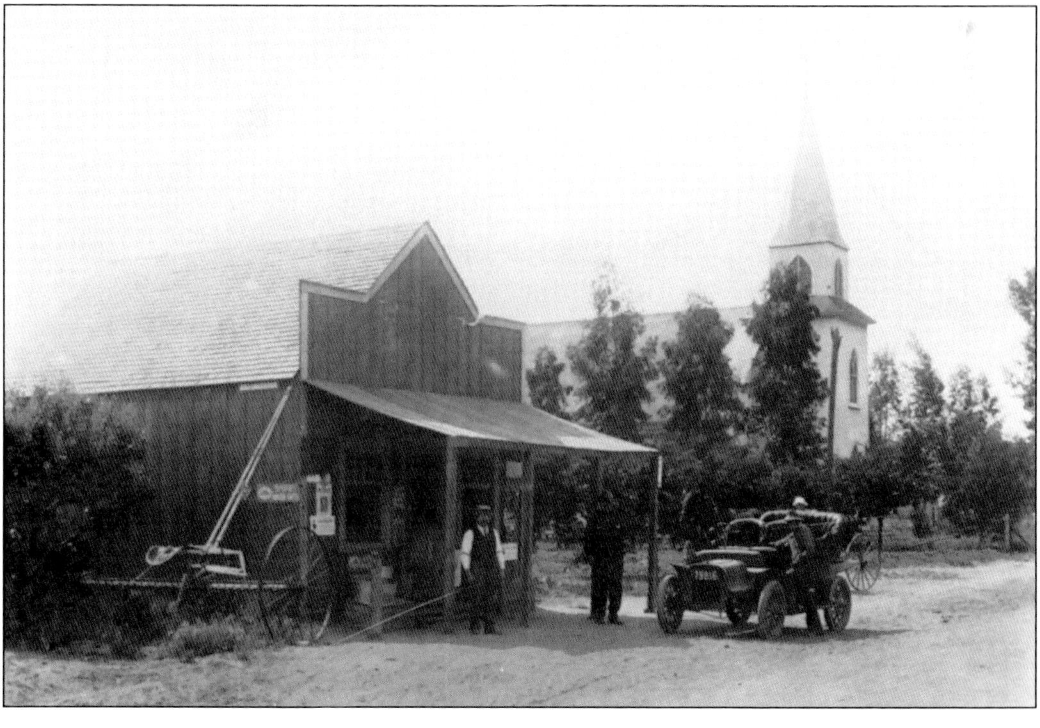

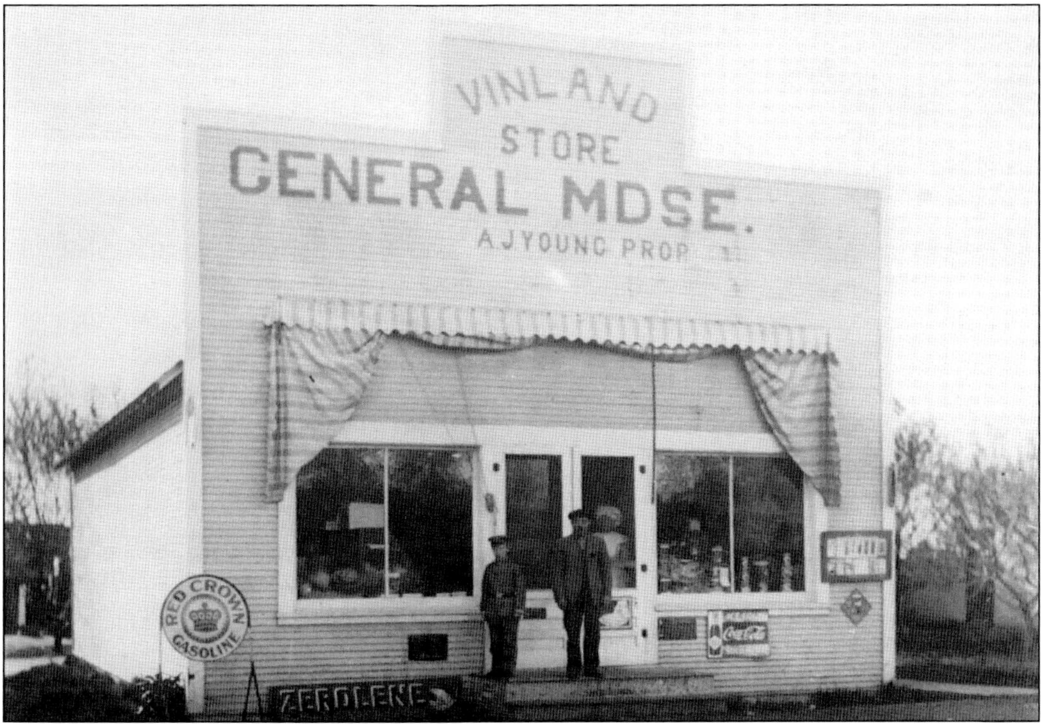

The Vinland Store is seen here some years later. Styles and products may change, but the need for a good grocery store will be there as long as people need to eat.

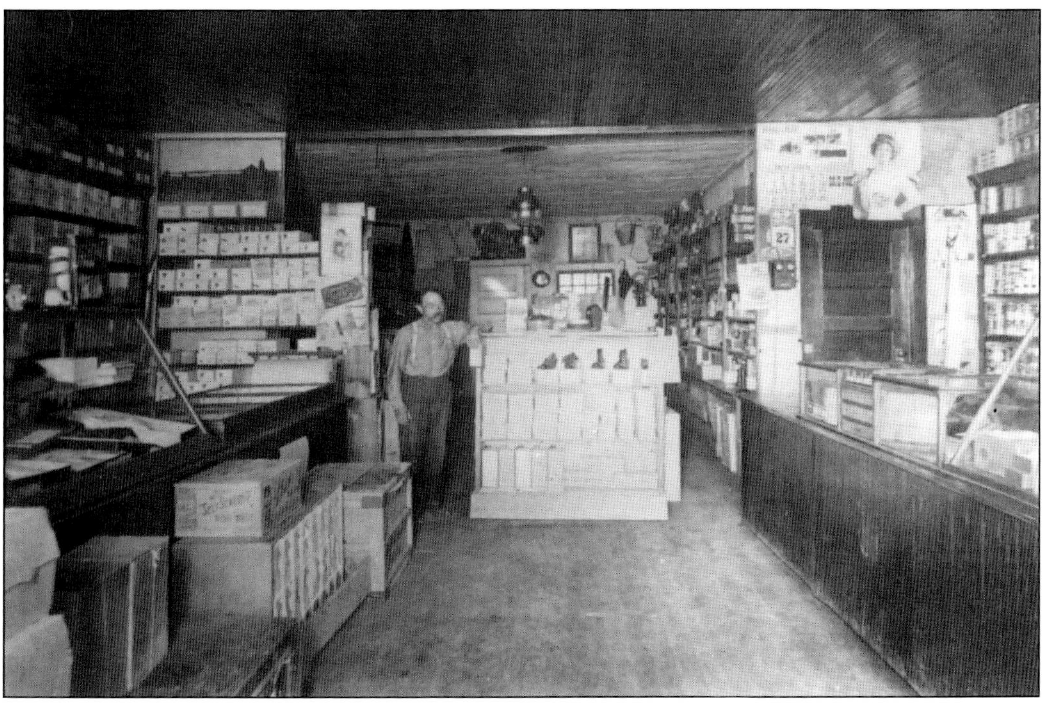

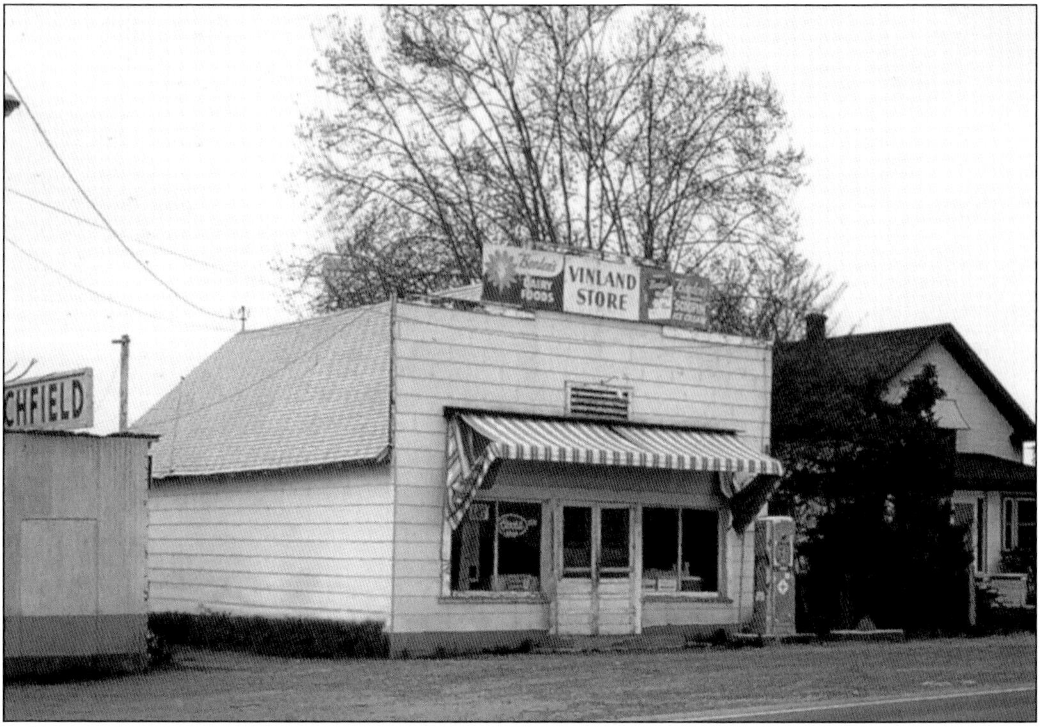

Fifty years later, the Vinland Store was still serving the community. Below, in the mid-1960s, Fritz Young was here to serve groceries and even gasoline.

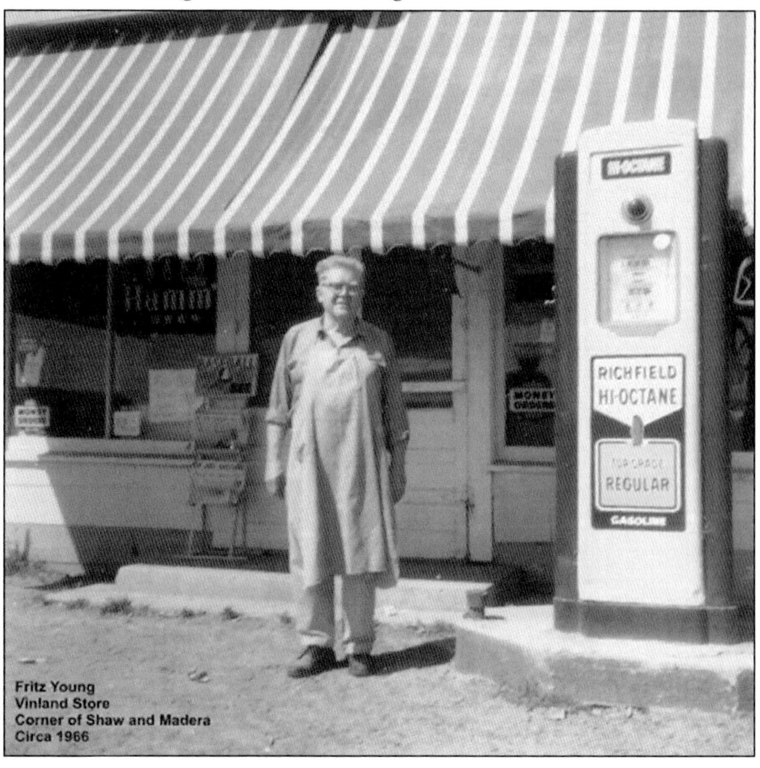

Fritz Young
Vinland Store
Corner of Shaw and Madera
Circa 1966

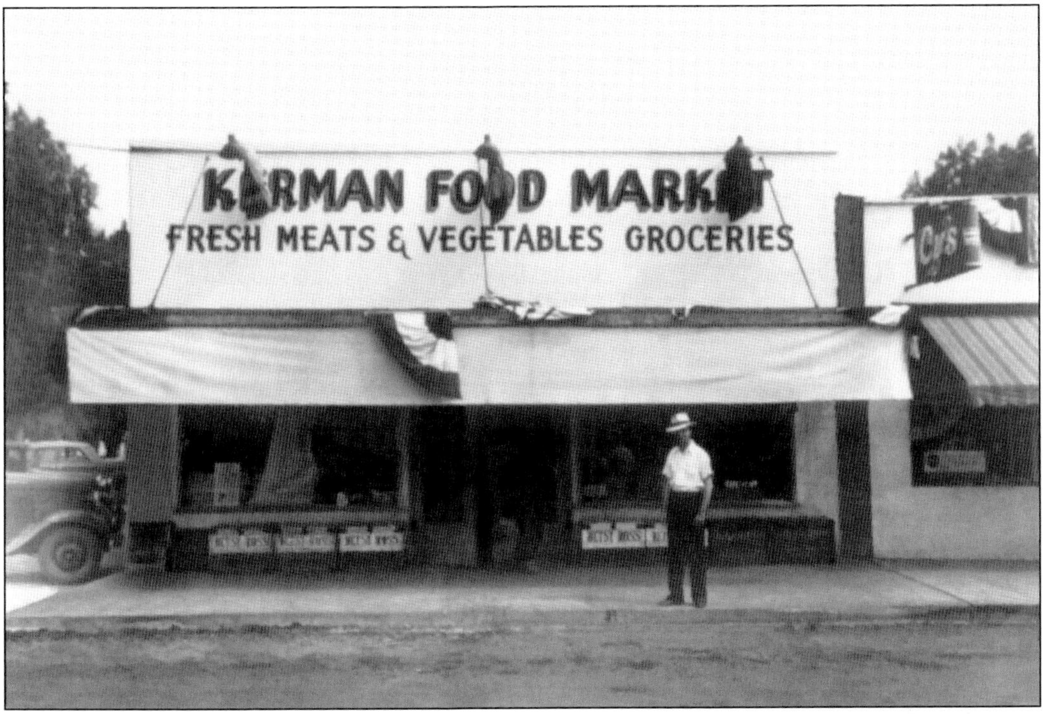

The Kerman Food Market and the Kerman Meat Market were there to serve Kerman in the early years. Kerman has a long history of offering fresh meat from local farms and ranches. Butchers like Corky Lindsey helped prepare and provide fresh beef, pork, lamb, and chicken for decades.

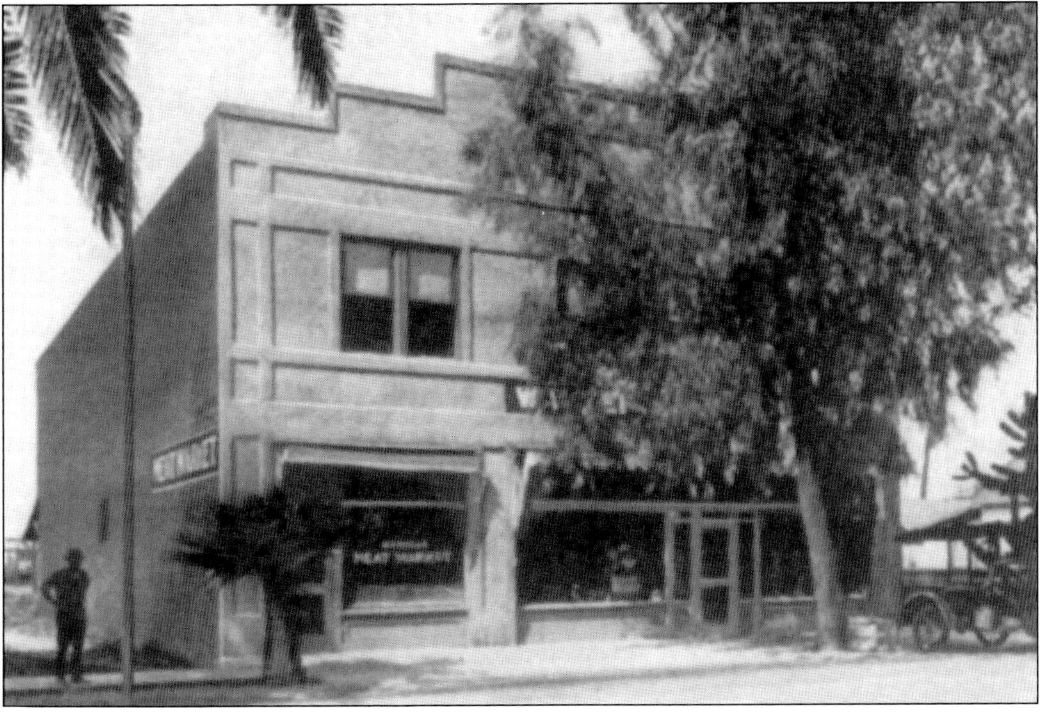

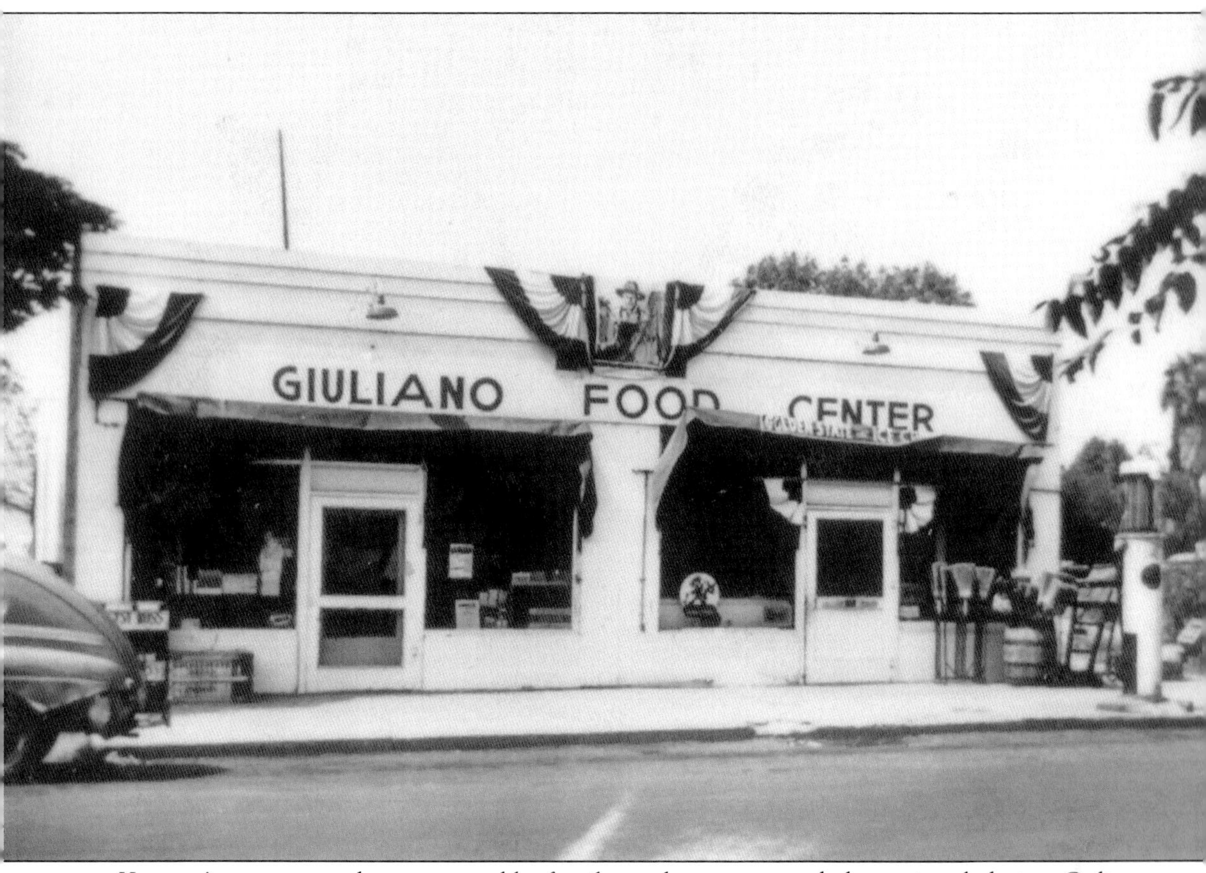

Kerman's grocery needs were served by family markets, not merely by national chains. Guliano Food Center, Lewis, Barker's, Miller's, and Epperson's may not be familiar names to many current residents of Kerman, but they served the community for generations.

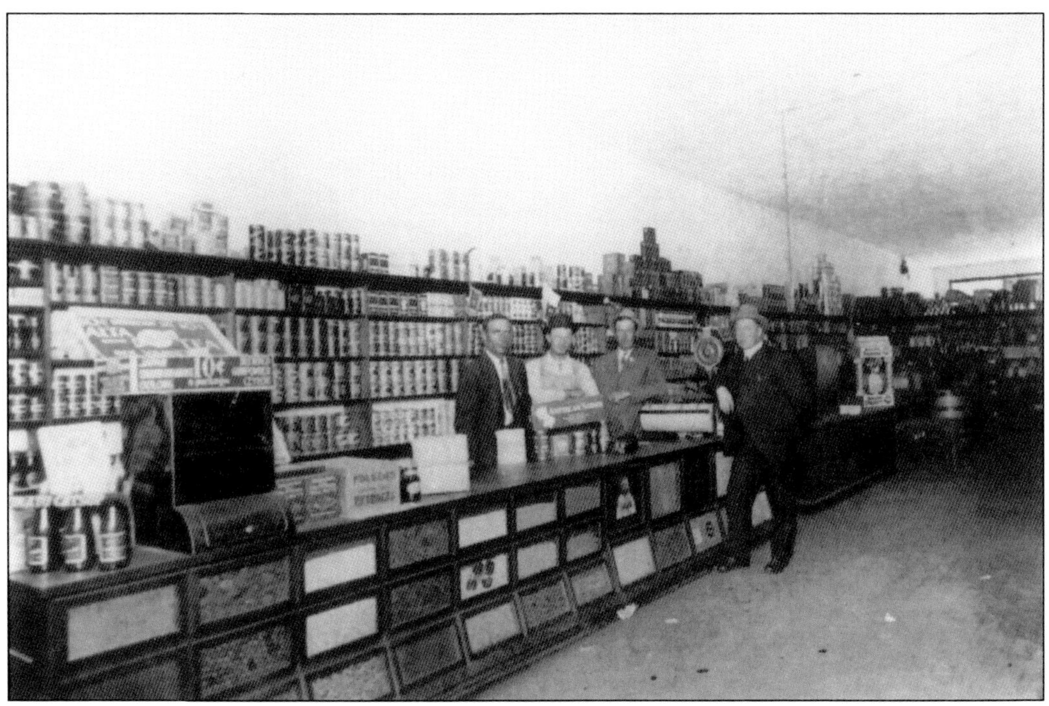

The above view inside Duke's offers a glimpse of a grocery store in 1919. Below, the view inside Miller's shows how some things stay the same: the Danish Creamery sign at right has the same logo used on the company's labels today.

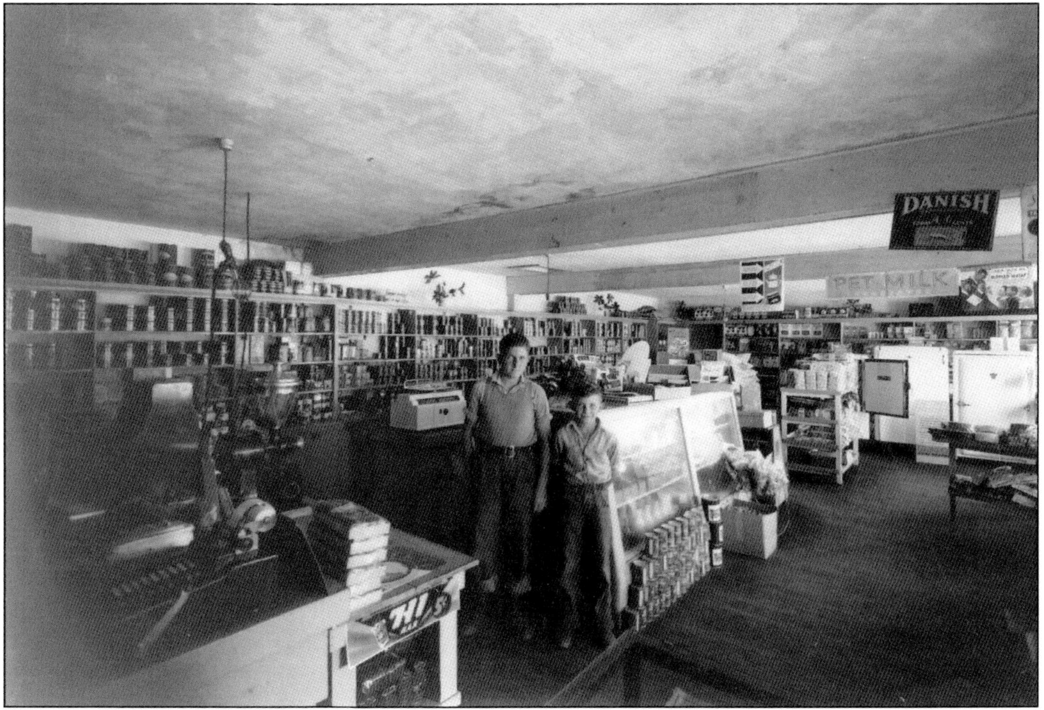

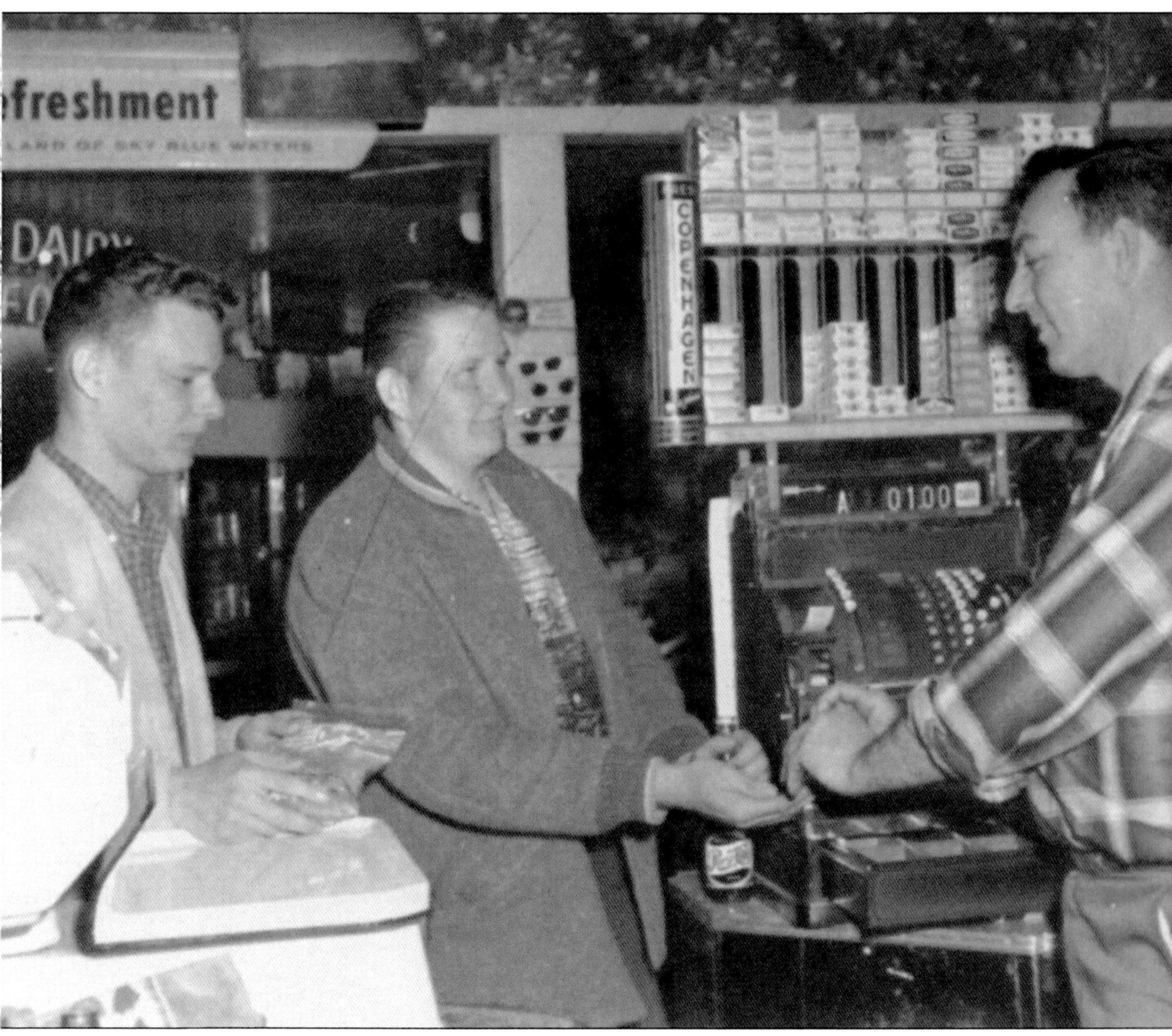

This photograph shows how personal service was dispensed in local stores like Epperson's for generations. Local grocers would often extend credit to farmers, who would pay after their crops came in. That sort of service is rare today.

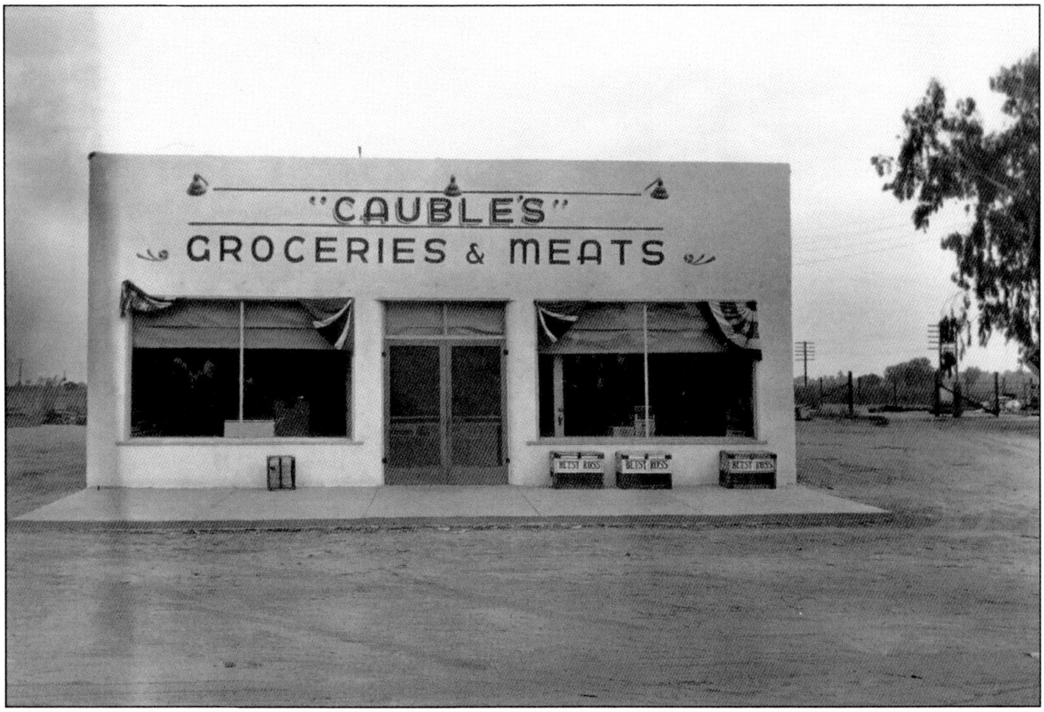

Cauble's Groceries & Meats was located on the southeast corner of Madera Avenue and E Street. Cauble's may be long gone, but Valley Food Center has served the community since 1955. Today, the Yep family provides local service that can never be replaced.

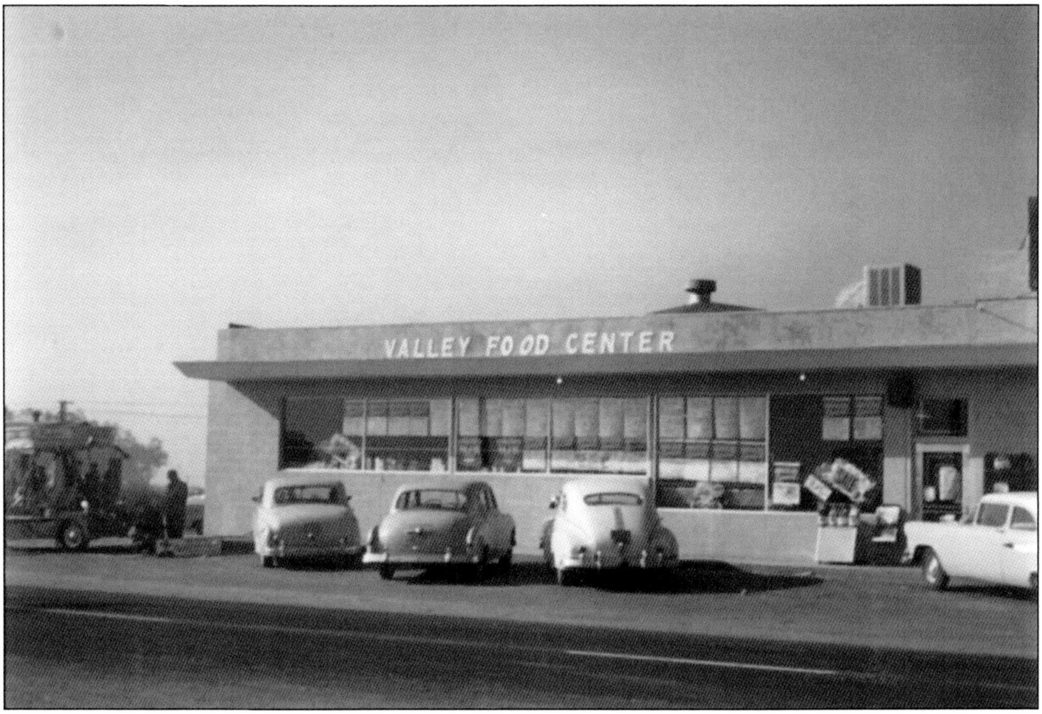

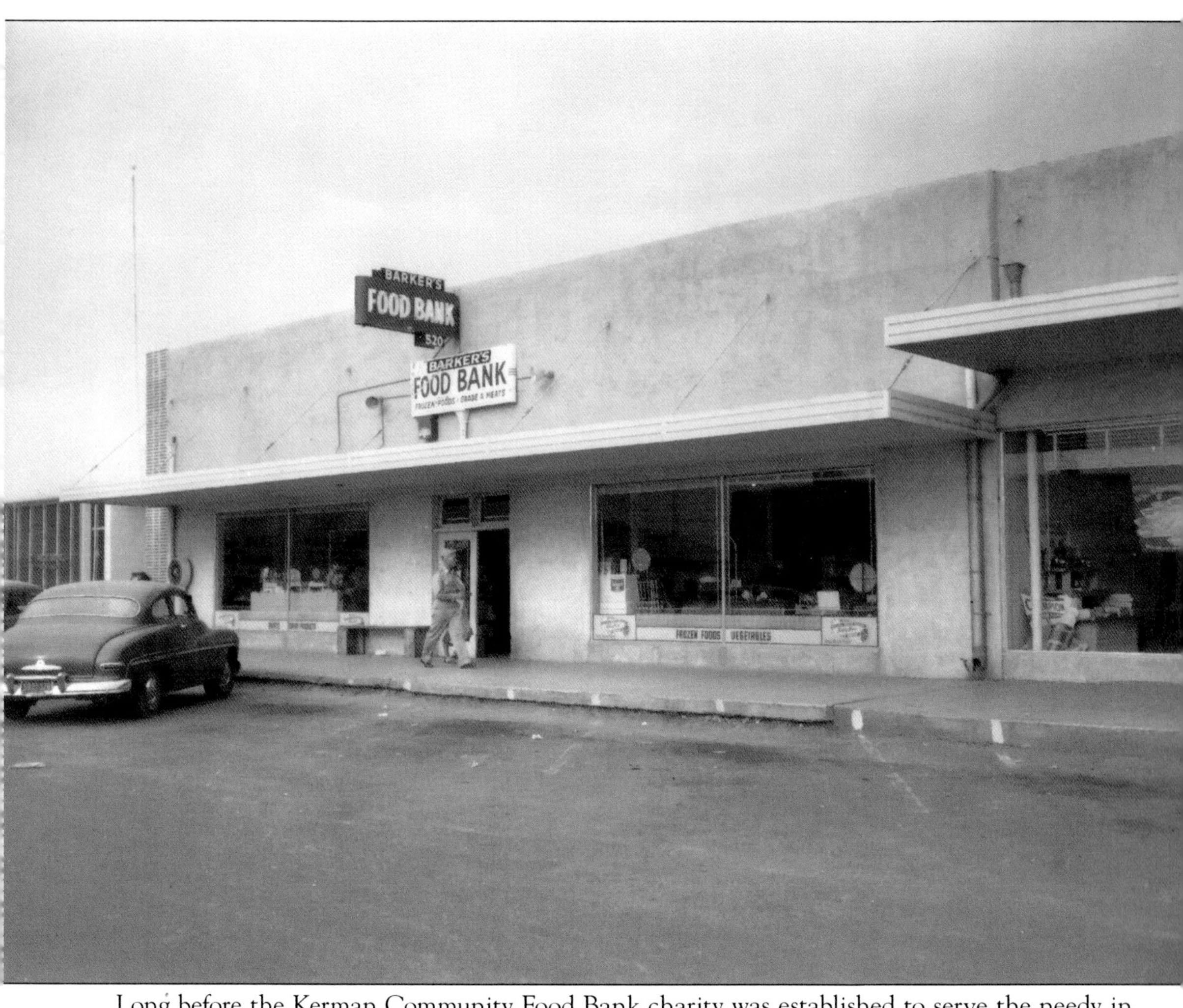

Long before the Kerman Community Food Bank charity was established to serve the needy in 1983, Barker's Food Bank was a grocery store selling food for the community.

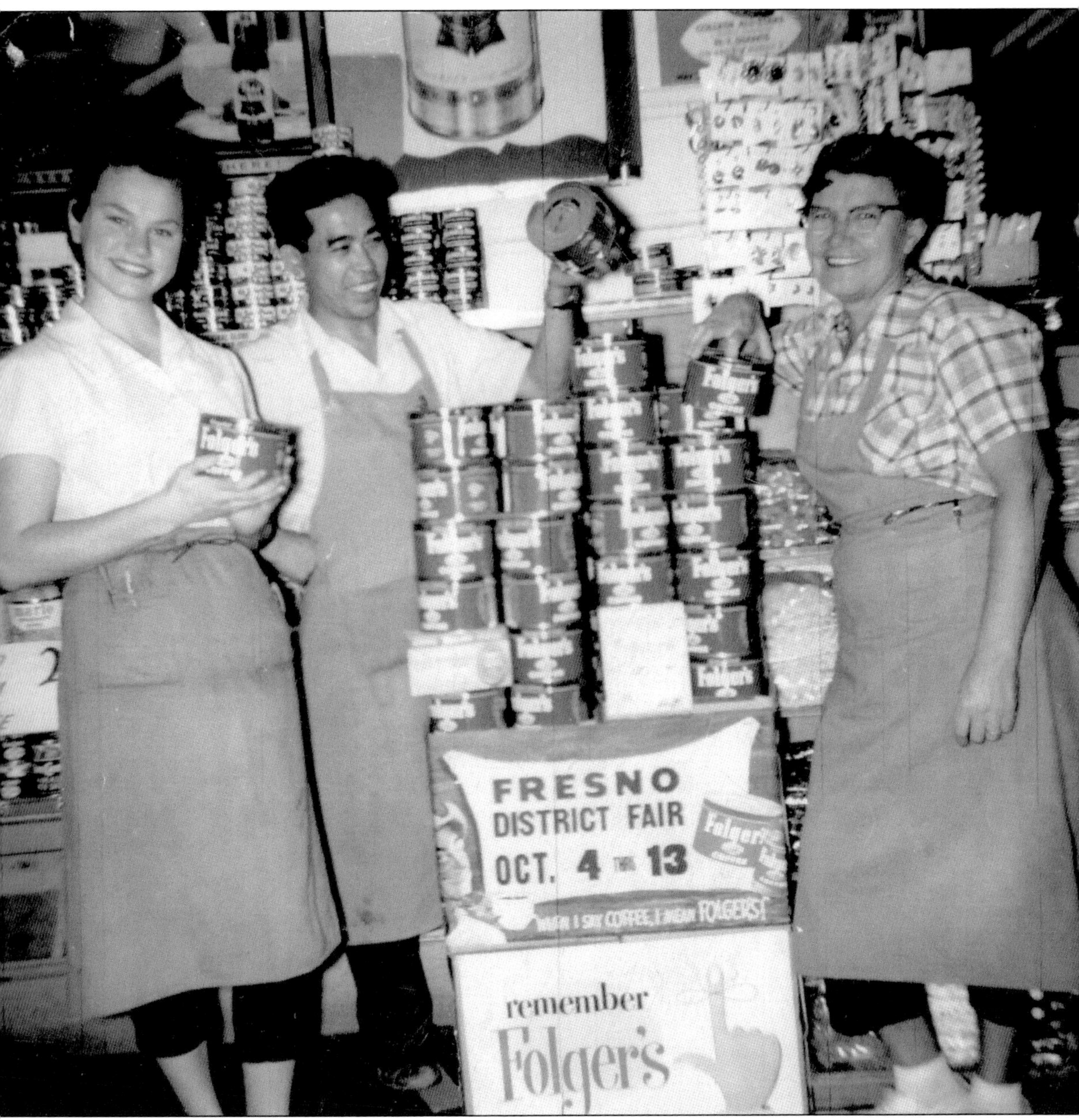

Good service never goes out of style. The fine folks at Ace Supermarket were always there with a smile and fresh products for Kerman shoppers.

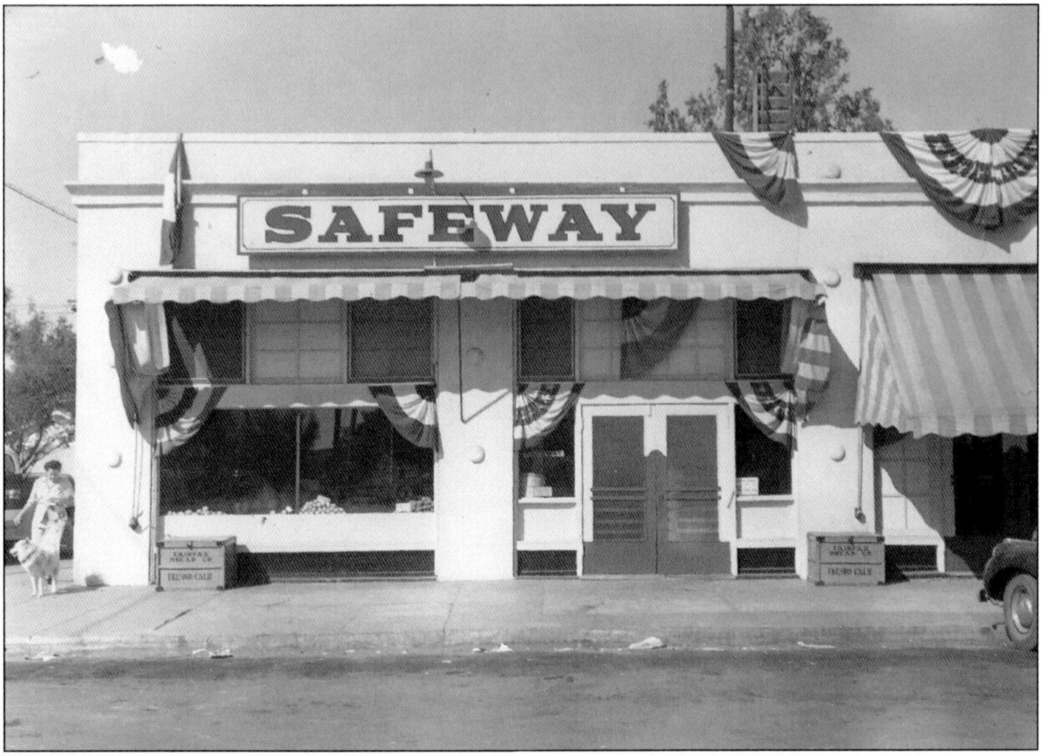

Over the years, different families and companies have served the community including Safeway and the Kerman Meat Market. The Safeway store was located in the Dakota Building on the west side of Madera Avenue, between D and E Streets.

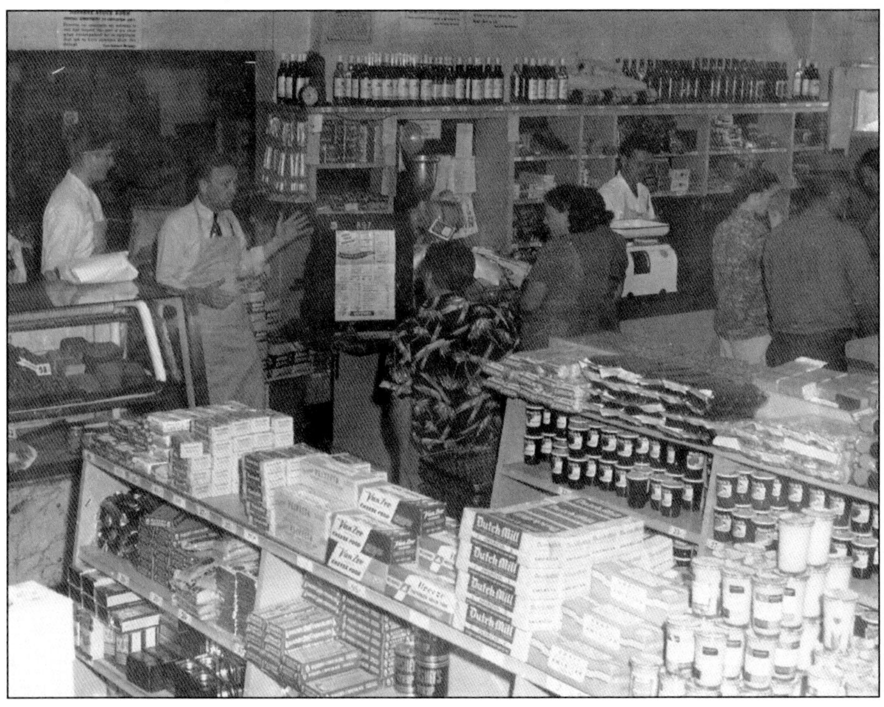

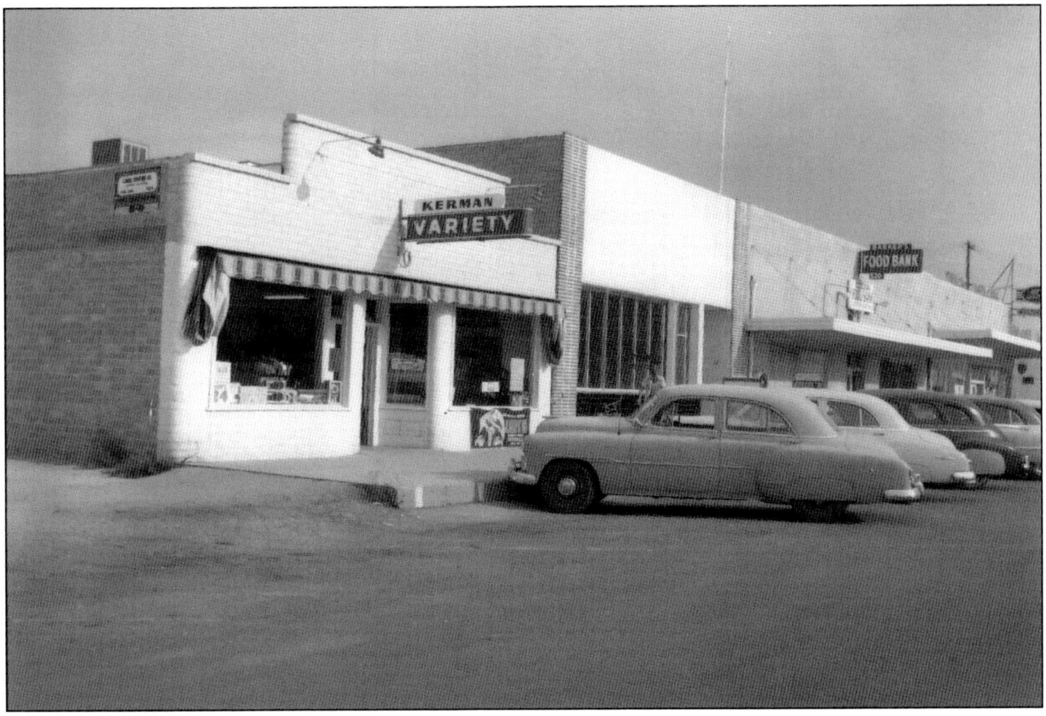

By the 1950s, Madera Avenue had filled up from Plaza Park all the way north to Kearney Boulevard. An electric sign had been put up at Madera Avenue and Route 180 in 1925 to point people toward the downtown. Slowly, the town was growing north to the Route 180 intersection.

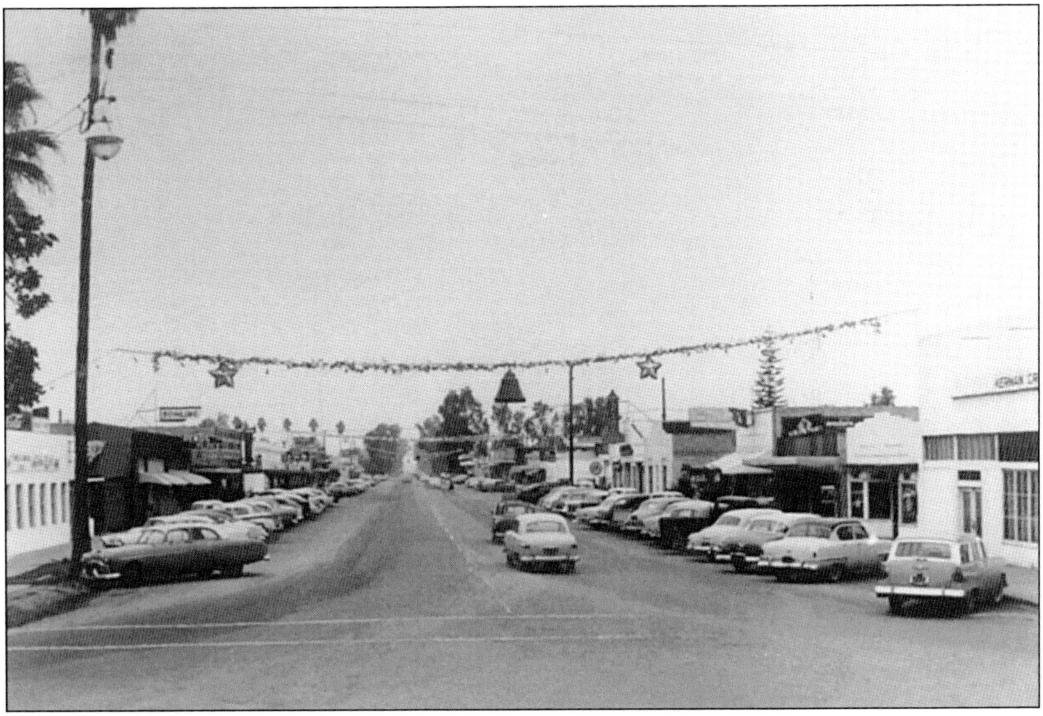

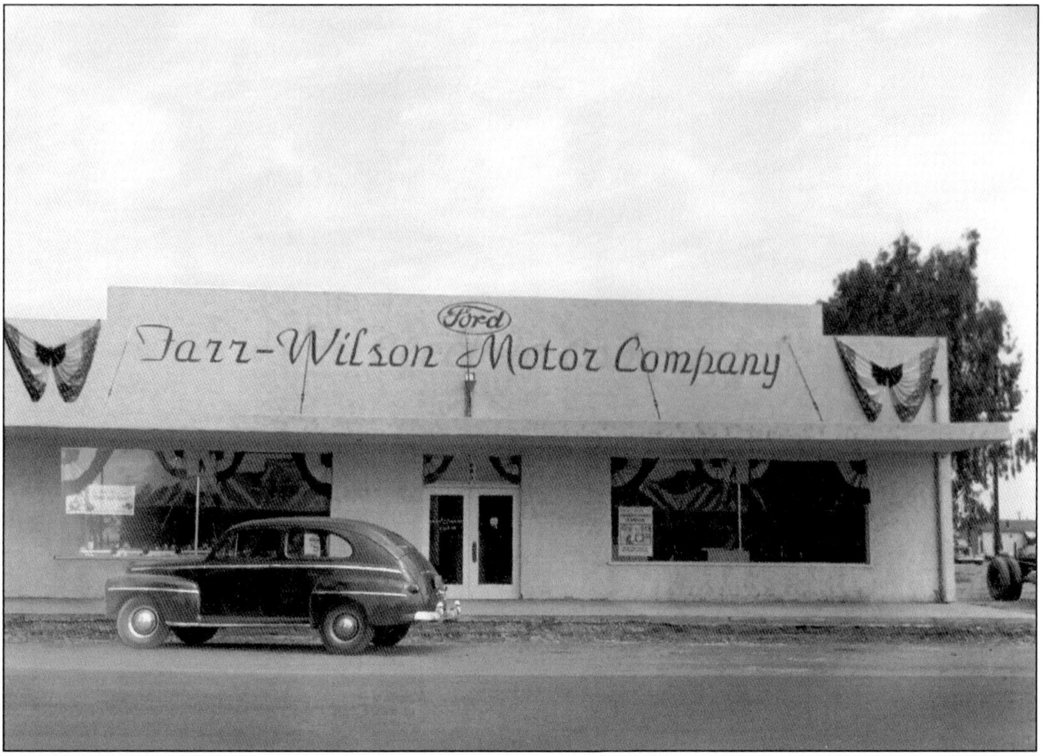

Today, there is only one car dealership in Kerman: H&J Chevrolet. In the past there were others, including Farr-Wilson Motor Co., which sold Fords, and Heims Motor Co., which sold Kaiser and Fraser automobiles. The Heims dealership was at the northeast corner of Madera Avenue and E Street.

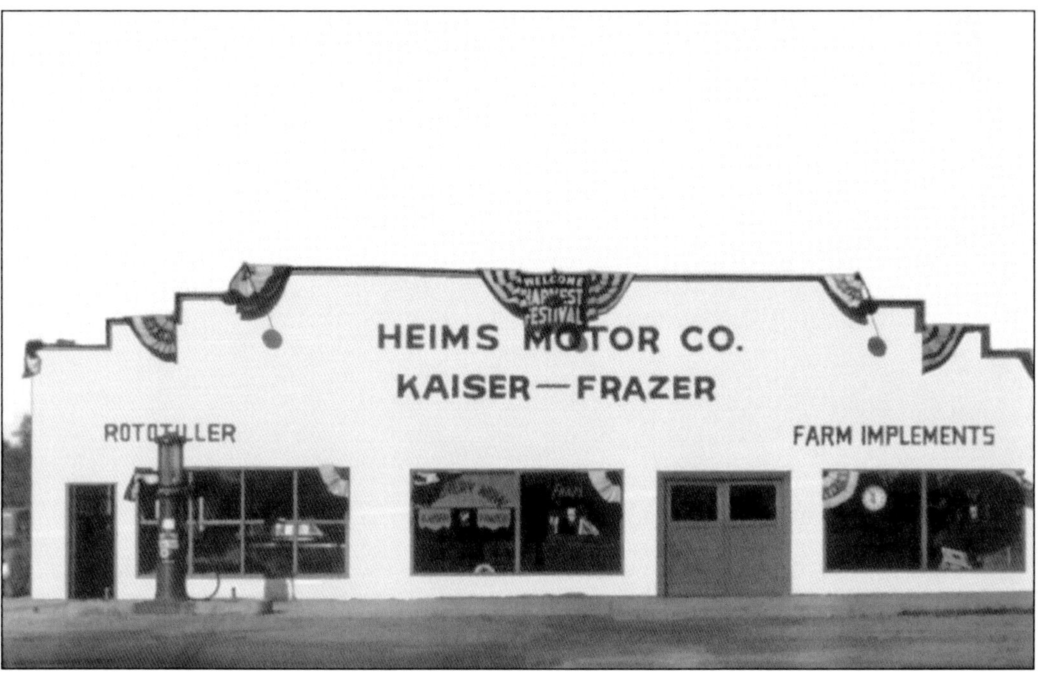

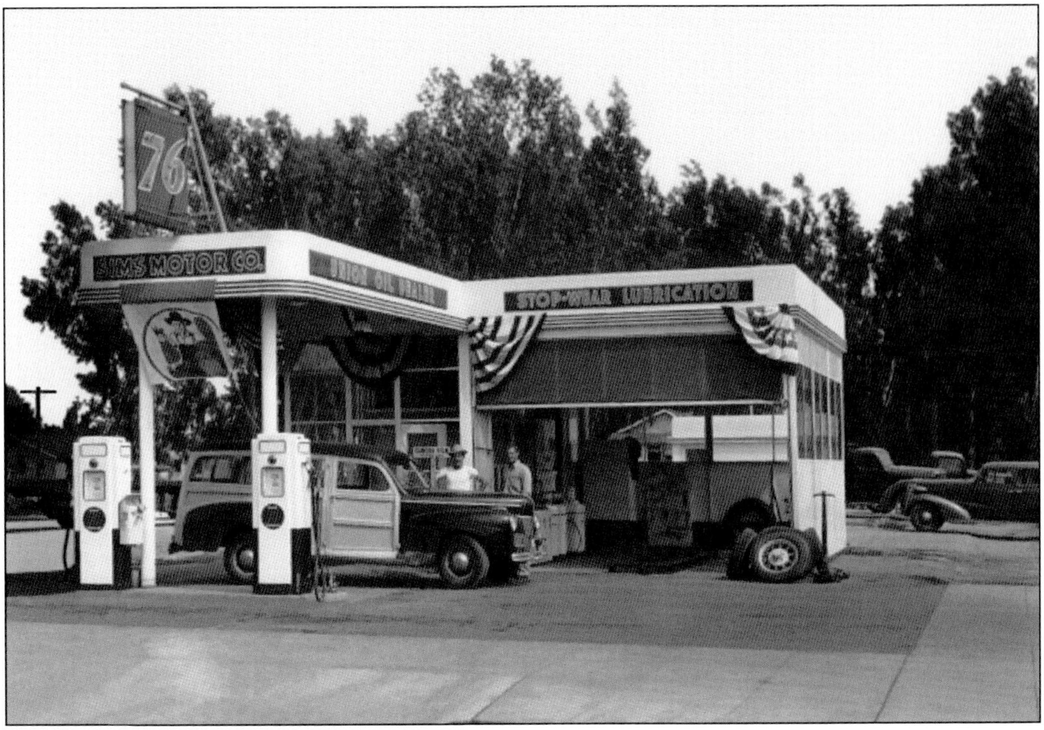

Sims Motor Co. was located on the southeast corner of Madera Avenue and D Street and became a car dealership. M.W. Steffen not only serviced cars, but the station also served as the Greyhound bus depot for Kerman.

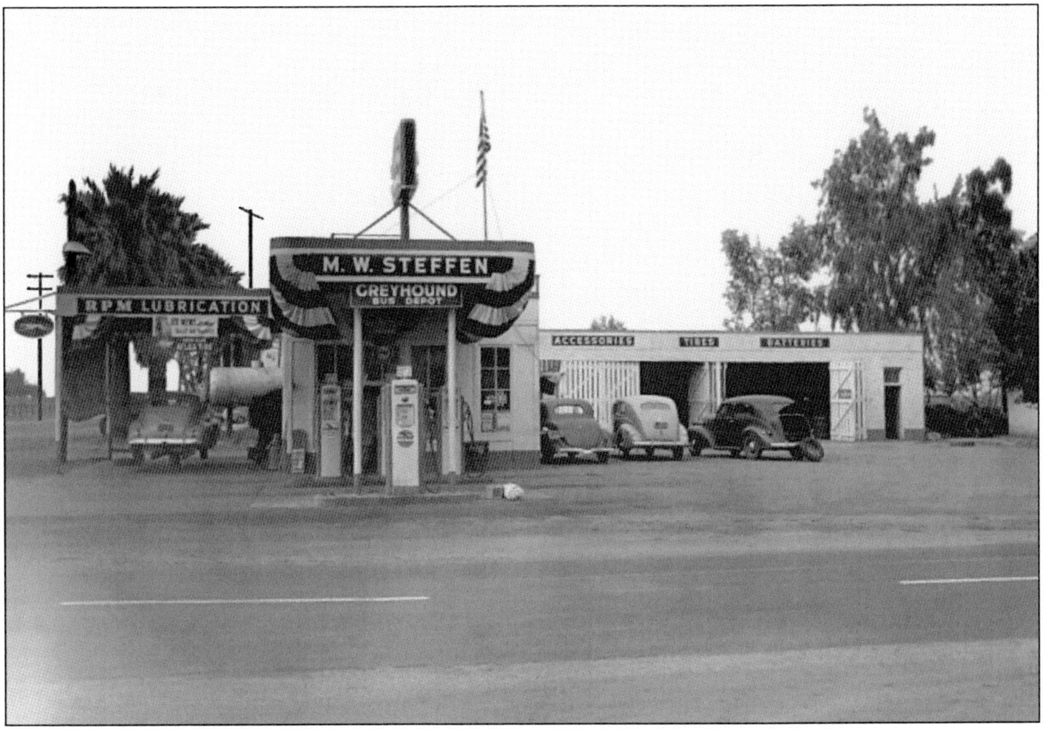

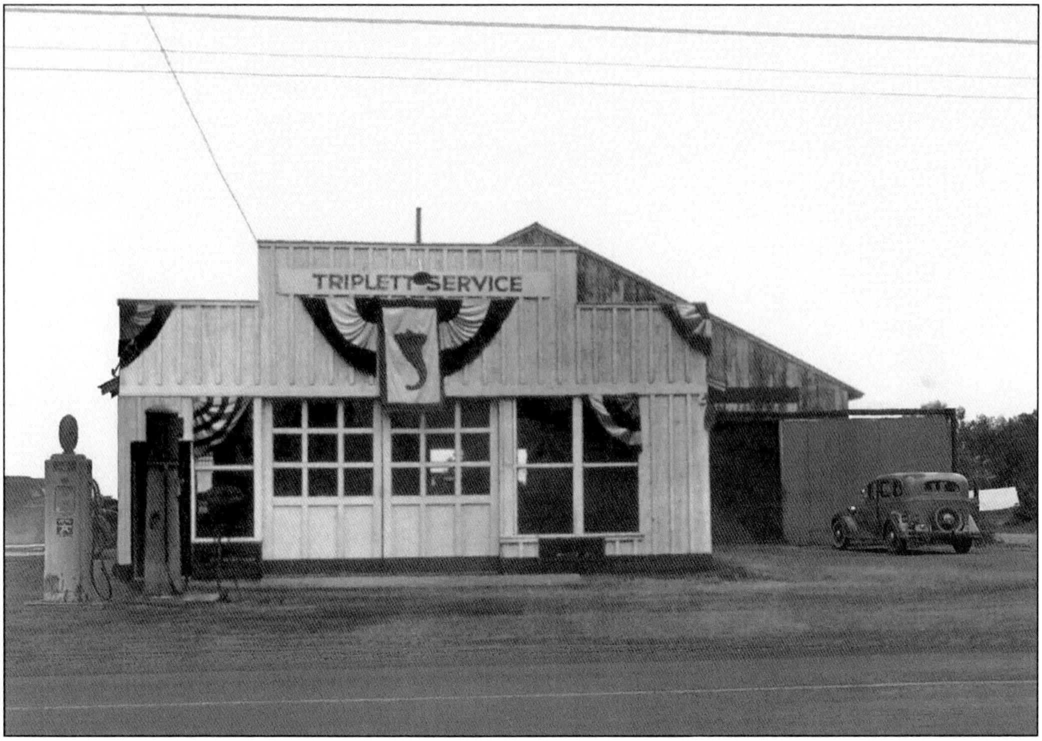

Above, the Triplett service station was located on the east side of Madera Avenue north of Kearney Boulevard. Below, judging by the laundry hanging behind V.E. Jones's service station (at left), the family must have lived nearby.

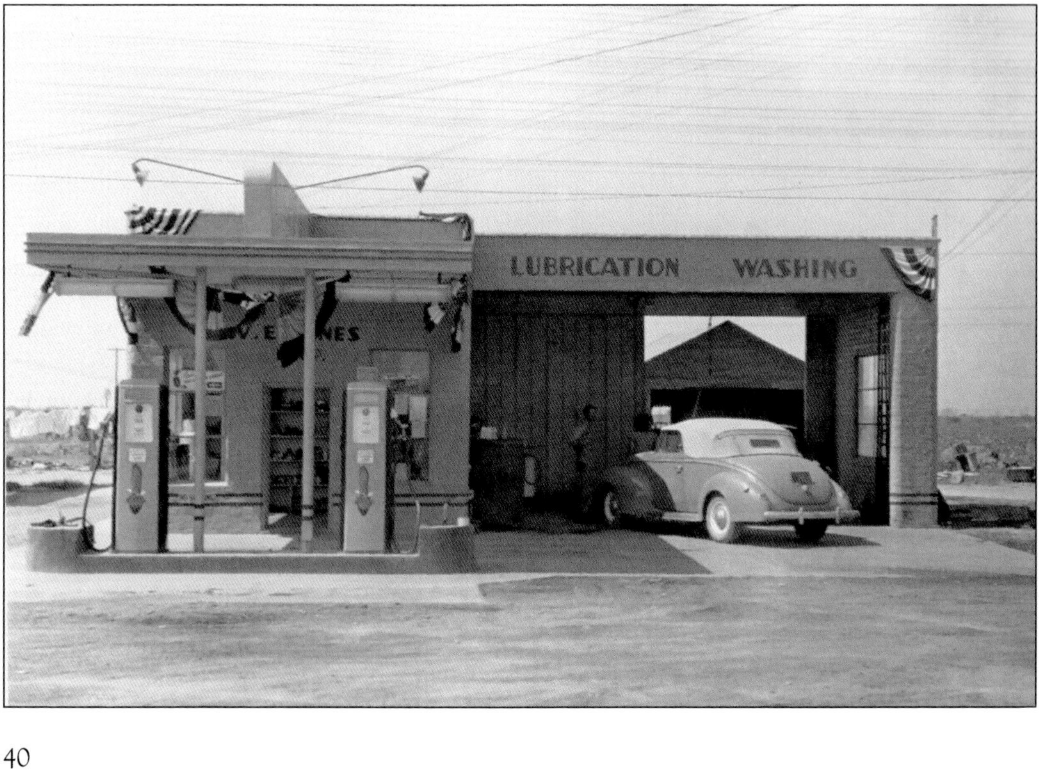

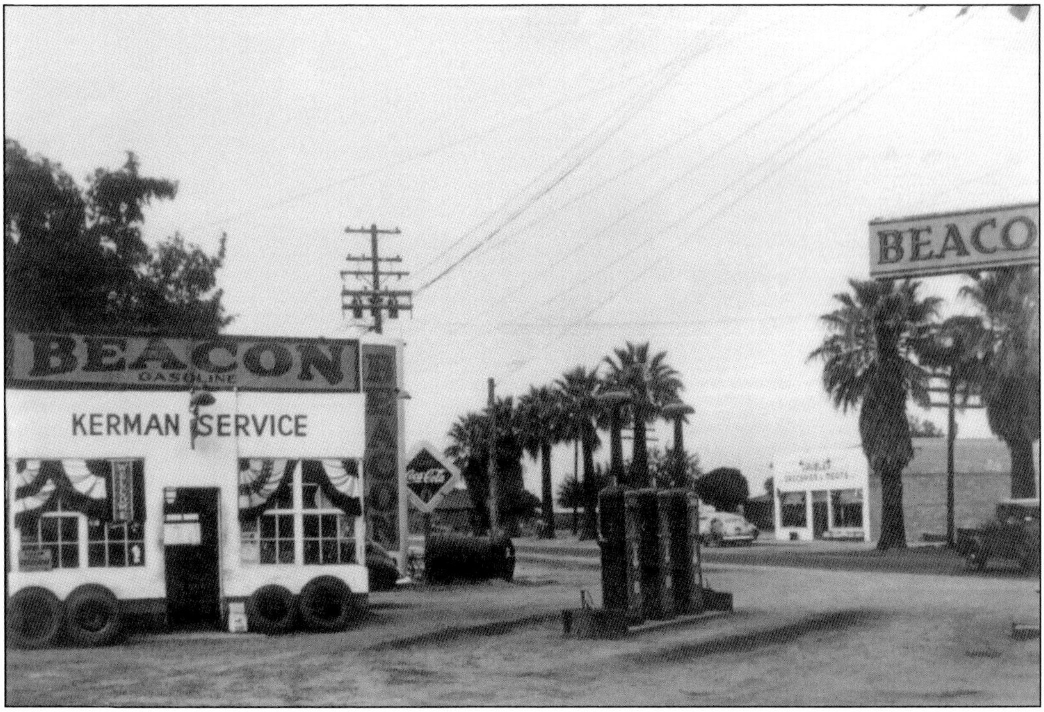

In these pictures, the progression of cars and gas stations over the years is evident. Miller's Service Station was north of town at Madera Avenue and Shields Avenue. Note the old-style hand-pump gas pumps.

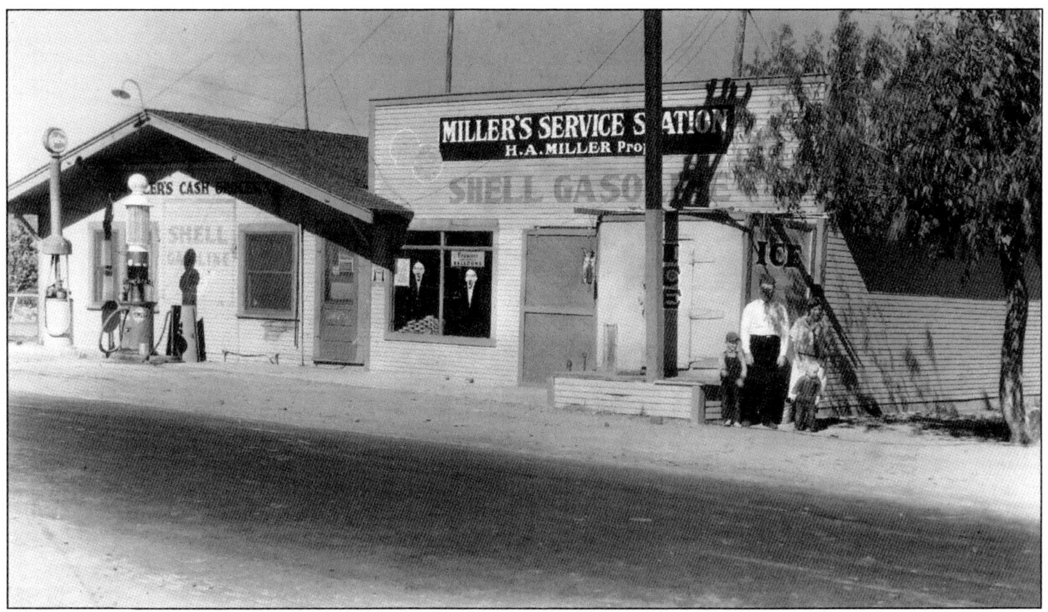

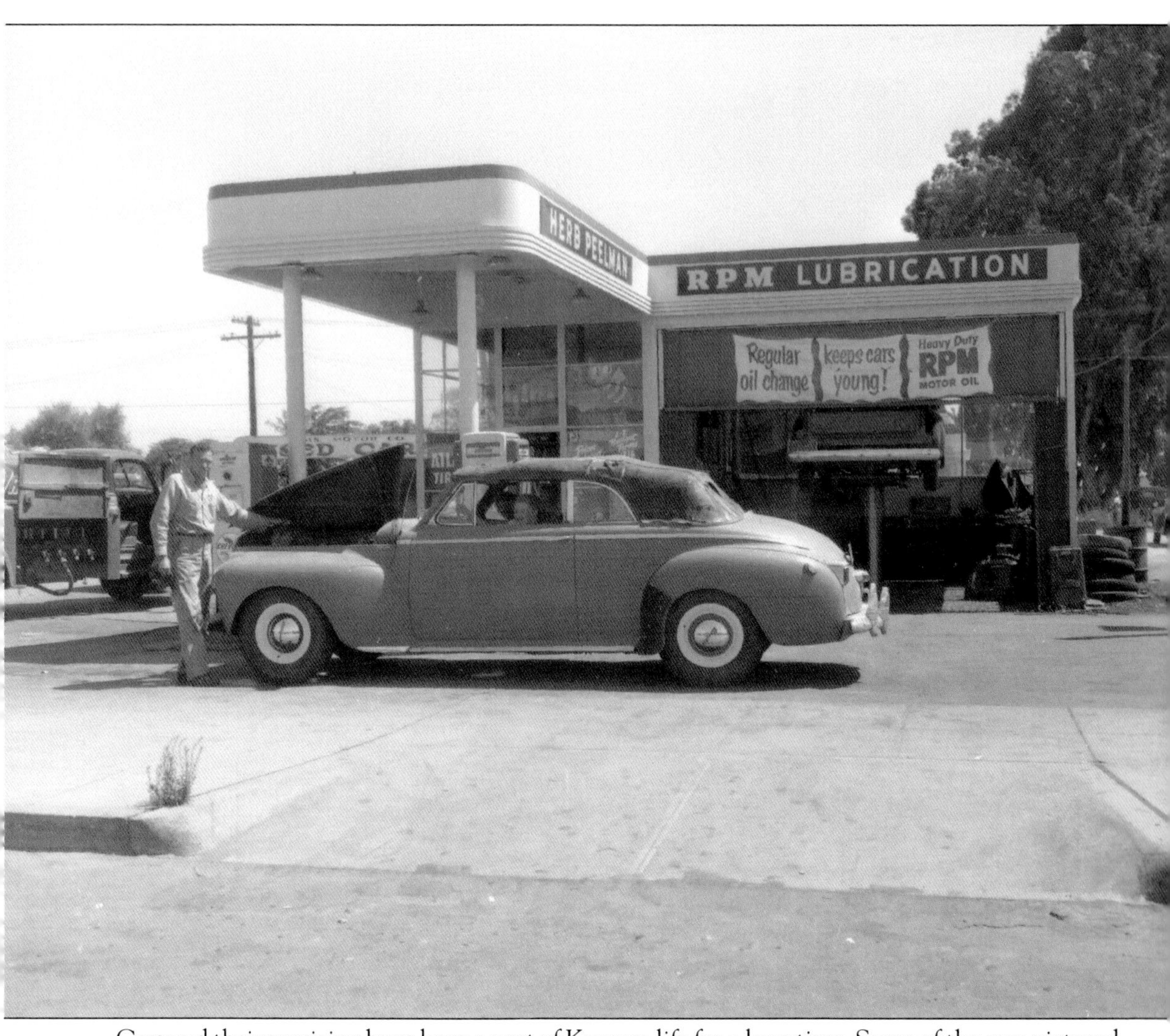

Cars and their servicing have been a part of Kerman life for a long time. Some of the cars pictured in this book have been restored by their original owners and can still be seen on the streets of Kerman today. Old-time Kermanites Vernon May and Harry Pederson worked at Peelman's Service Station (pictured) when they were young men. Pederson eventually become mayor of Kerman.

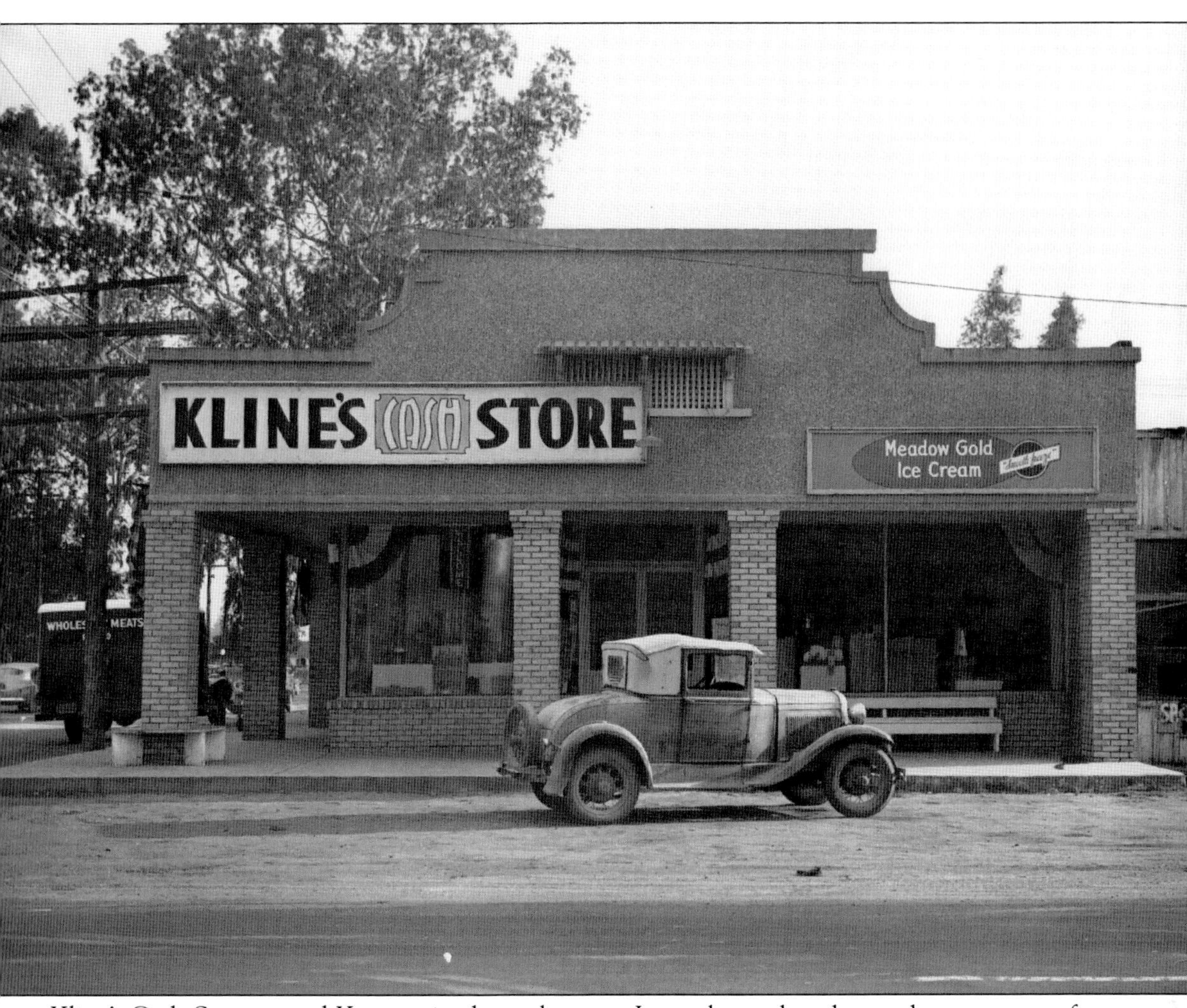

Kline's Cash Store served Kerman in the early years. It was located at the southwest corner of Madera Avenue and Whitesbridge Road.

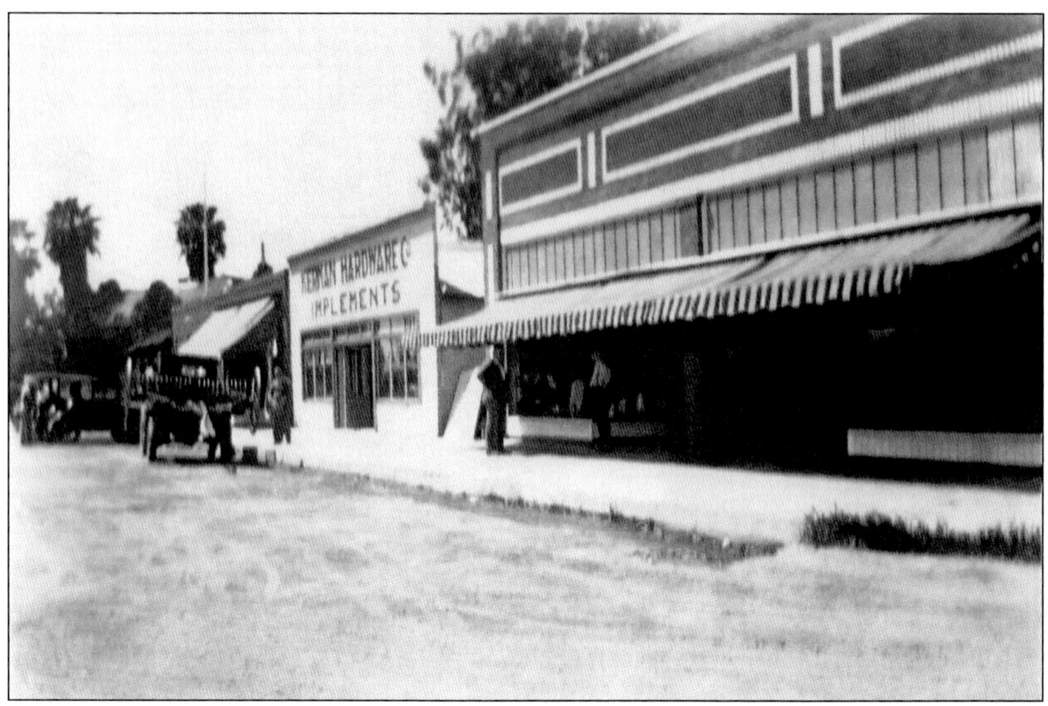

In the old days, everyone was a do-it-yourselfer, and the local hardware store was where one went for supplies for those projects. Below, wood stoves for sale are pictured inside one of these stores. The hardware store and five-and-dime were descendants of the old general store. In the days before Internet shopping, small-town residents had the world's goods brought to them in places like Kerman Hardware.

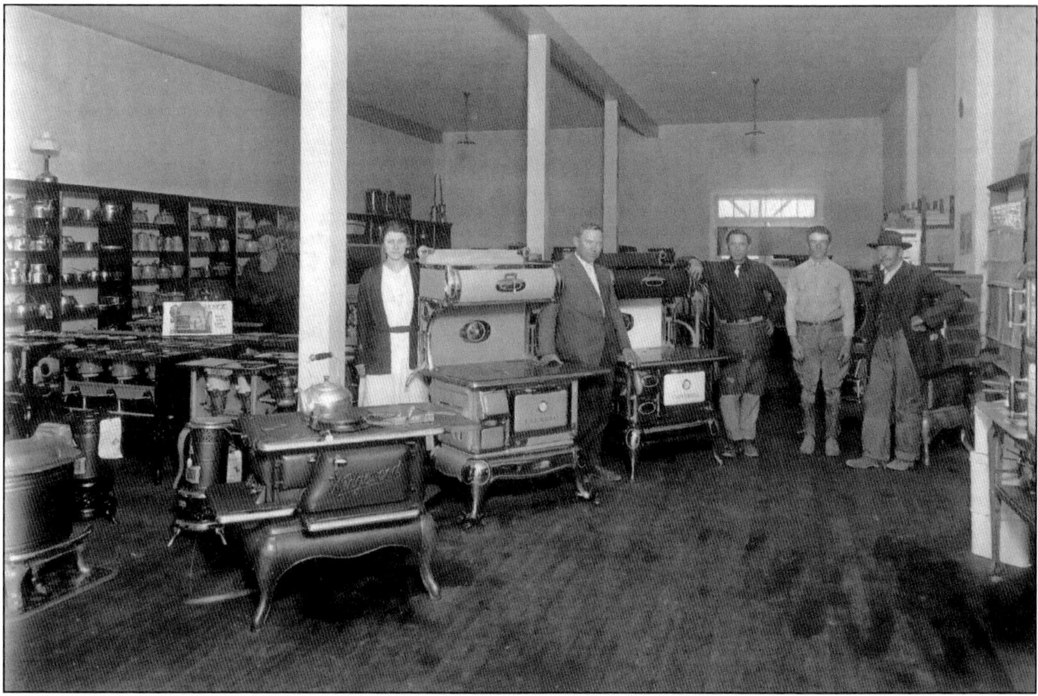

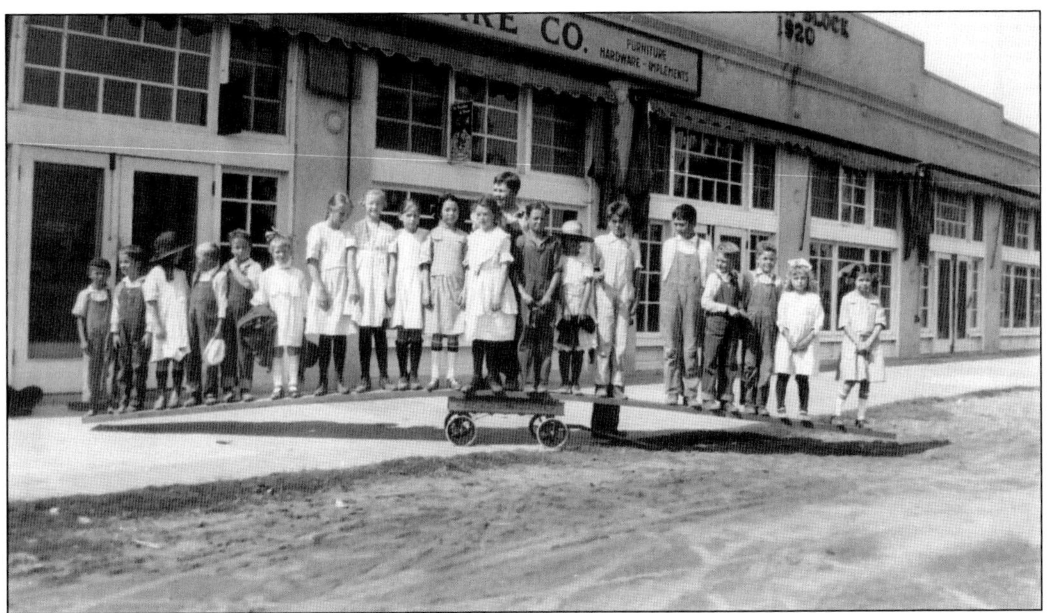

It was not all work, even at the hardware or lumber stores. Pictured above is an amazing acrobatic feat. All of these children had to be still at the same moment to maintain balance. Below, generations of Kermanites have gone to Reno's for their hardware needs.

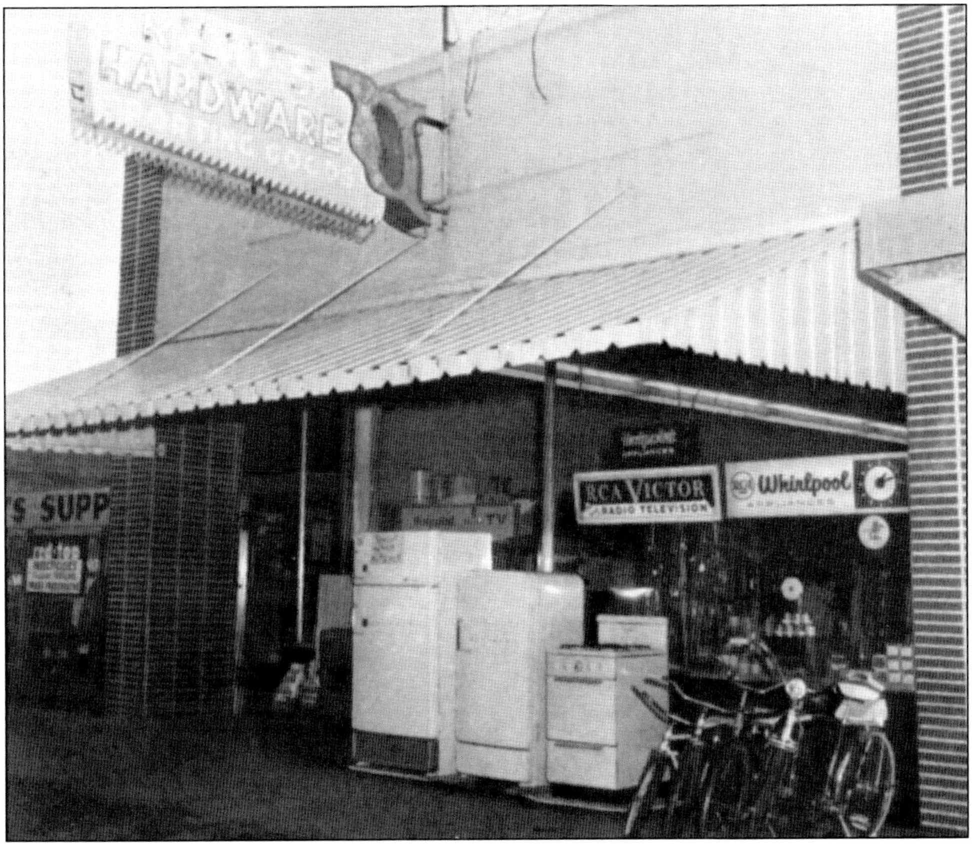

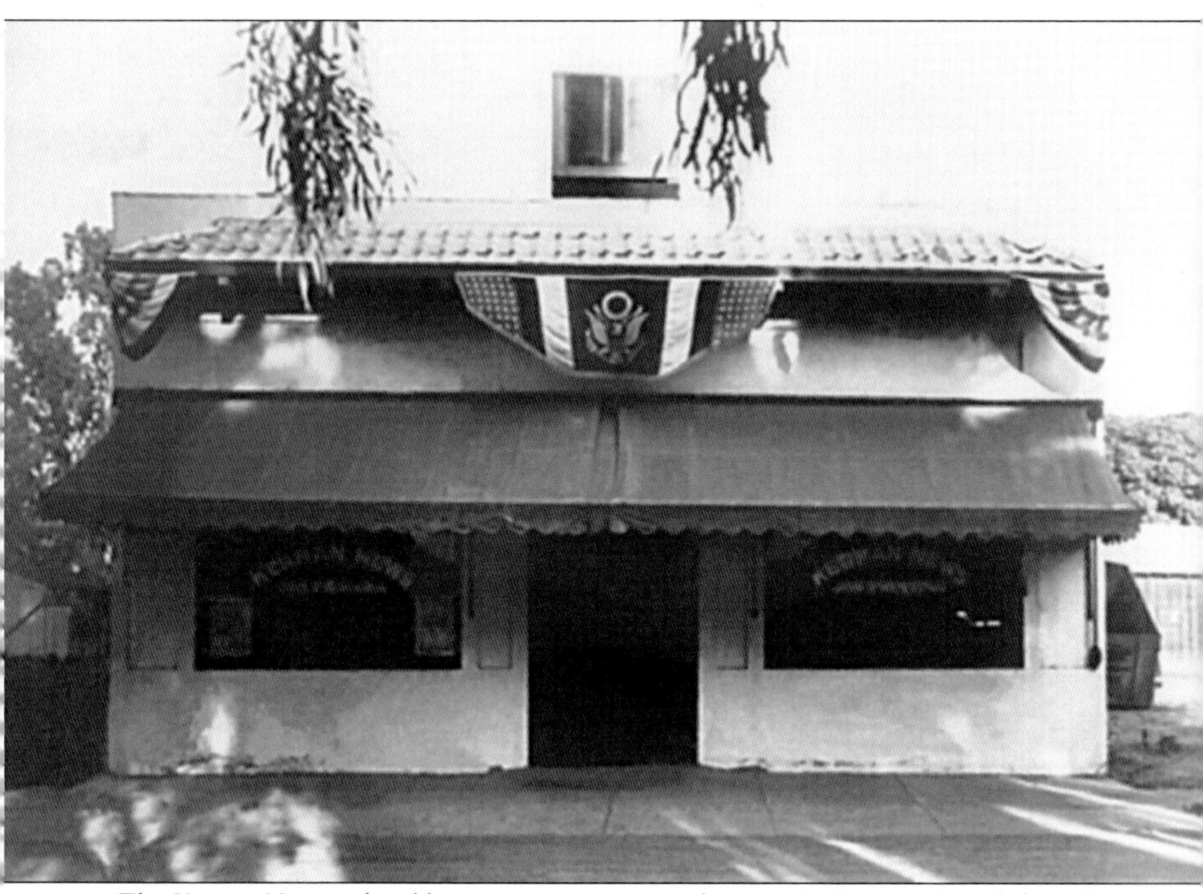

The *Kerman News* is the oldest continuous running business in Kerman. Founded in 1906, it has faithfully reported on events in town for over a century. The first office was on the edge of Plaza Park and then it moved uptown. The world has changed quite a bit, but the *Kerman News* is still here.

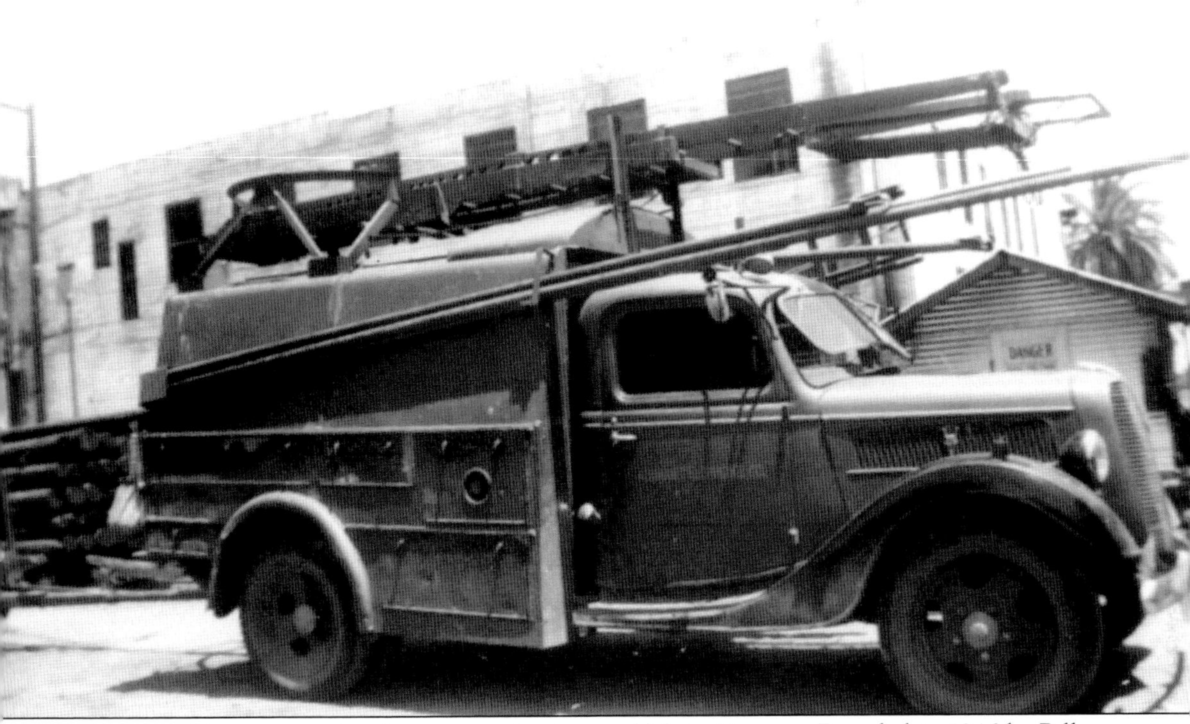

Kerman Telephone is another business at the heart of life in Kerman. Founded in 1946 by Bill and Katie Sebastian, the phone company has grown beyond Kerman and beyond telephones, but is still run by members of the Sebastian family. The family and employees of Kerman telephone generously support many of the activities in Kerman's schools and community.

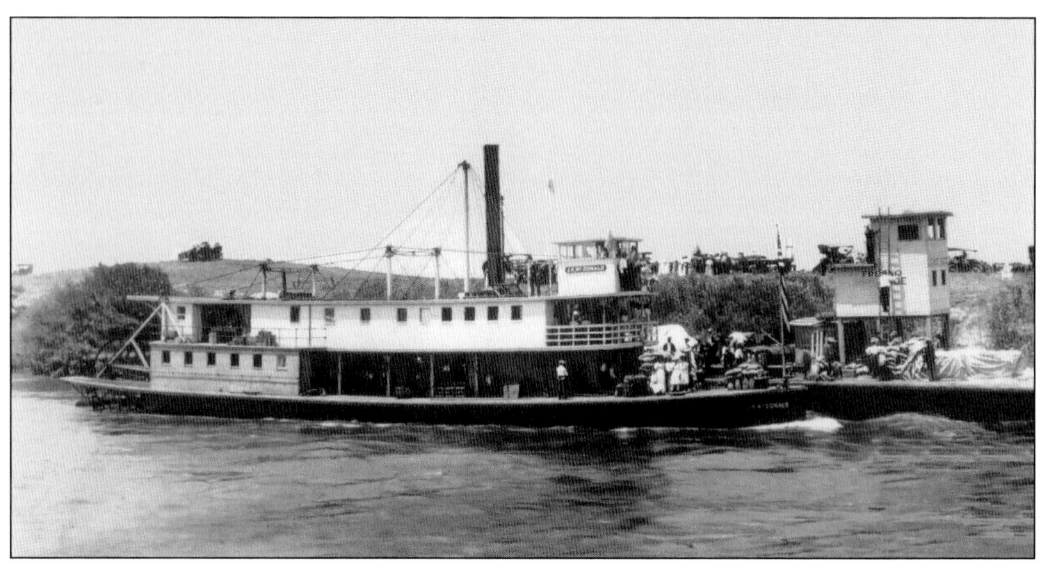

Steamboats worked the San Joaquin River near Kerman from 1852 to 1896. On June 13, 1911, Captain C.P. McCurty brought the *J.R. McDonald* up the river to Skaggs bridge towing a barge. The barge, named *East Side*, was to be the dock for restored ferry service to Kerman. On the way back down river, the *J.R. McDonald* got stuck for a few hours on a sandbar. It floated free when irrigation district managers opened the gates to allow more water flow, but that was the end of riverboat service to Kerman; however, the story has a happy ending. The people who met at the riverside that June day decided to make a tradition of it, and thus began what became the Kerman Harvest Festival, held each year in September.

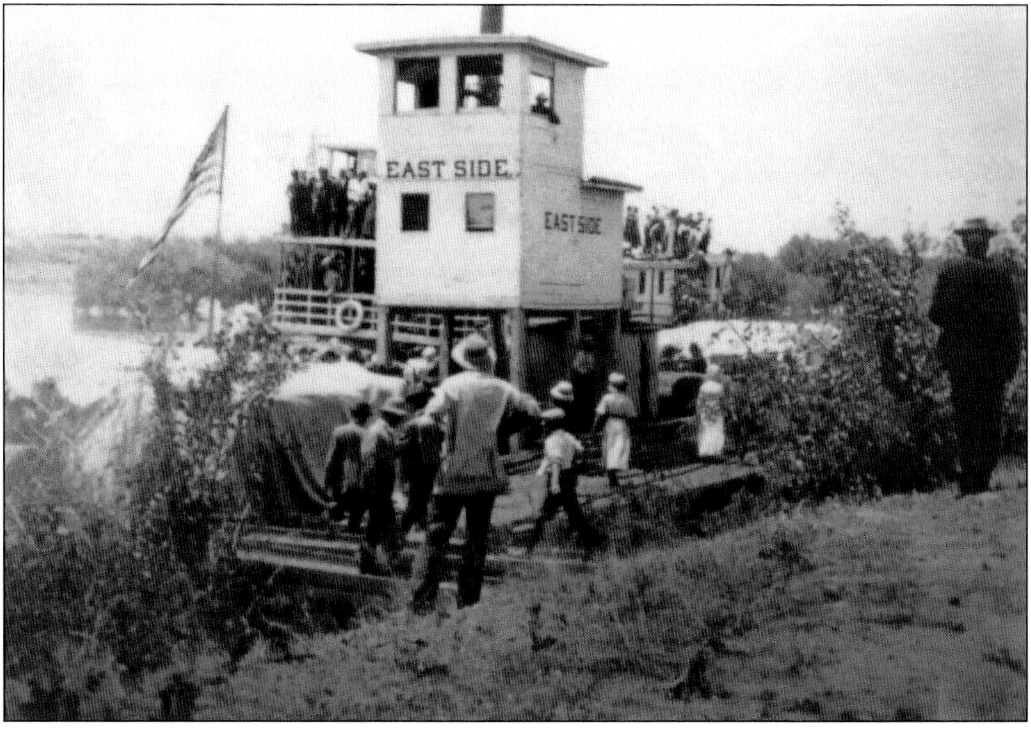

Two

Farming

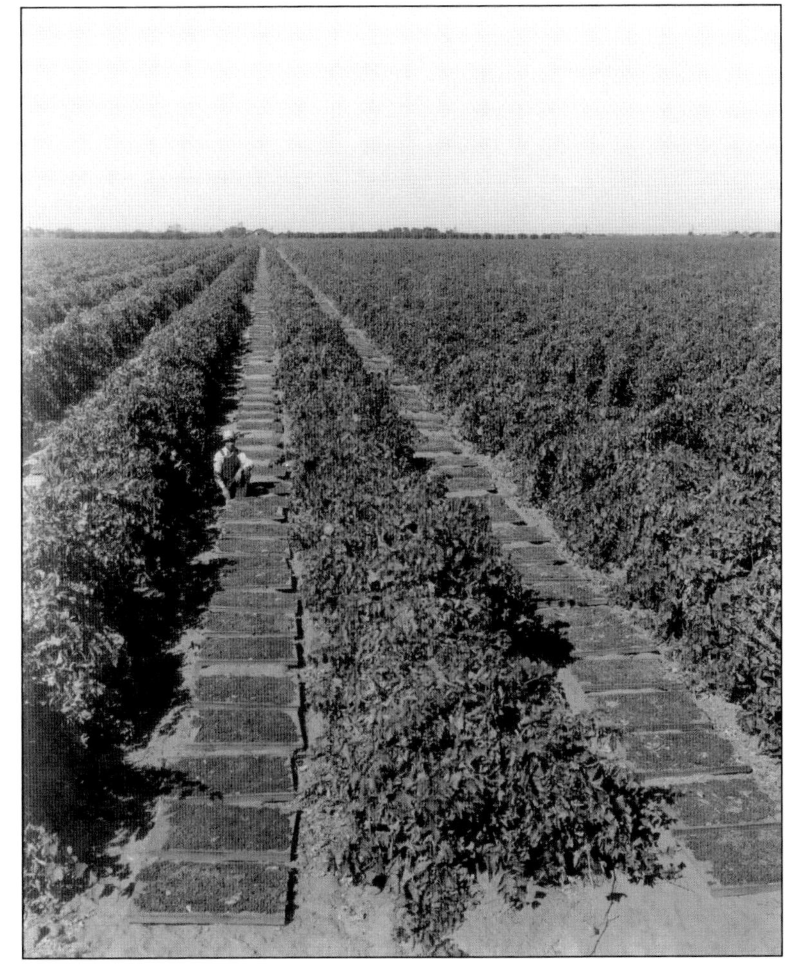

While Kerman began as a train stop, it has always been a farming community. Abundant sunshine and a Mediterranean climate make for fabulous farming conditions. Over the years, different crops have dominated as market conditions changed. Among the stable crops over the years are cotton, grapes, alfalfa, and dairy. Over 300 different crops are grown in the valley, with many of them found here in Kerman. Here, grapes are drying in wooden trays.

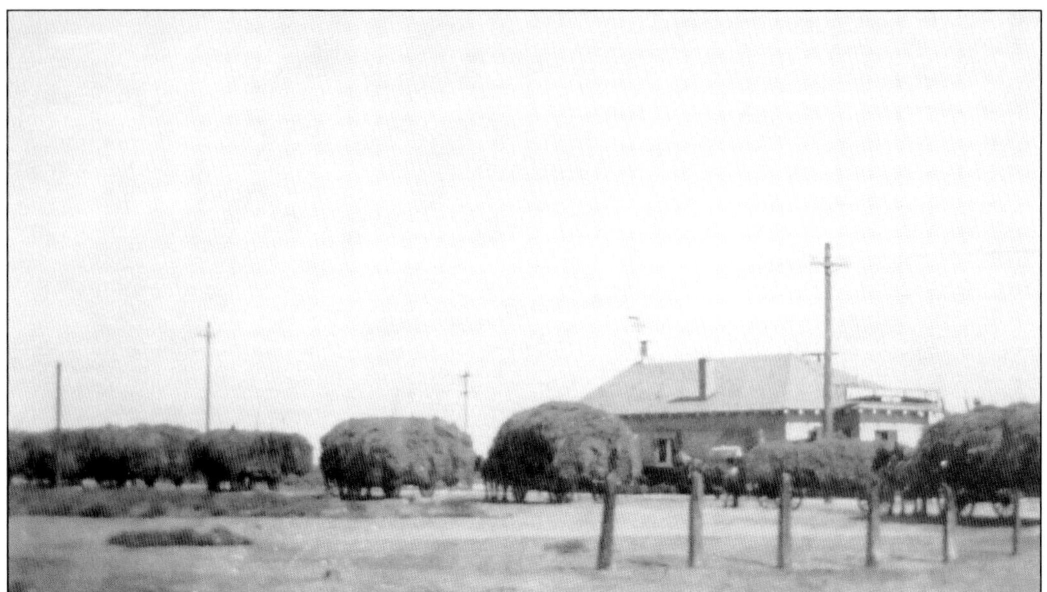

One of the first crops grown in the area was alfalfa. Horses and mules were still used in the fields in Kerman's early years. Dairy production also began in the early years, so there was plenty of demand for alfalfa as a livestock feed. These days we are used to hay in bales, but for many years, hay was hauled loose and thrown up into barns by pitchfork. Pictured above are wagons of loose hay waiting to be weighed and delivered. Below, hay waits to be baled at the yard.

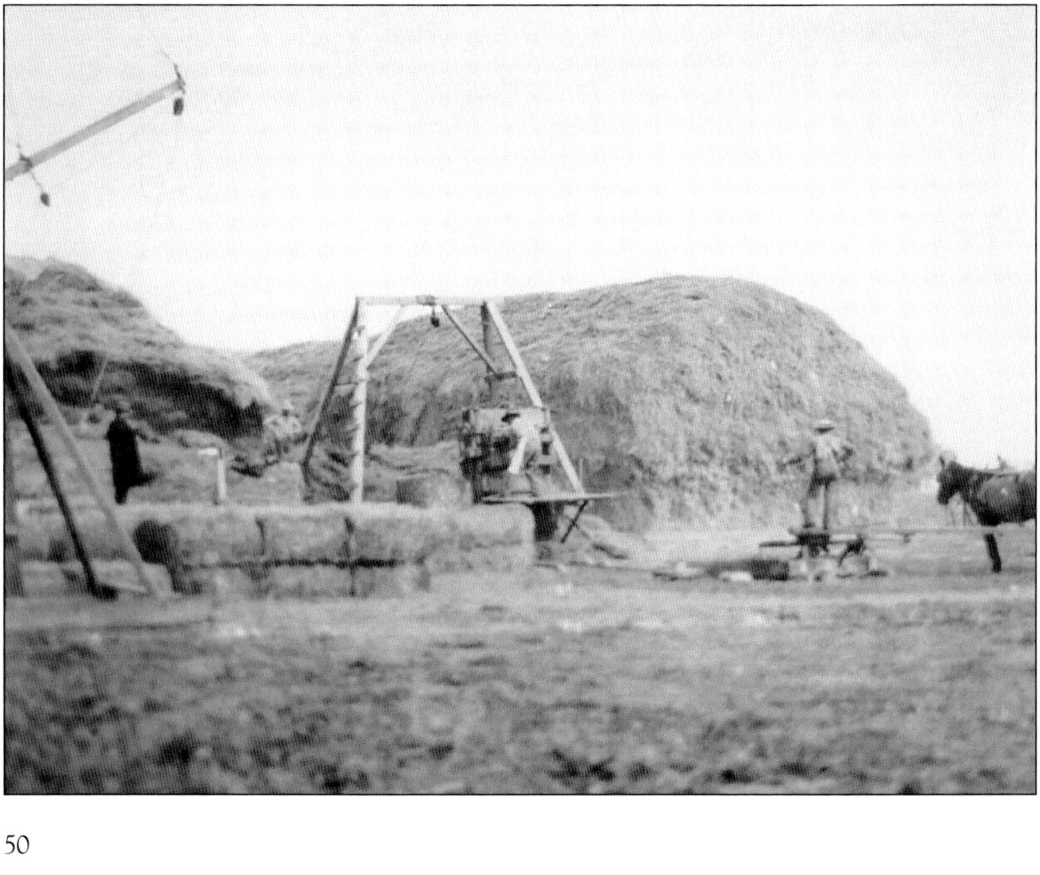

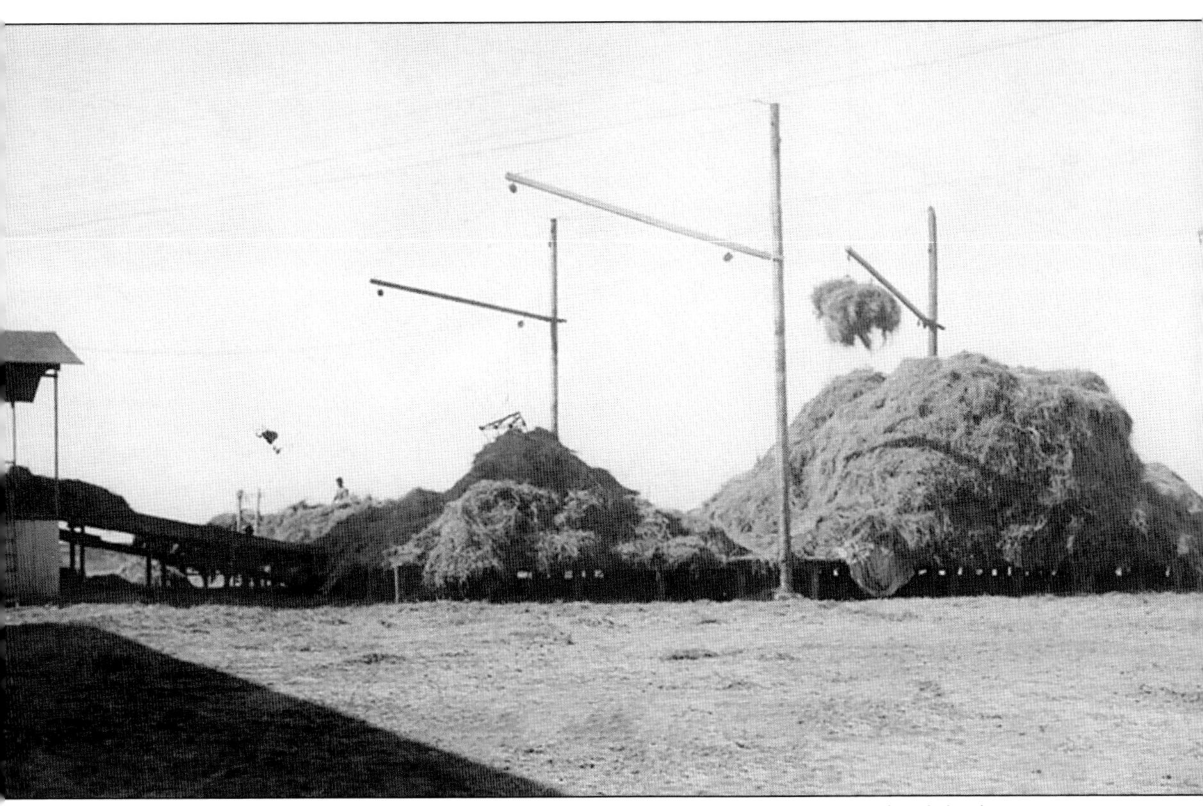

Even though baling equipment had been invented in the 19th century, much of the hay grown in Kerman's early years was loaded and shipped loose. It was then pitched up in to barns by hand. The hay was stored in the top of the barn, then pitched down to the cows below. Hay is grown during the hot summer months, and one farmer's son remembers that at the end of the day, his jeans could stand up by themselves after being soaked through with sweat.

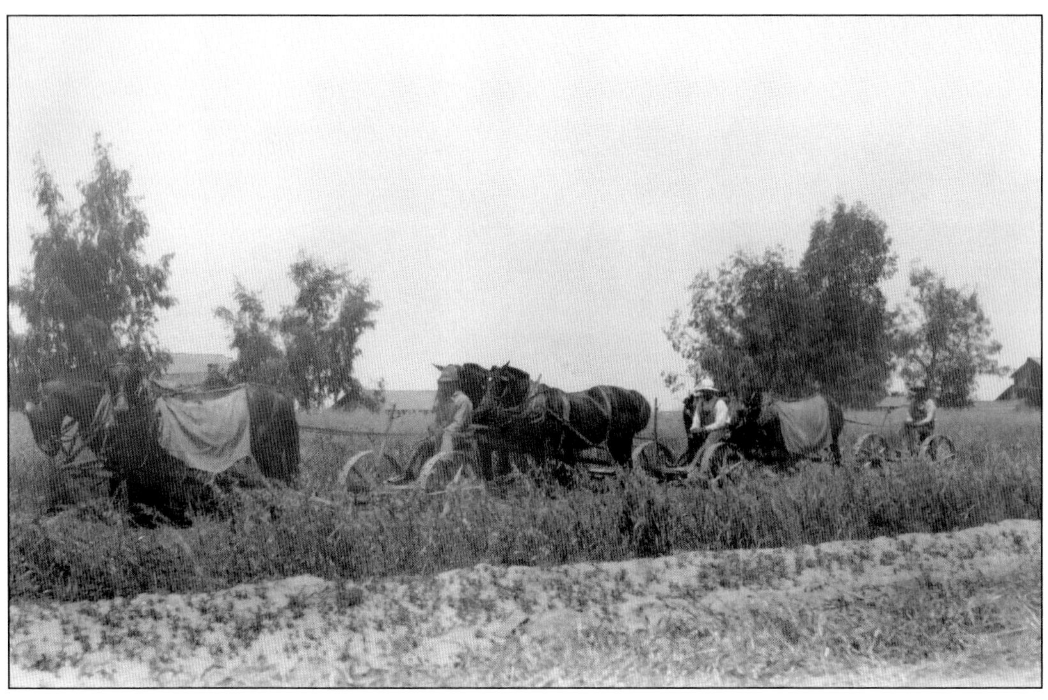

All that hay was put to work on local farms. For centuries, farming was done by horsepower and manpower. Here, three men and three horses plow together. Before steam power or diesel engines, this is how work was done. Below, two horses pull a plow in a vineyard.

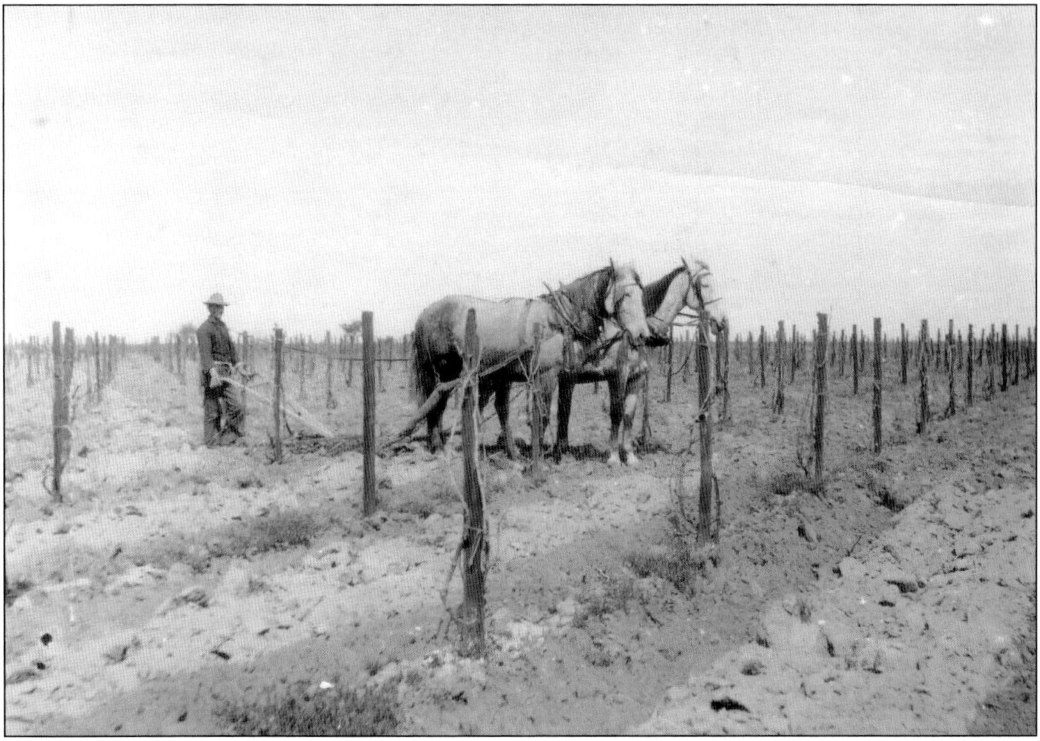

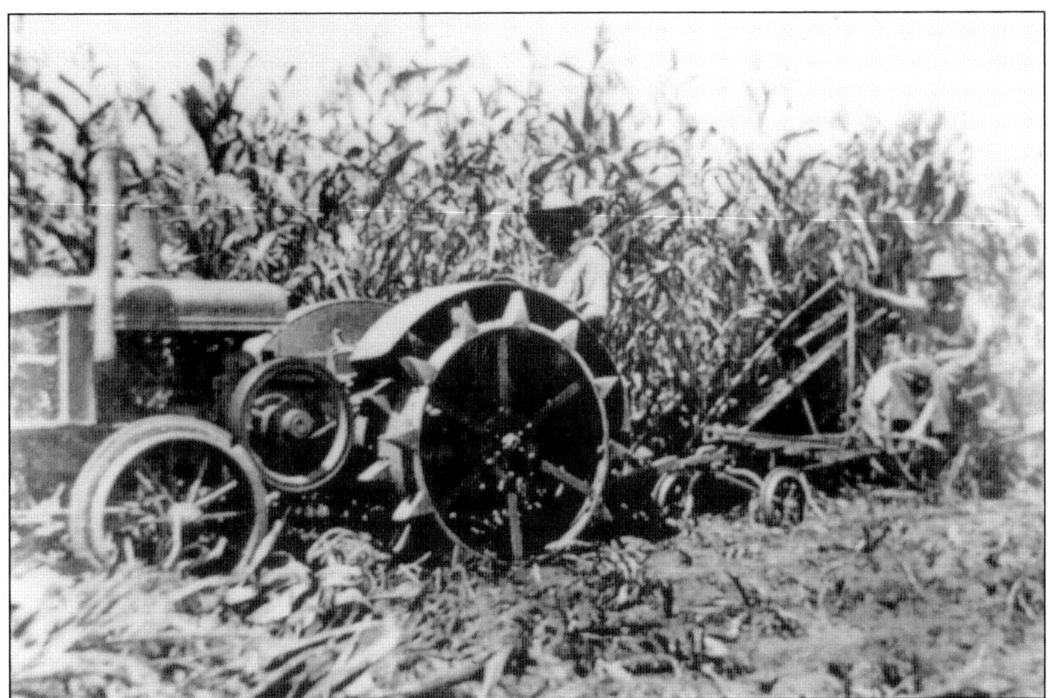

Farm equipment has seen many changes over the past century. One of the first major shifts was from horse to steam power. The tractor below is from 1908. In addition to the steam engine, note the steel wheels. Steel wheels are great for traction, but of course, they cannot be driven on the road from one field to another. They probably are not as smooth riding as rubber tires, either.

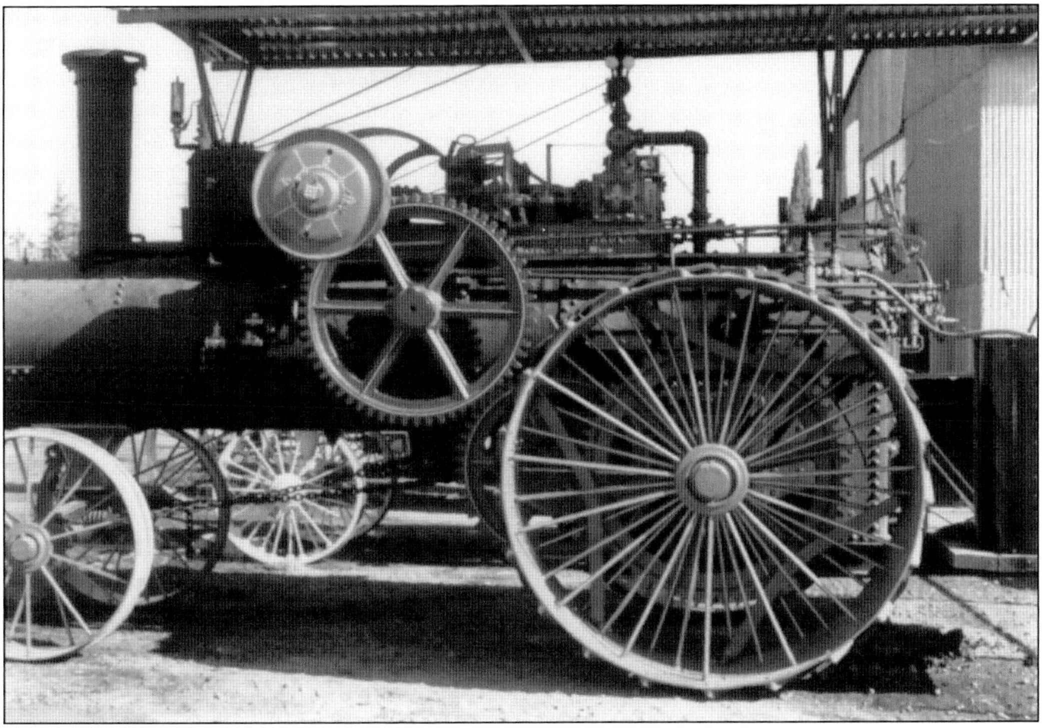

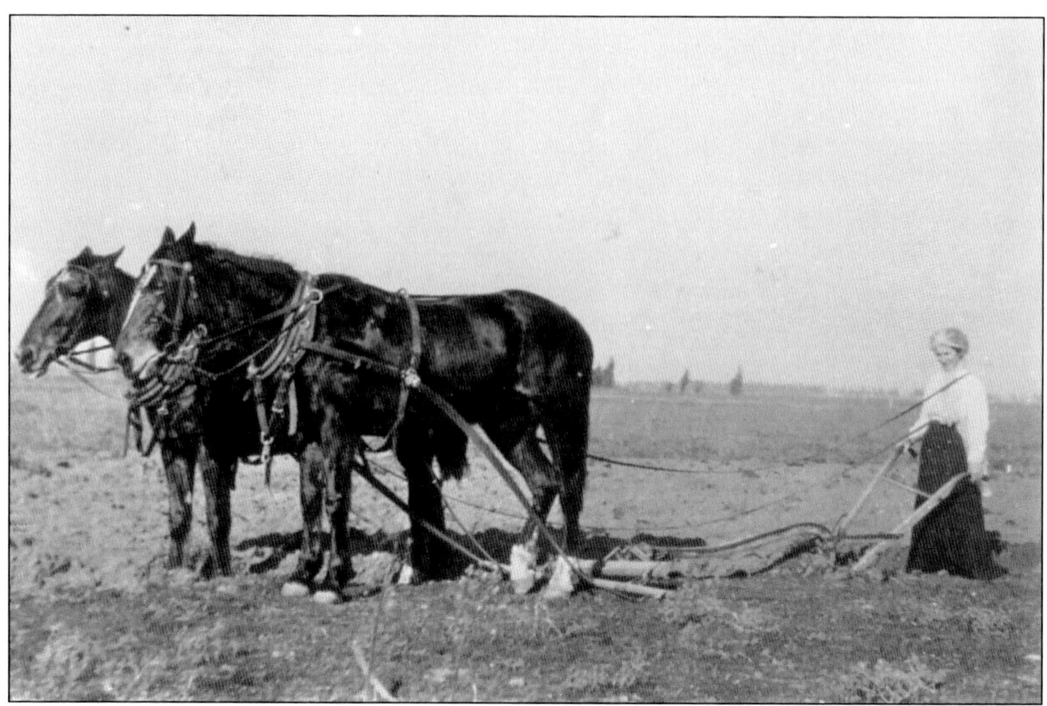

Women have always been a key part of keeping the farm going. Pictured above is a woman with a two-horse team and a plow. That would be a full day's work for the strongest of men. New equipment, like the steam-powered land leveler seen below, was a welcome change from horse-drawn implements. The first tracked equipment, like the leveler below, were created a few hours north in the Sacramento Delta.

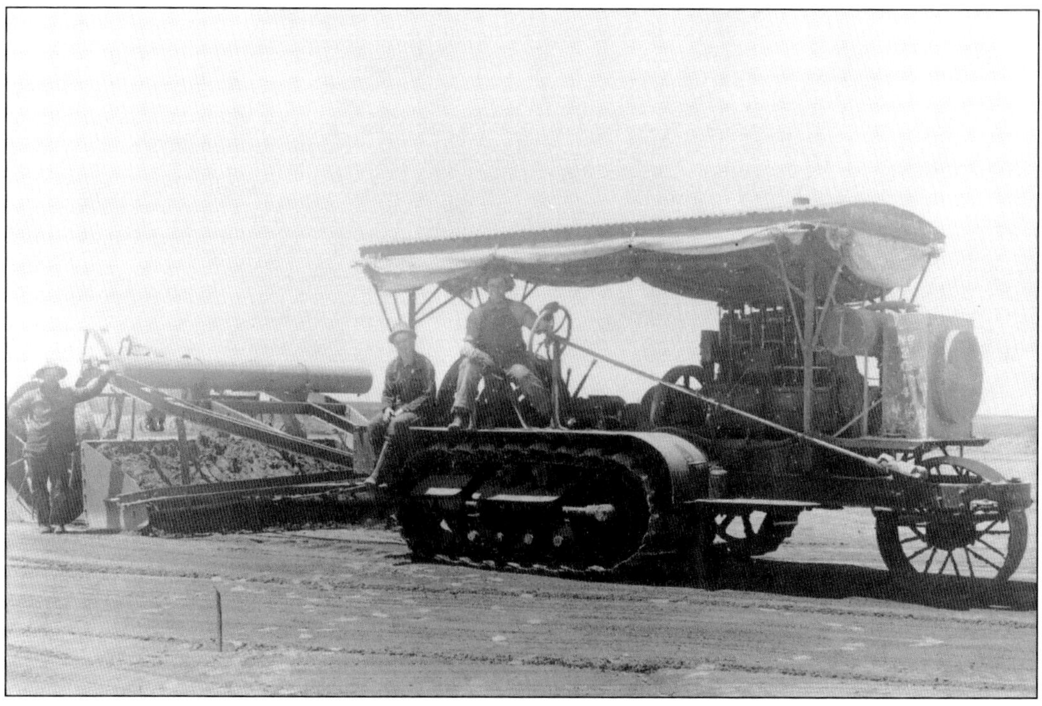

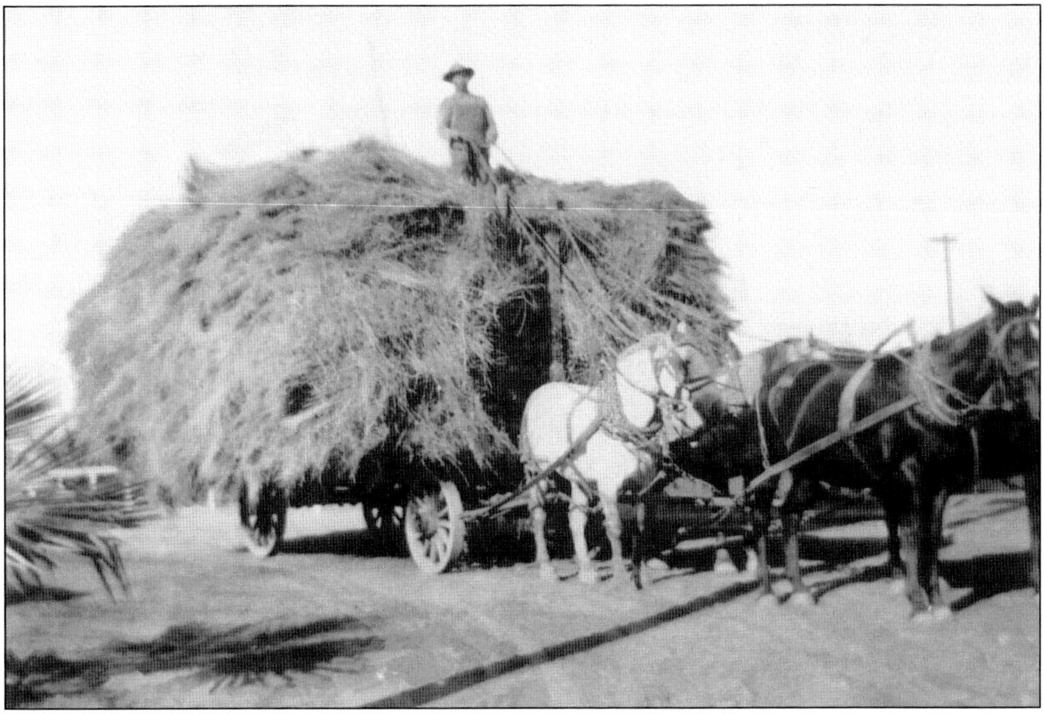

At first, loose hay was moved by horse-drawn wagons. In later years, farm trucks moved hay. As late as the 1940s, it was not unusual to see wagons of loose hay moving down the middle of the road, blocking traffic in both directions. Produce was also moved from the field to packing sheds by horse-drawn wagon.

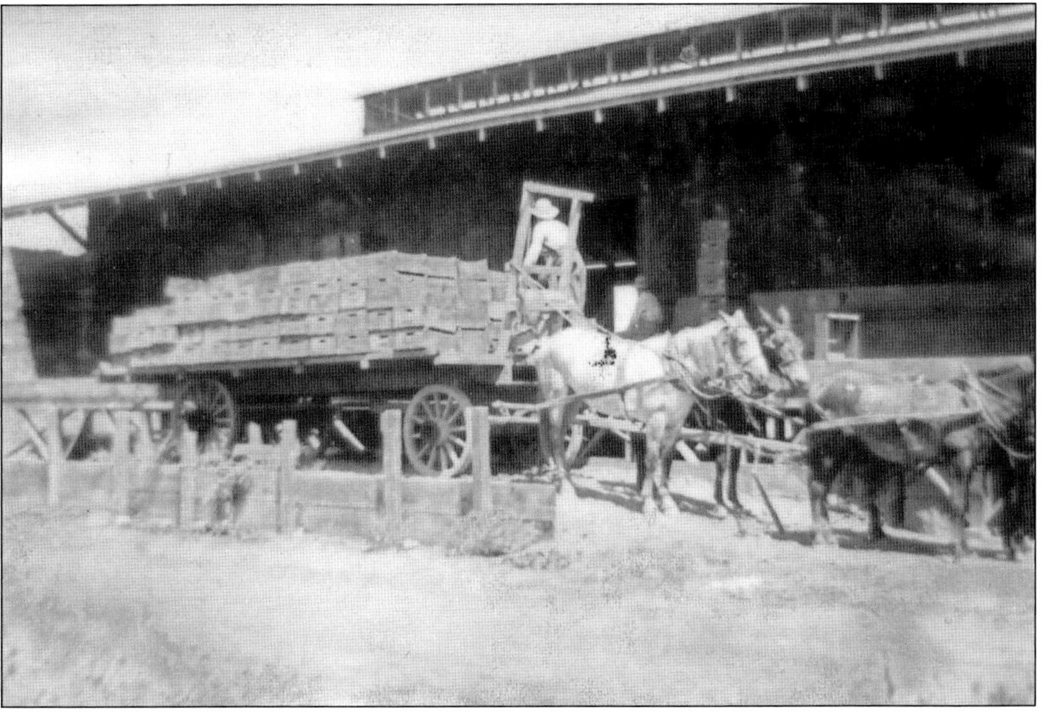

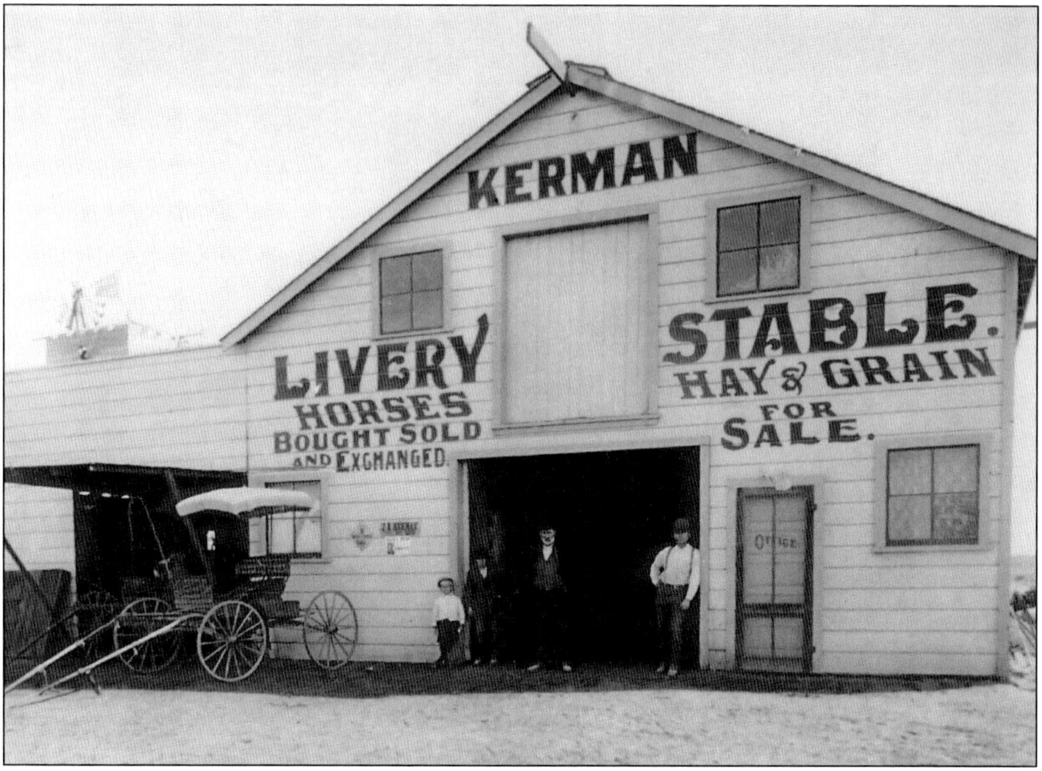

Of course, all that horsepower required feed and supplies. Since everyone used horses, the Kerman Livery Stable was one of the hubs of social life in the early days.

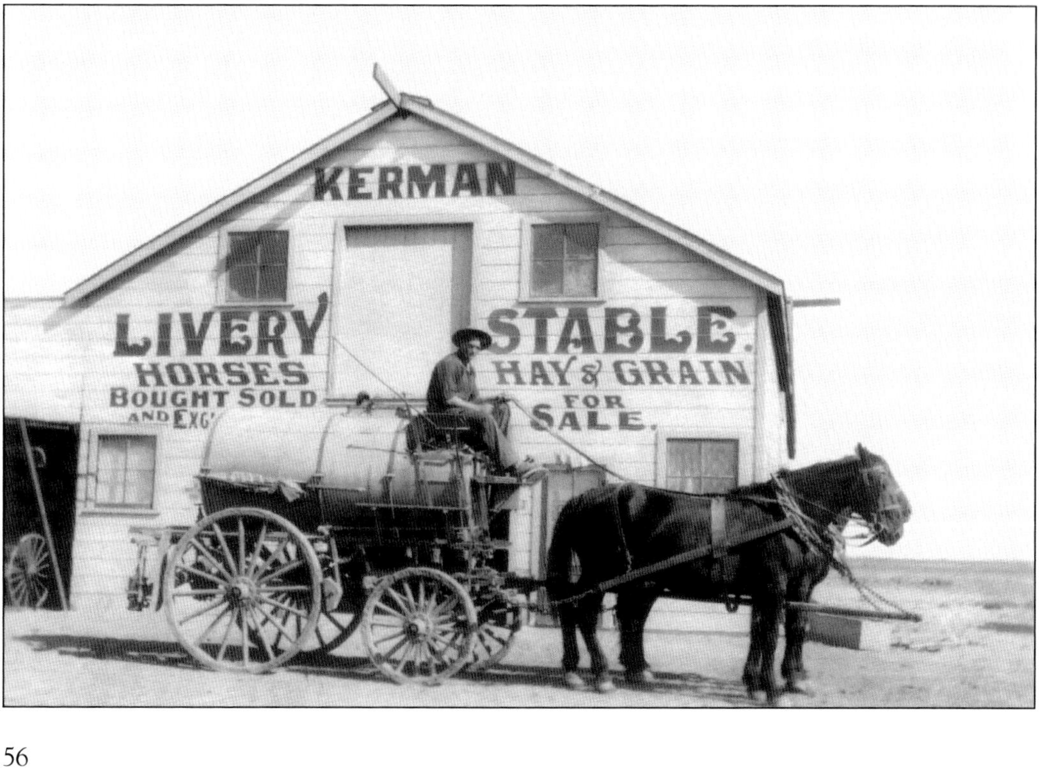

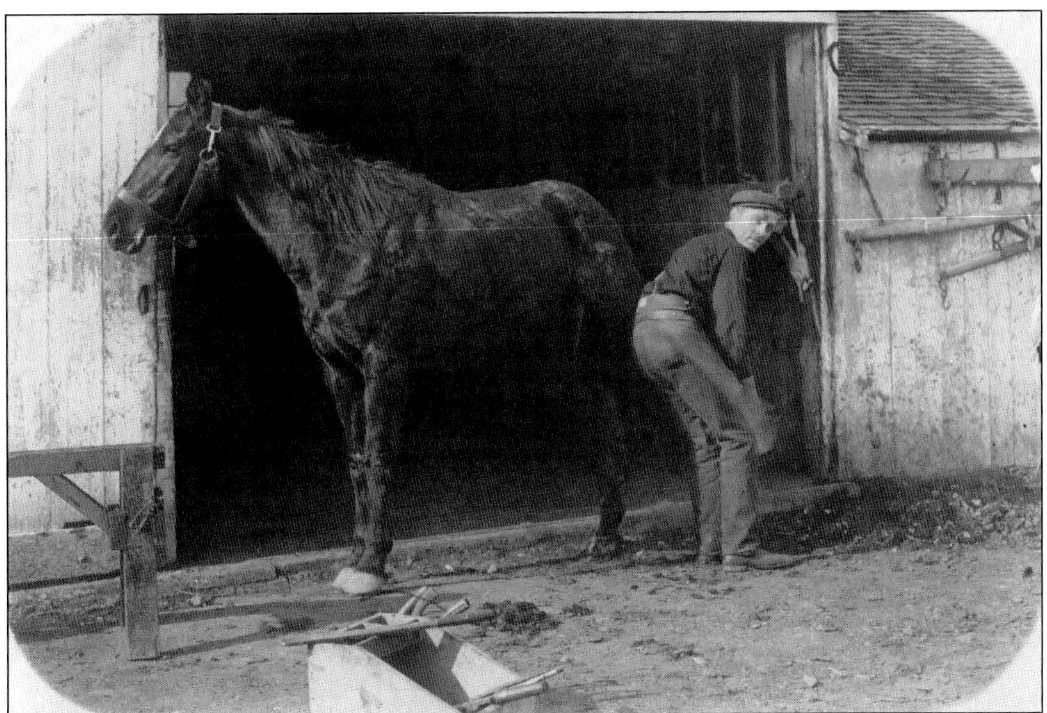

All those horses went through a lot of horseshoes. George Helsem moved from Los Banos, where he had been the head blacksmith for the Miller and Lux Land Company. He and his brother Charly opened a blacksmith shop in Kerman. In recent years, the original shop was moved into town, next to the original Kerman Elementary School. A mural on the side of the shop celebrates Kerman's early years.

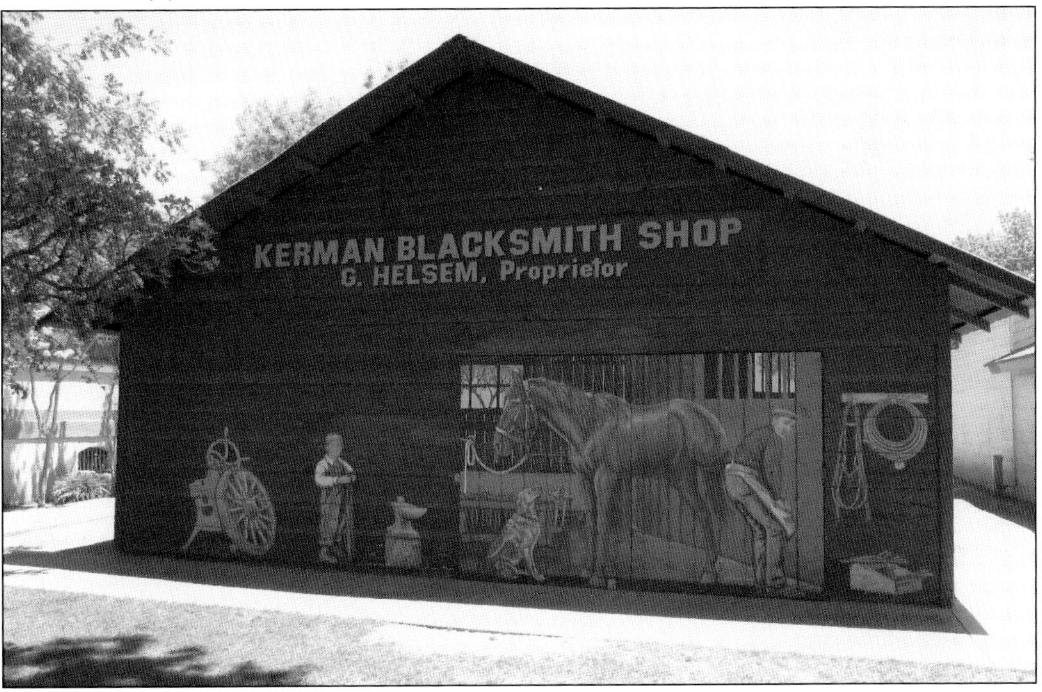

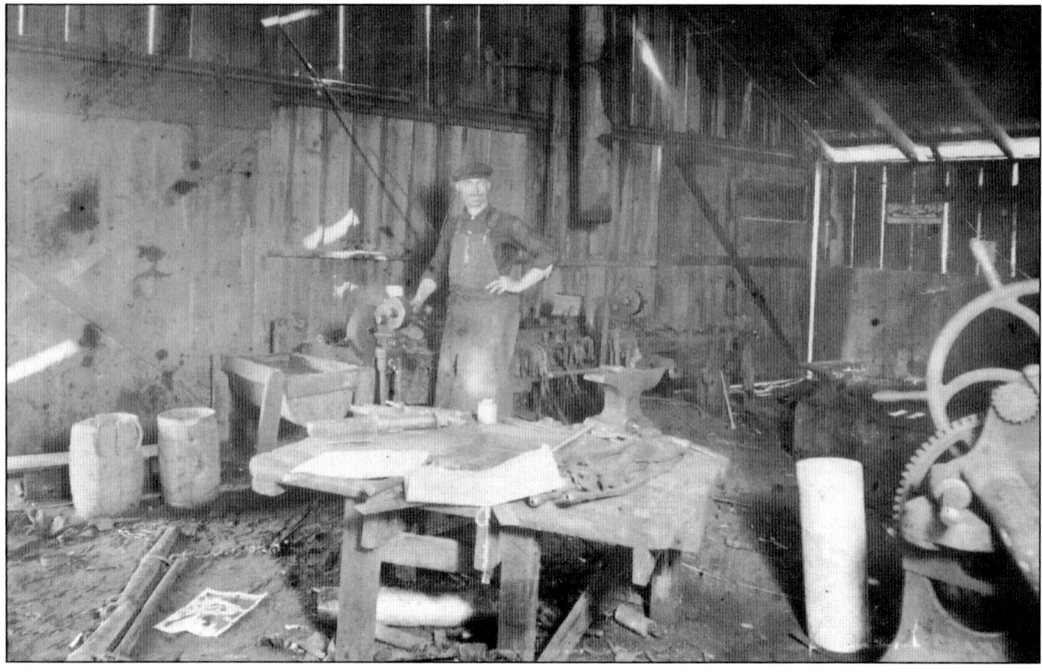

Above, George Helsem is pictured inside his blacksmith shop. Note the rough plank walls and lack of insulation; it must have gotten warm in the summer. Pictured below is an early motorcar. Blacksmiths did repairs on these horseless carriages, just as they did for their horse-drawn predecessors.

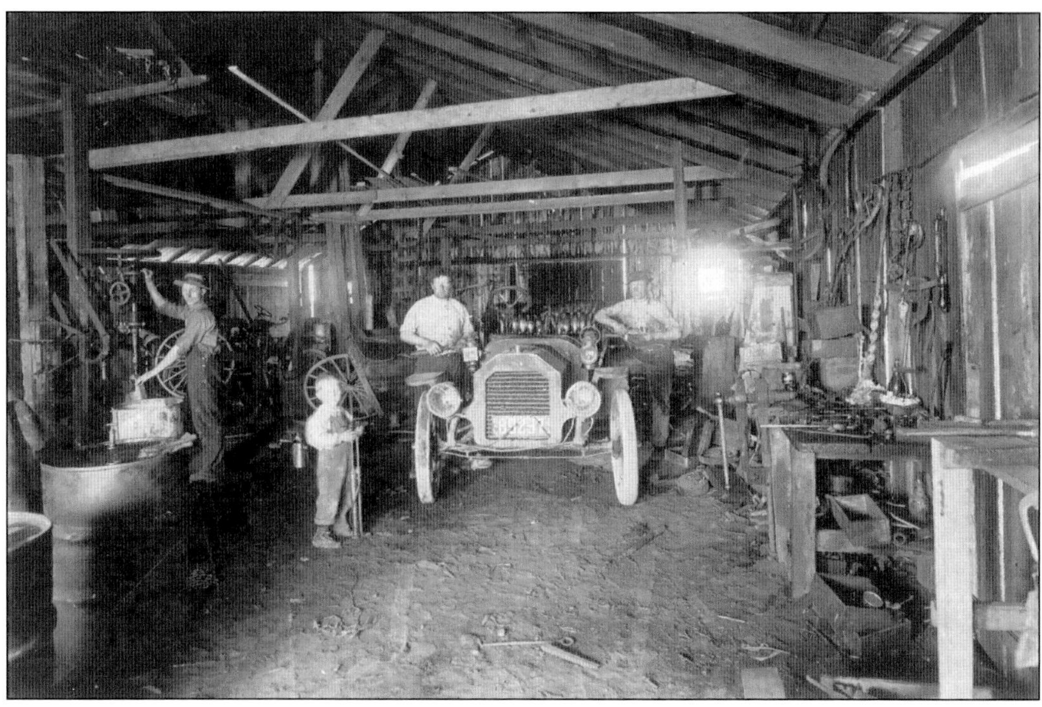

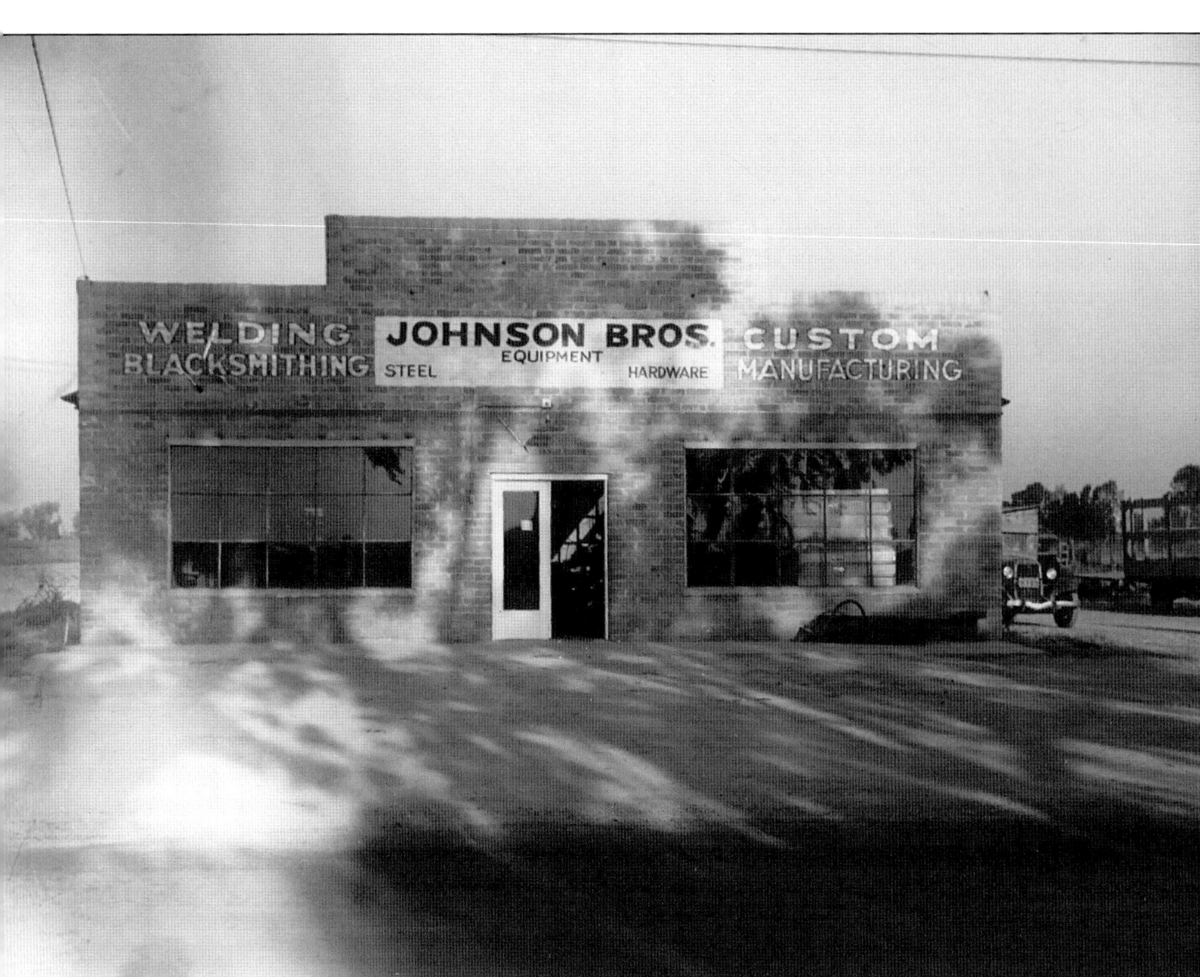

George Helsem was succeeded by the Johnson brothers. Welding was added to the list of services and eventually replaced blacksmithing. In the 1940s, the Johnson Brothers opened a shop on Madera Avenue. Welding shops are still important in farm country. While most farmers can weld, they tend to leave the bigger projects to the professionals.

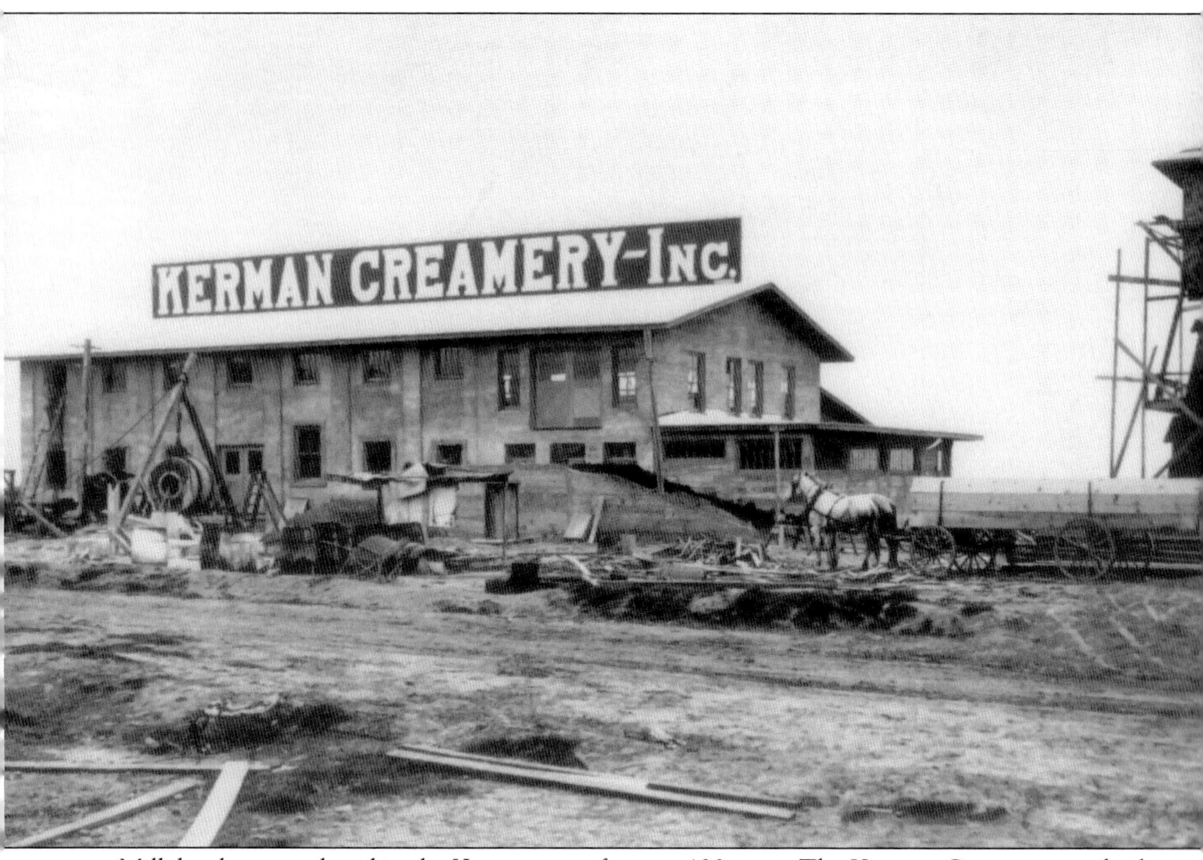

Milk has been produced in the Kerman area for over 100 years. The Kerman Creamery was built in 1904. Abundant sunshine, mild weather, and local alfalfa production attracted dairy families from the Azores, Denmark, and other places in Europe to bring their skills to Kerman and begin a new life.

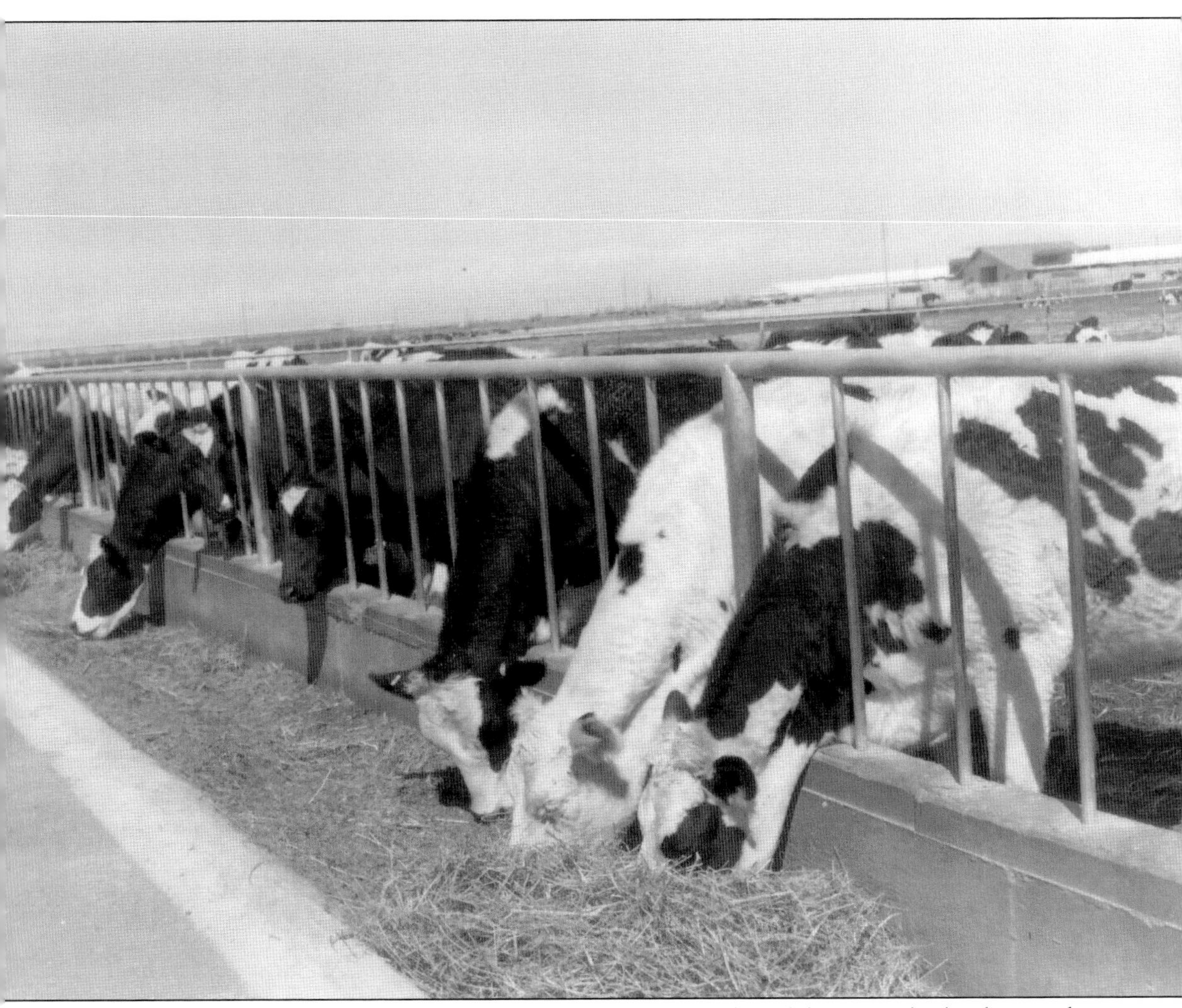

Cattle ranching in California goes back to the time of Spanish Californios. The land around Kerman was grazed by cattle before it was put under the plow or planted to become vineyards and orchards.

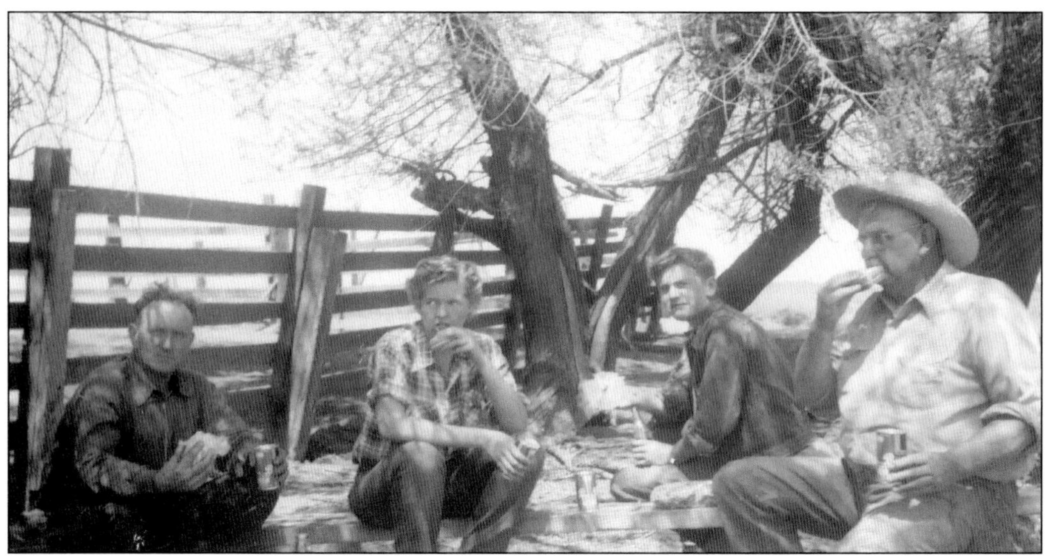

Roundups are traditionally known for big barbecues when the work is done. These feasts are known for some of the best cooking of the year. The tradition continues at many ranches around Kerman that still have end-of-year barbecues and also the Kerman Harvest Festival, where the whole community celebrates.

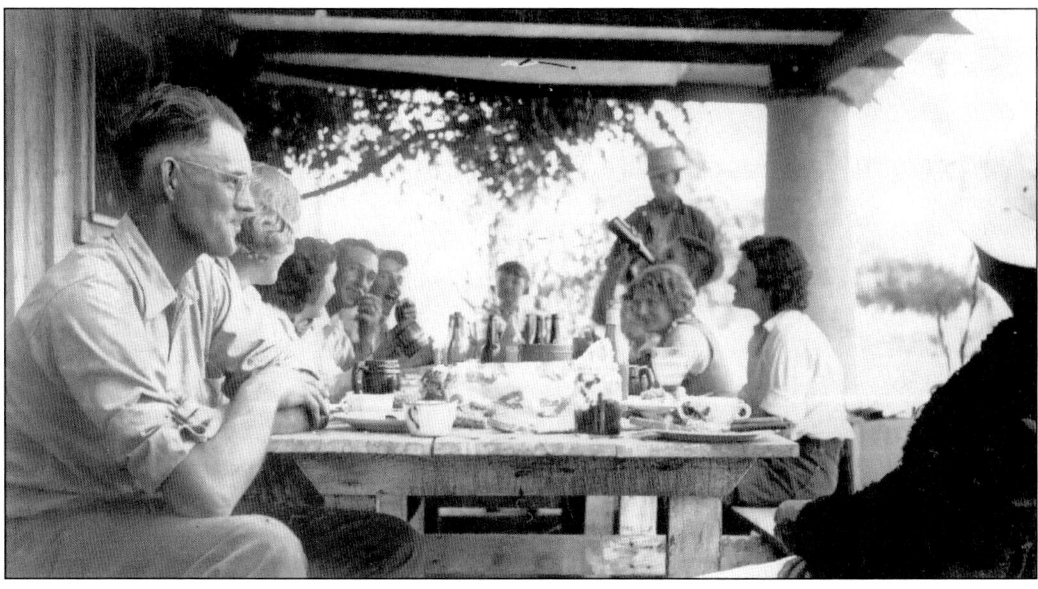

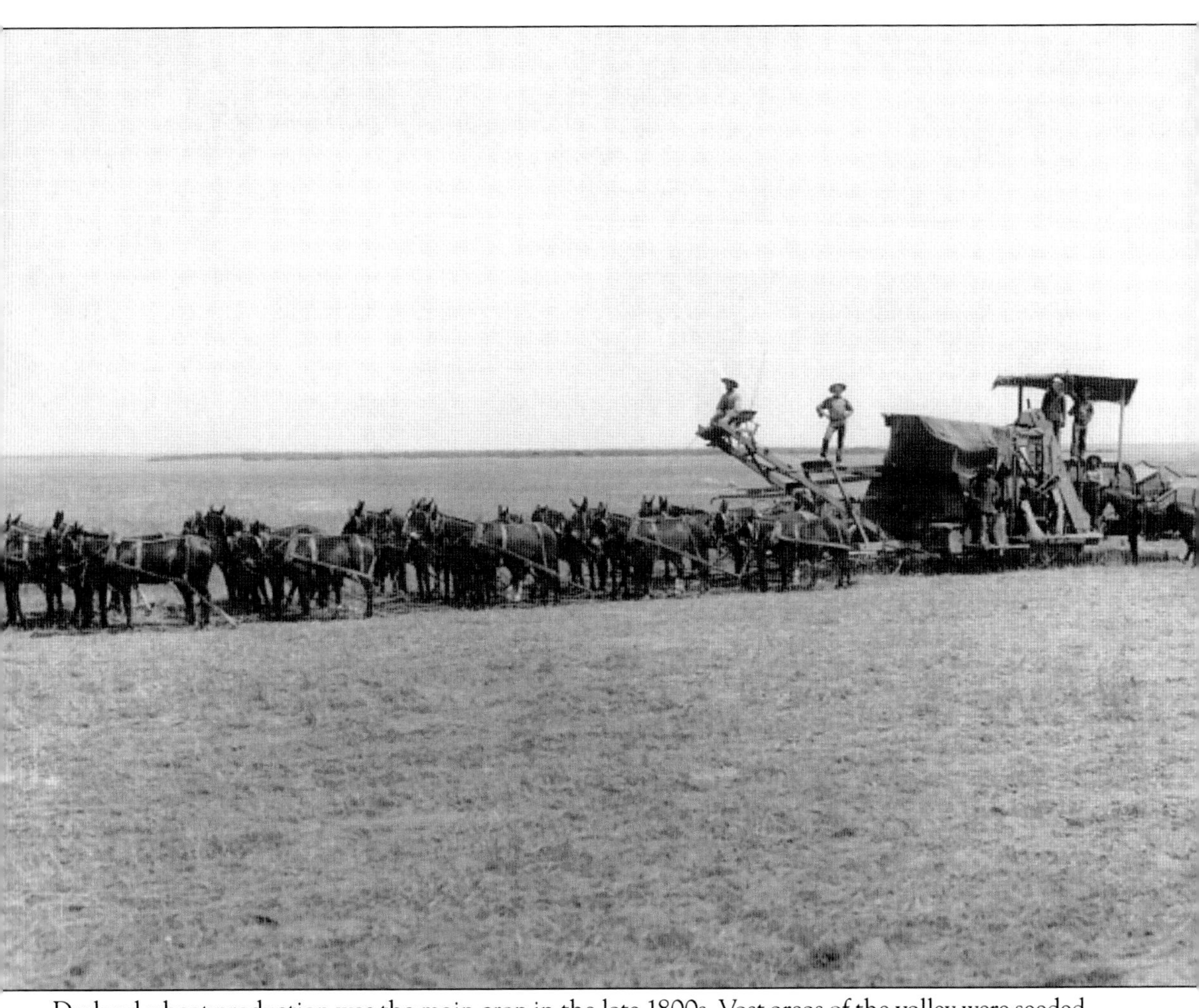

Dryland wheat production was the main crop in the late 1800s. Vast areas of the valley were seeded to wheat. Crews worked the fields with horse-drawn, steam-powered threshing machines.

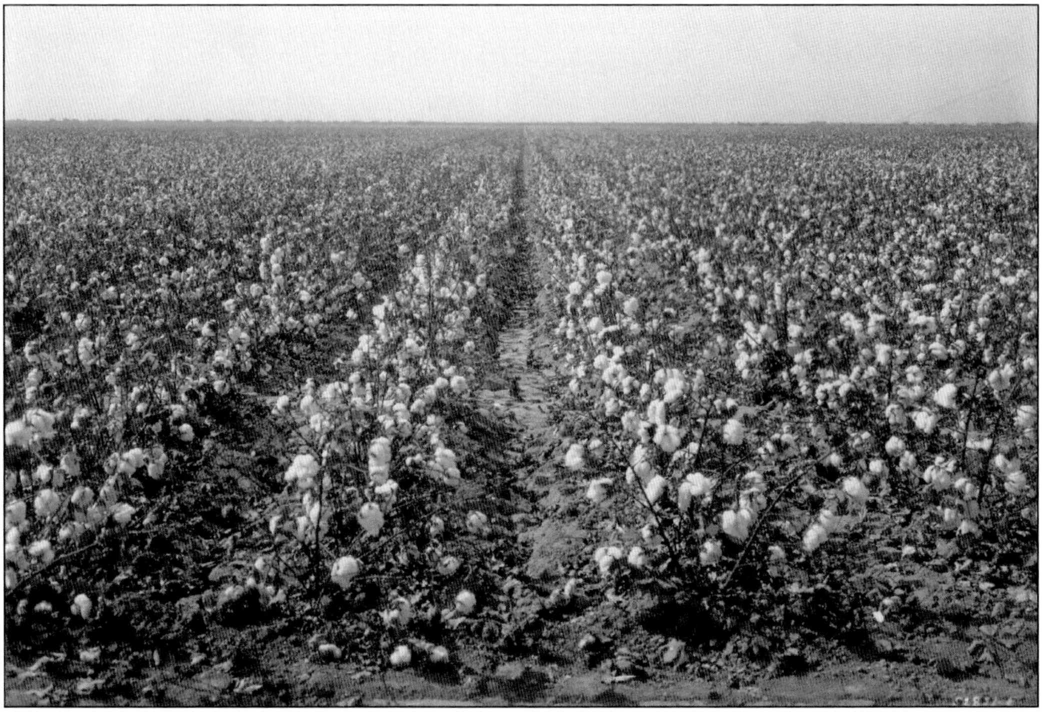

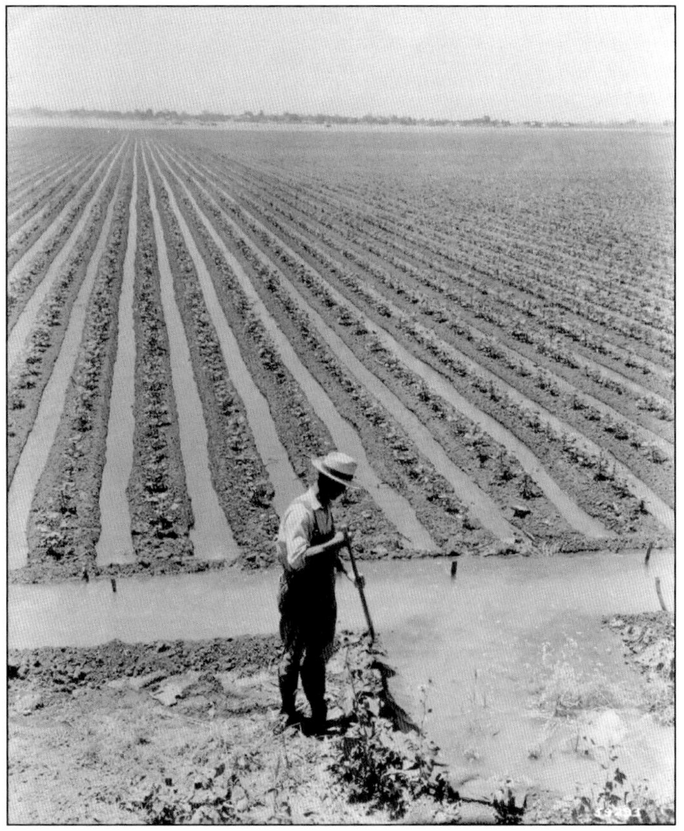

Cotton was grown in Kerman for generations before being slowly replaced with permanent crops like grapes and almonds. Cotton and alfalfa were grown in rotation, with cotton being grown for three years and then alfalfa for three years. As a legume, alfalfa built up the soil and fixed nitrogen for "king cotton."

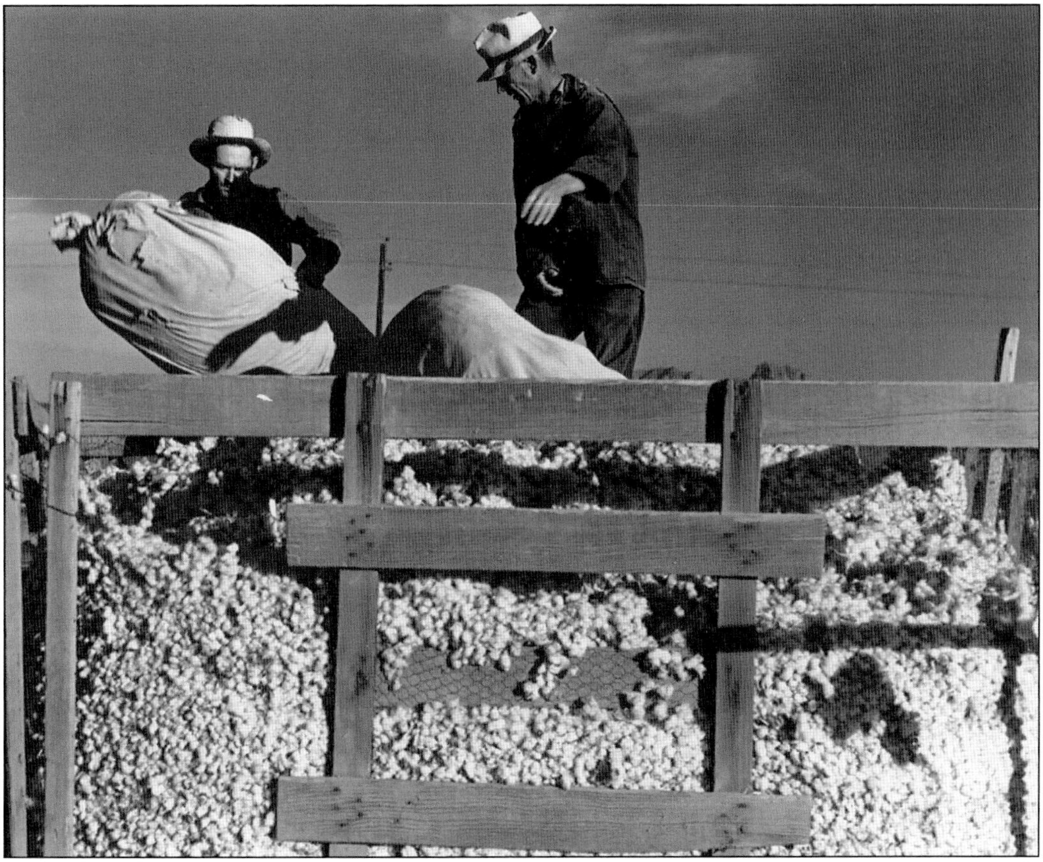

Before the advent of modern harvesting equipment, cotton harvesting was labor intensive. Hand-weeding crews would work through the area during the early summer. Labor camps would spring up in the fall and stay through harvest before moving to the next crop.

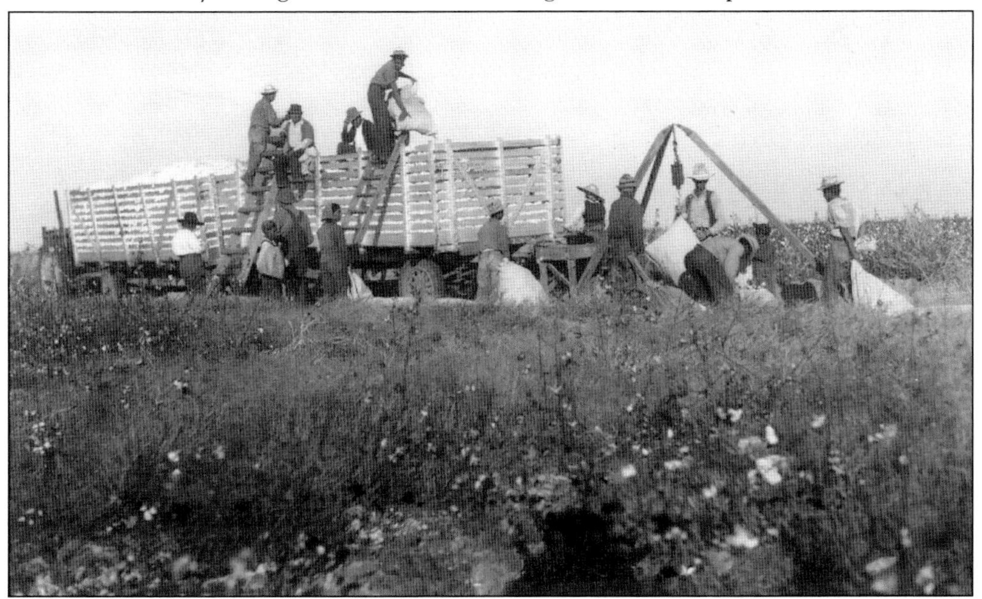

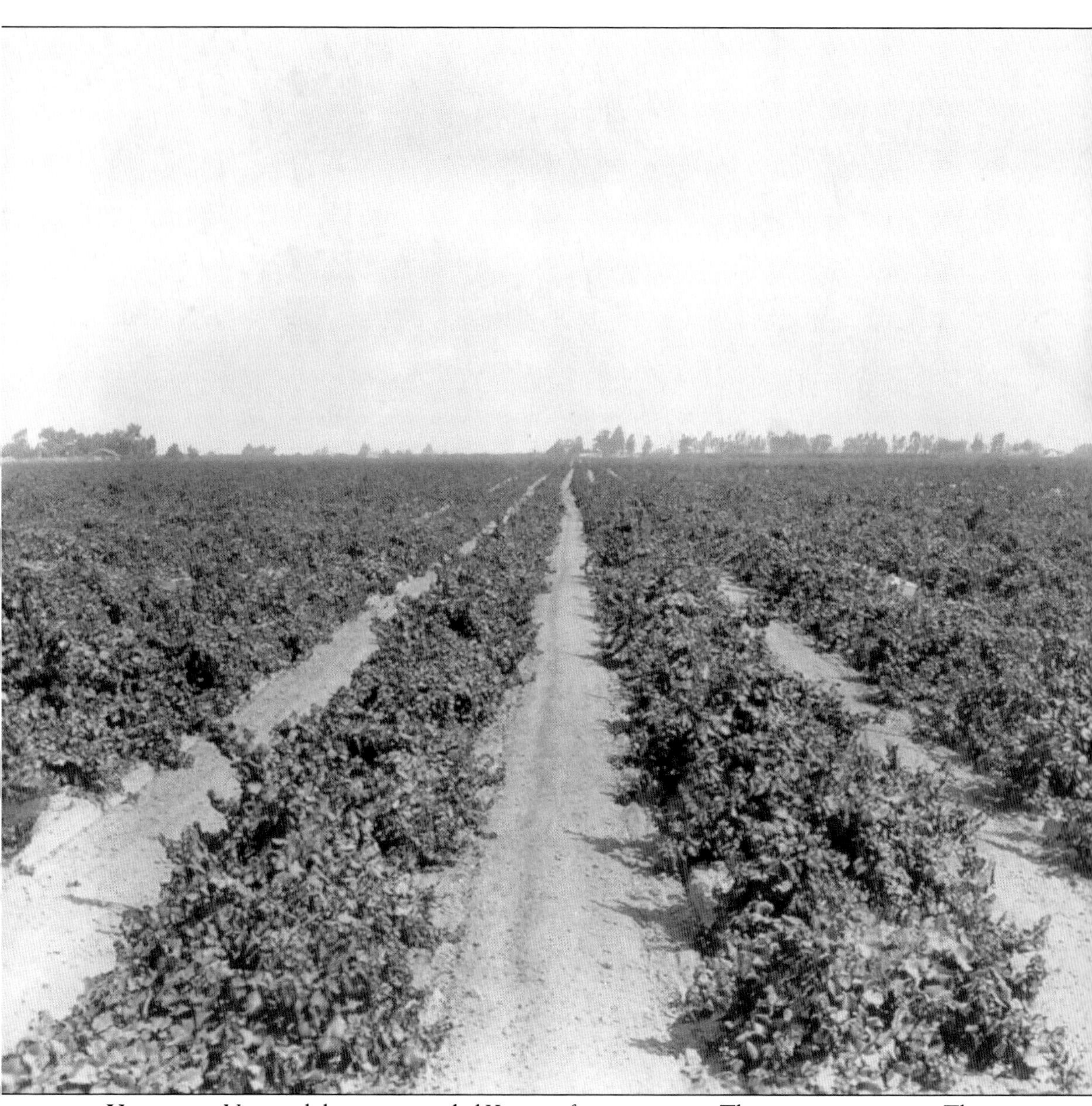

VINEYARDS. Vineyards have surrounded Kerman for generations. The vast majority grew Thompson seedless grapes, which could be used to make raisins, table grapes, or juice.

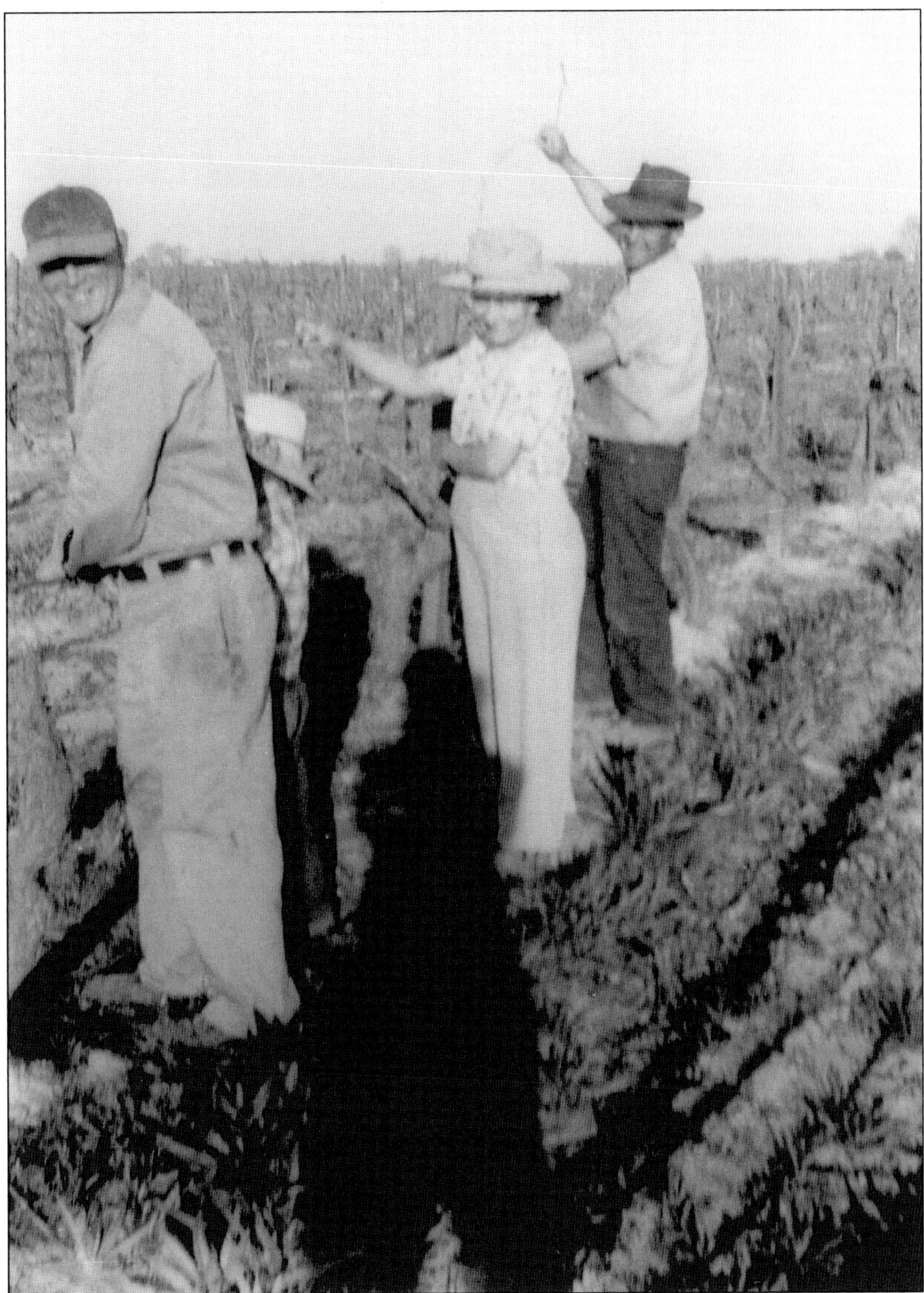

Harvesting Equipment. In recent decades, many vineyards have been converted over to wine grapes. Modern harvesting equipment has replaced hand labor to cut and lay down the grapes, but pruning and tying are still done by hand.

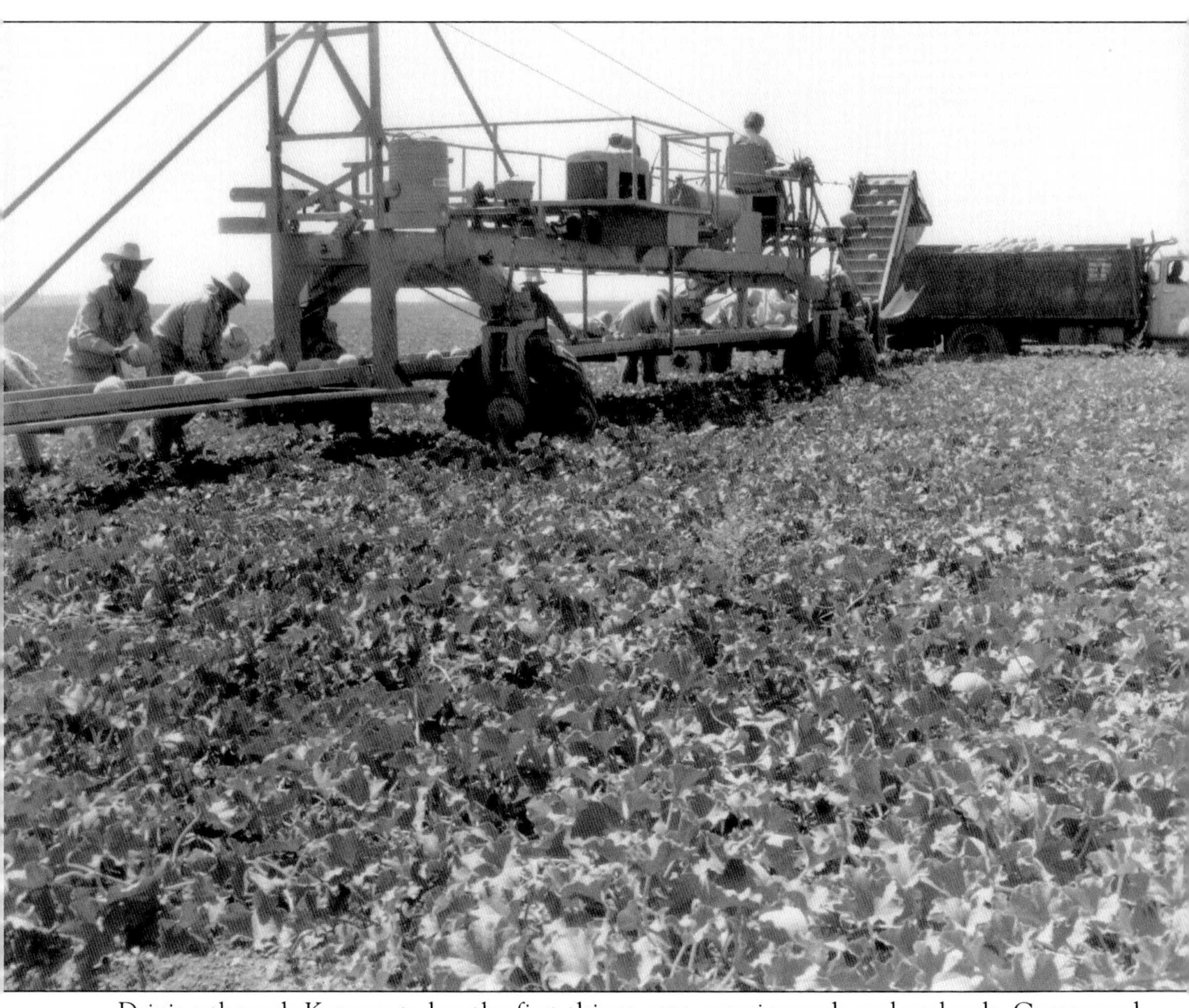

Driving through Kerman today, the first things seen are vineyards and orchards. Grapes and almonds are not the only crops that have been grown in Kerman.

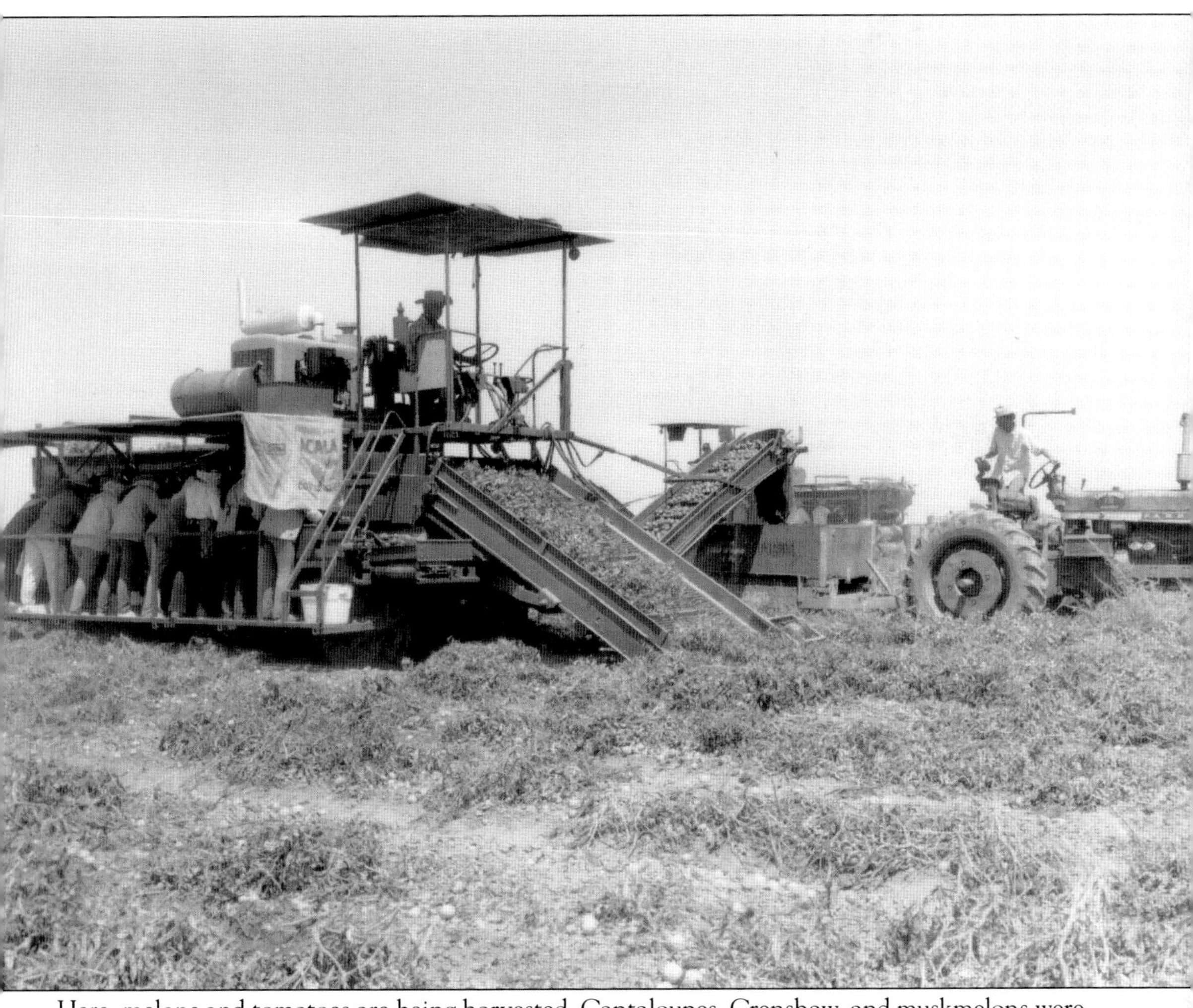

Here, melons and tomatoes are being harvested. Cantaloupes, Crenshaw, and muskmelons were harvested years ago. Both processing and fresh tomatoes were also harvested.

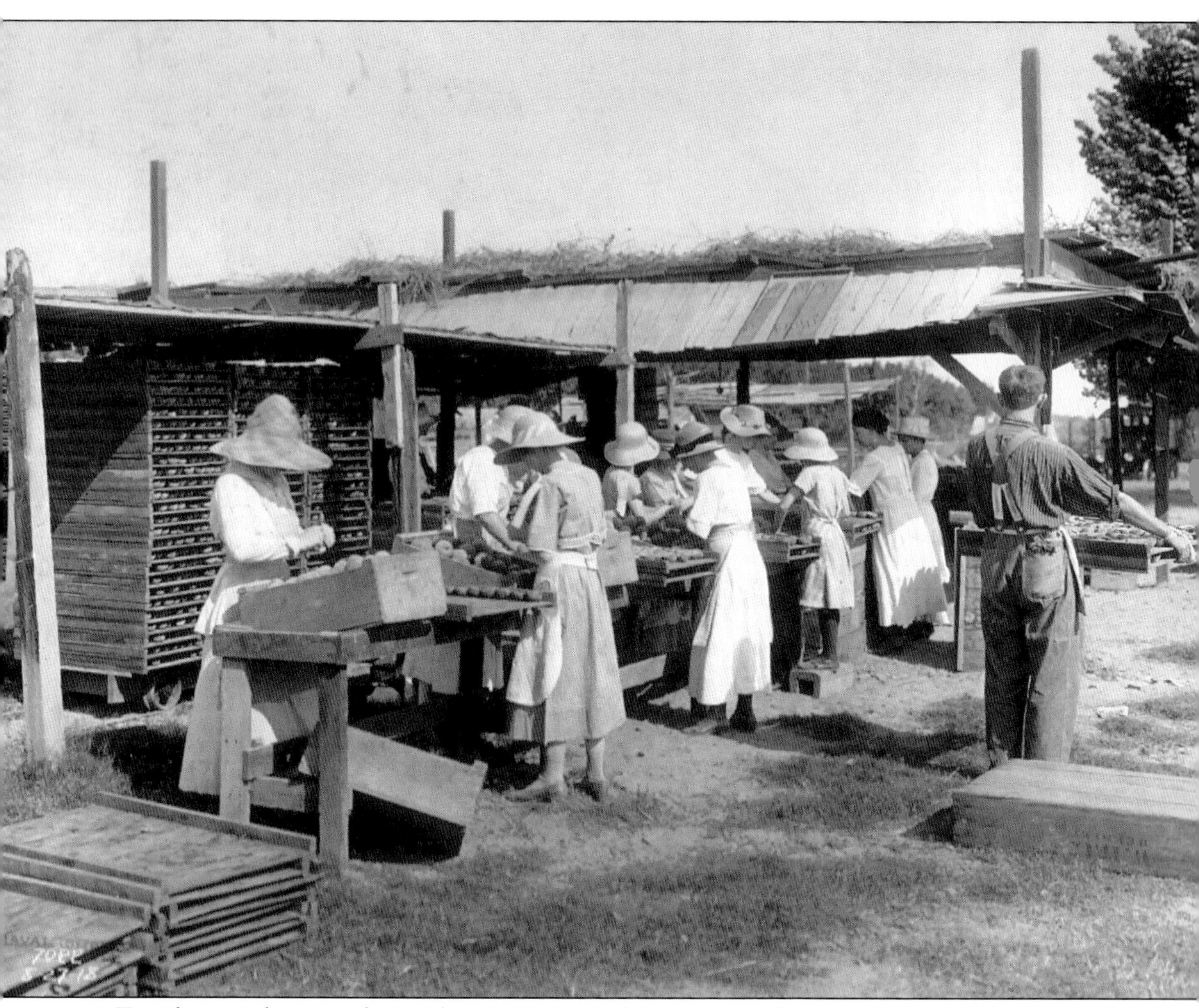

Tree fruit, such as peaches and apricots, were also grown in the area. Often, they were dried in the valley's warm fall weather. Frequently, family members would come out during harvest to get the crops in and processed. More than one farmer's wife helped cut peaches or roll raisin trays.

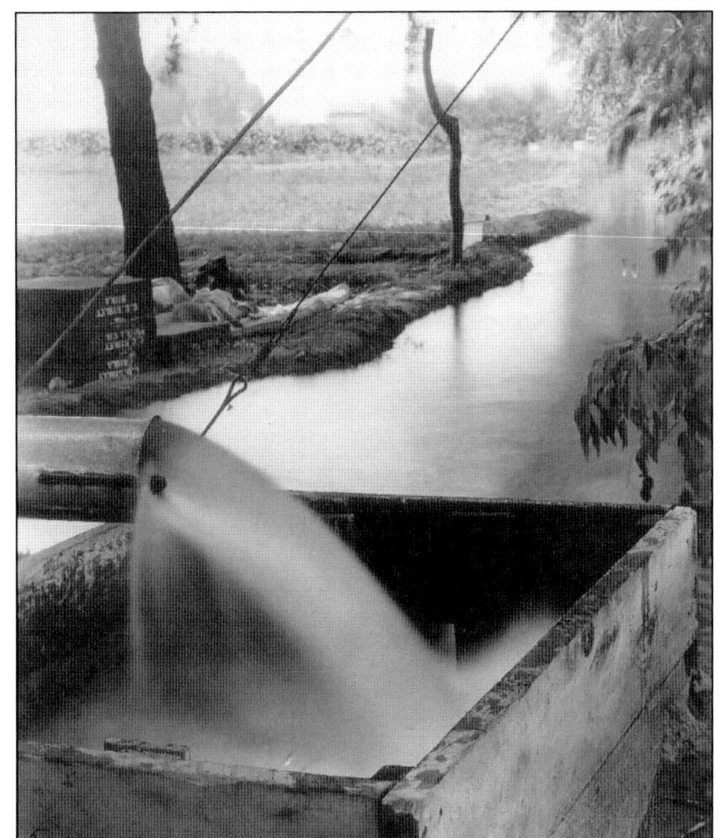

Summers are long and hot in Kerman. The Mediterranean climate helps grow over 400 crops in the valley, but they need water. Beginning in the 19th century, irrigation projects were begun in California. In the words of Pres. Theodore Roosevelt, "The purpose [was] reclaiming . . . areas of the West by irrigating lands . . . and thus creating new homes upon the land."

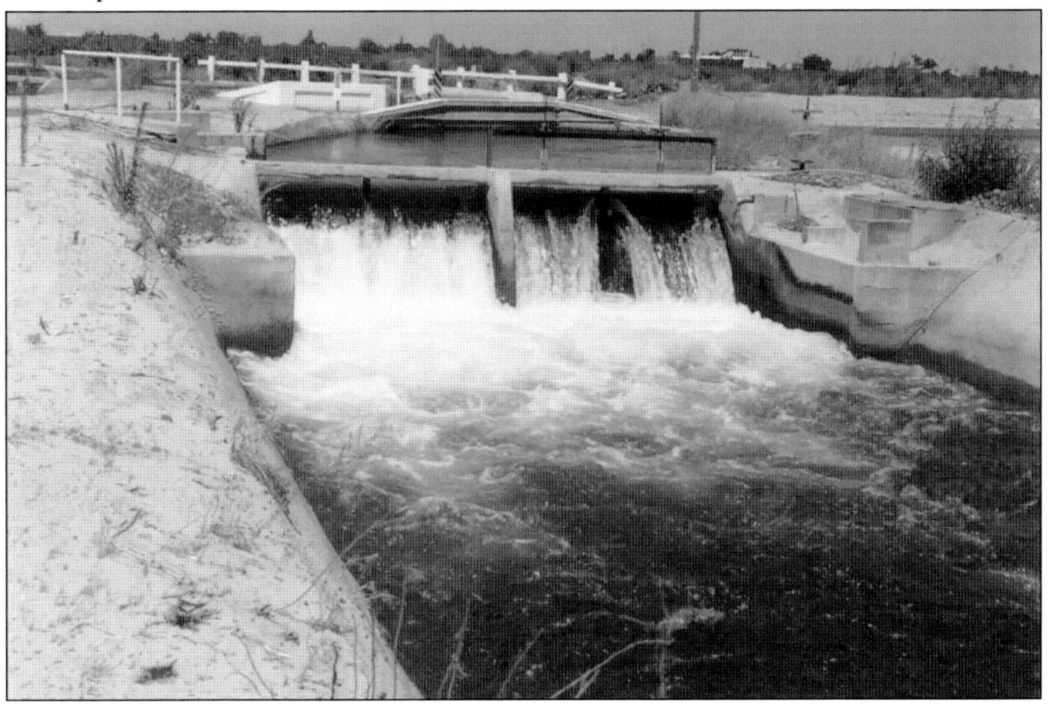

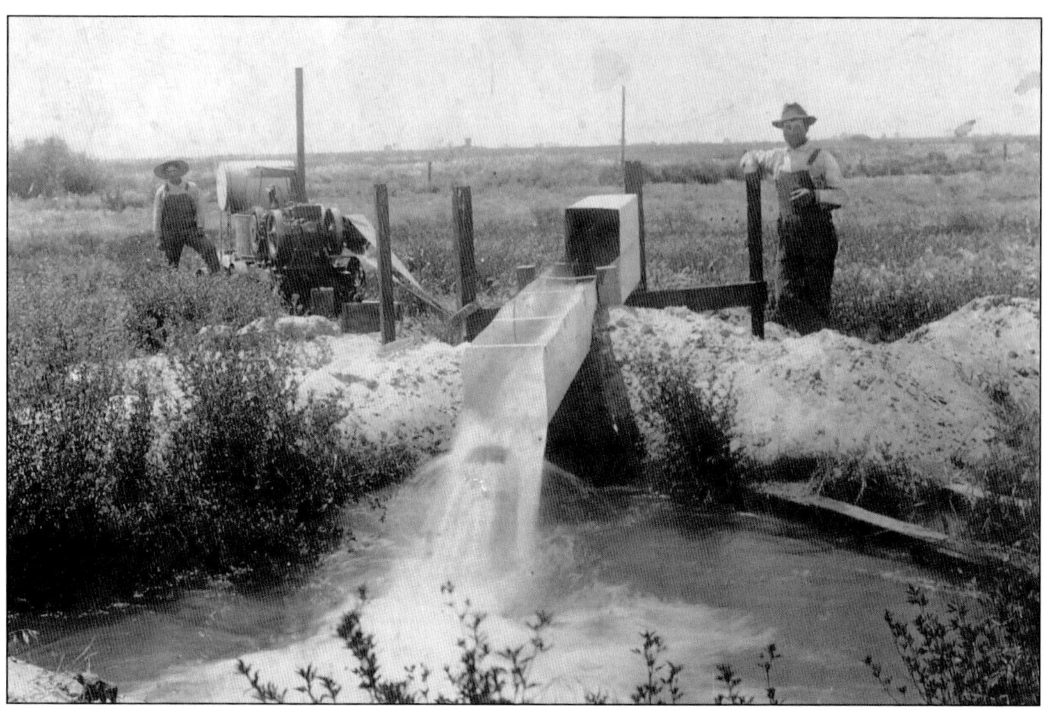

One of the great inventions of the 20th century was the vertical turbine pump. When canal water is not available, farmers can pump groundwater to keep their crops irrigated. Modern pumps are now paired with drip irrigation to create highly efficient and productive systems.

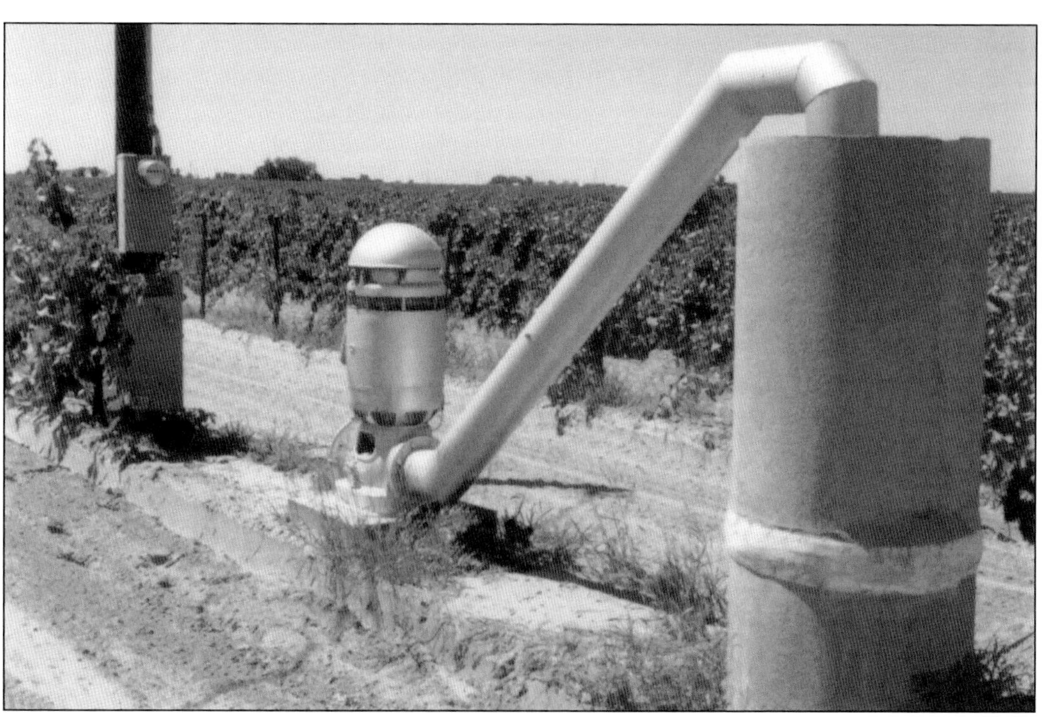

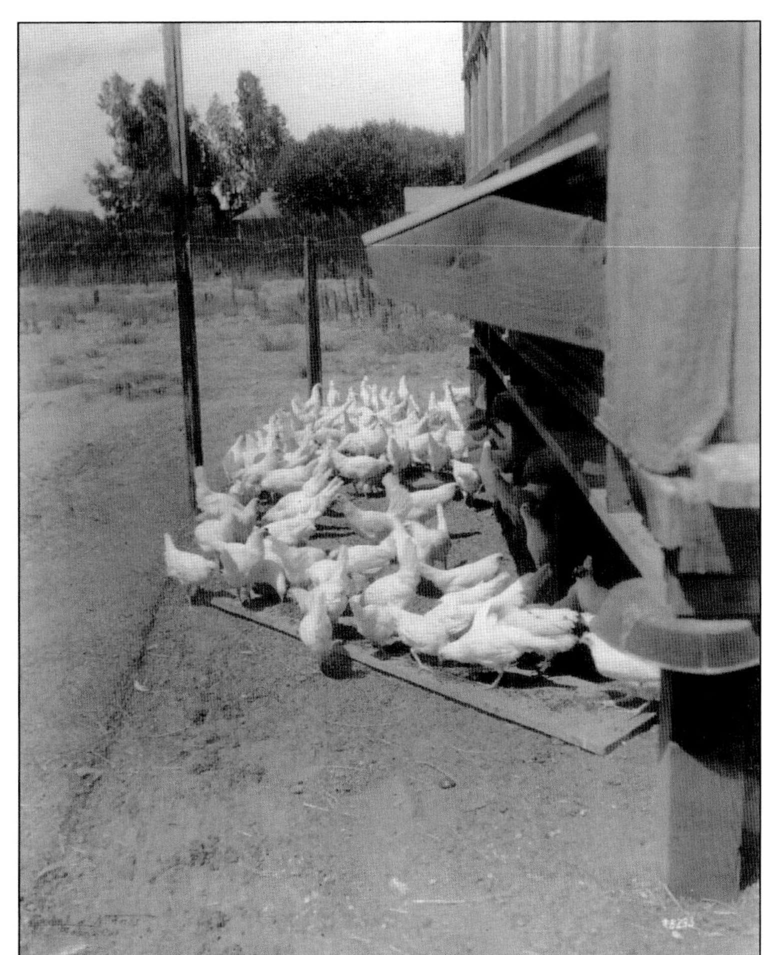

In addition to row crops, grapes, and tree nuts, livestock has been raised in the area since Kerman's founding. Chickens have been raised for meat and eggs. Turkeys and pigs were also raised.

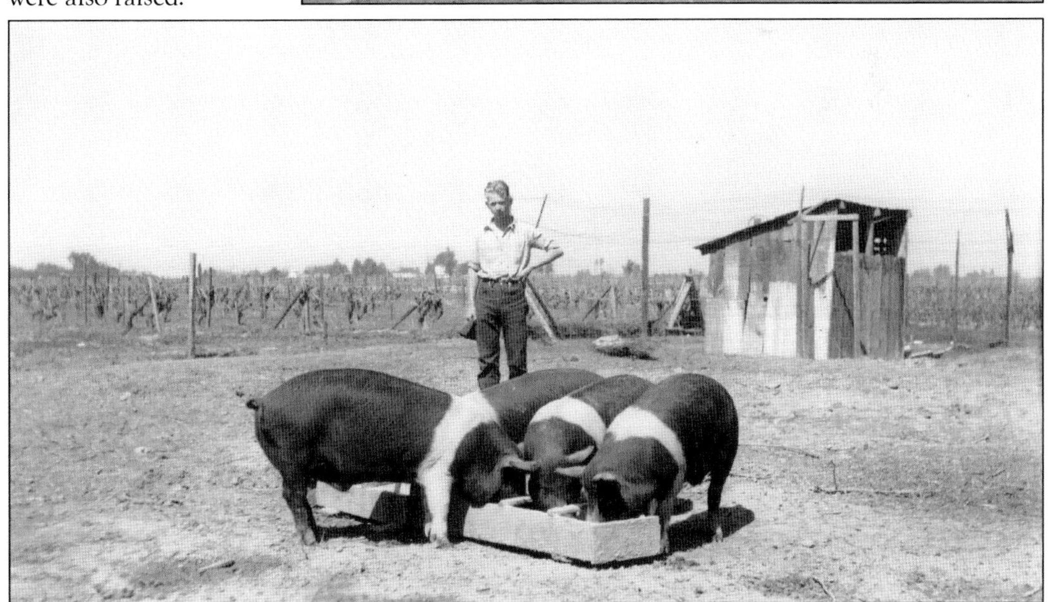

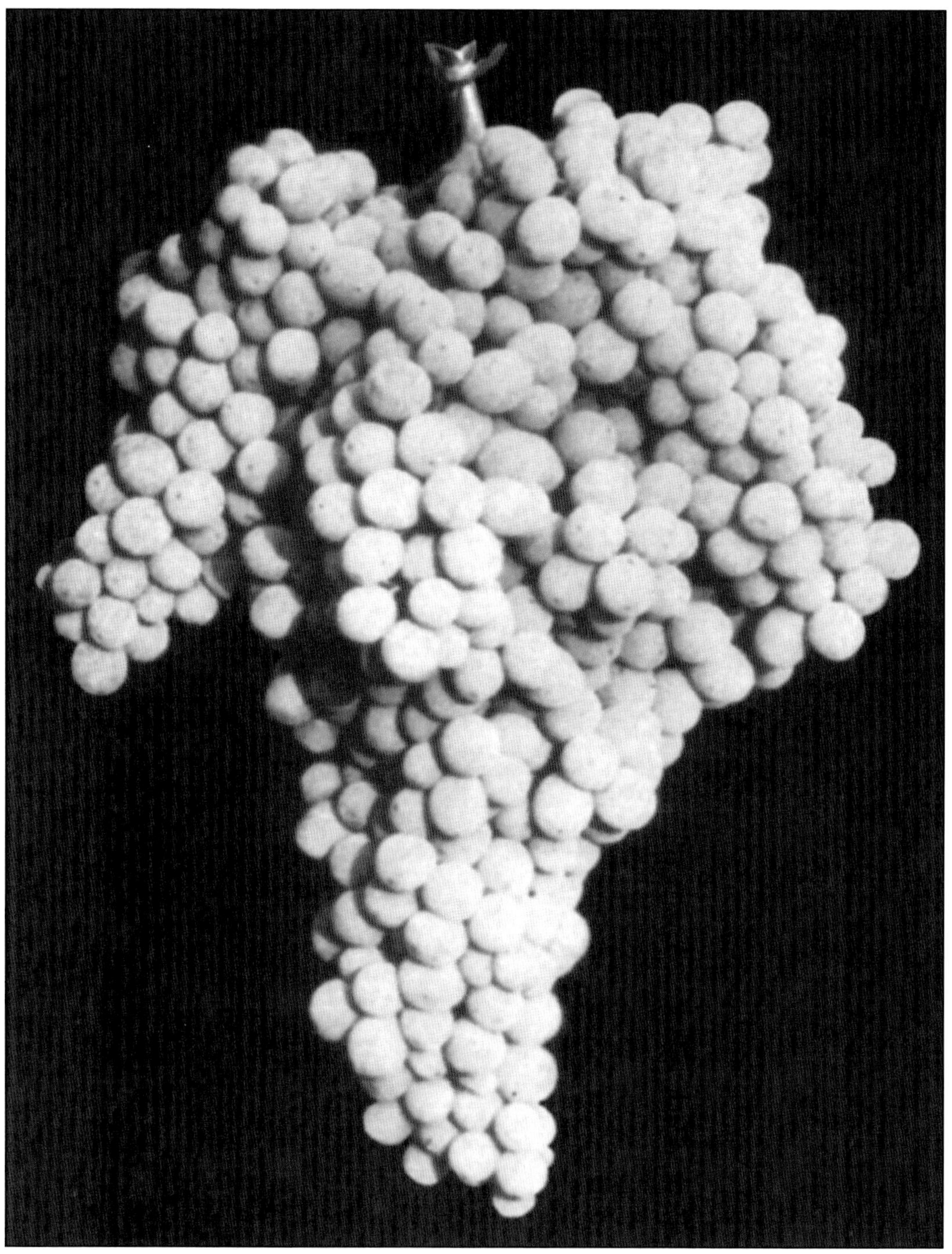

For generations, grapes have been at the heart of Kerman agriculture, especially the famous and versatile Thompson seedless grape. Other varieties have been grown for wine and table grapes.

Three

Churches

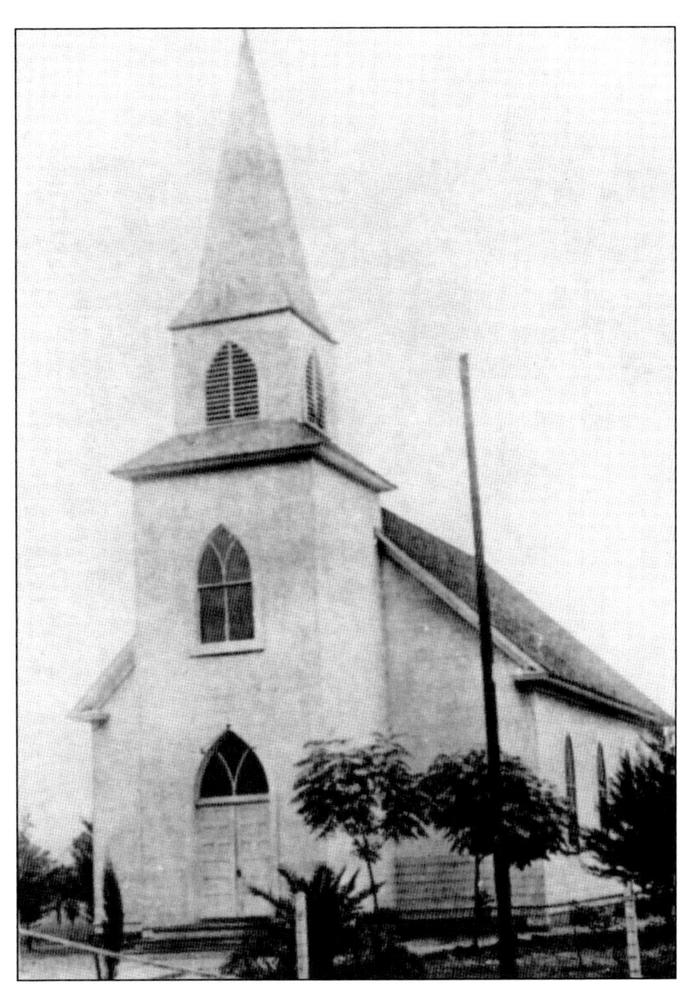

The congregation of Bethany Lutheran Church holds the honor of being the oldest congregation in Kerman. They have been meeting continuously in their building on Shaw and Madera Avenues, which was completed in 1909.

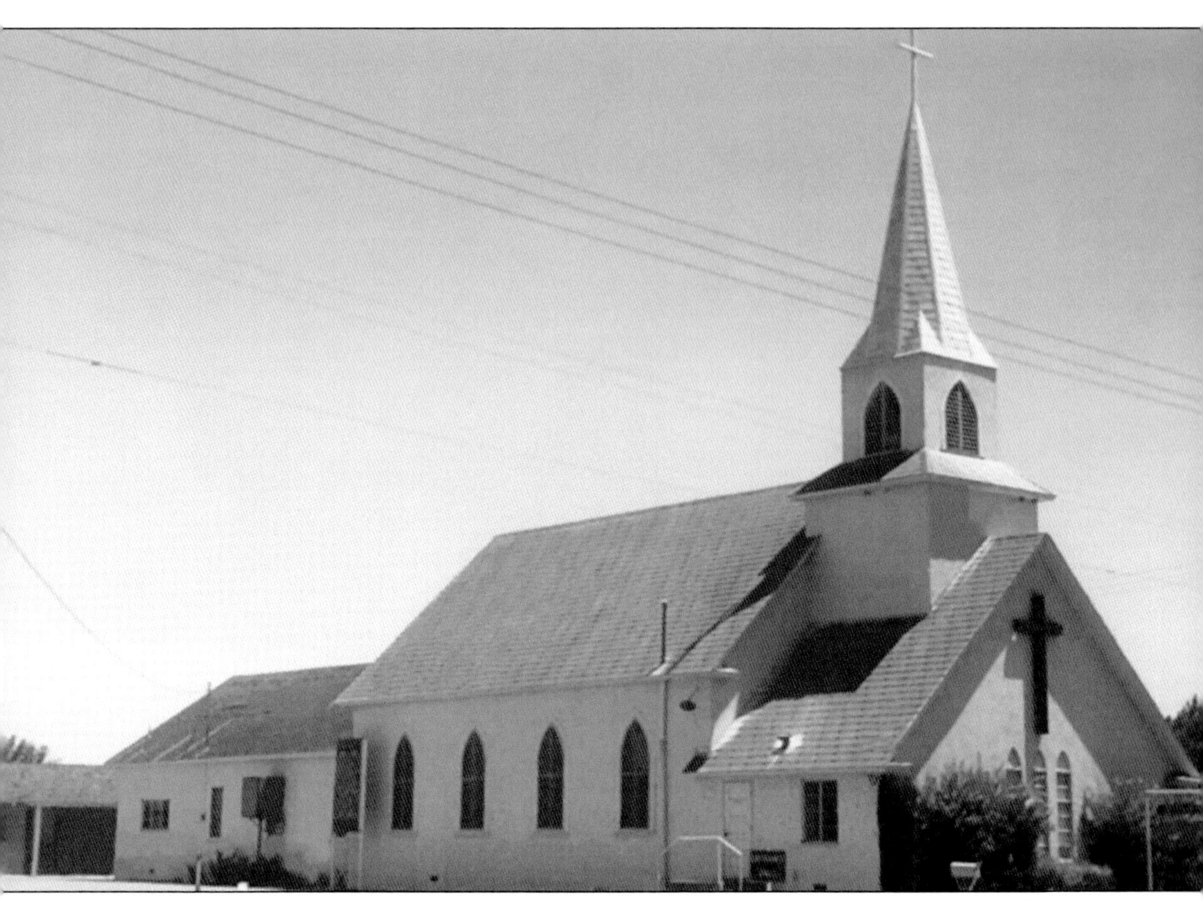

This photograph of Bethany Lutheran Church was taken 75 years after the one on the previous page. There have been minor modifications, but it is the same building. Even though the city of Kerman has grown, there is still a strong need for churches in the countryside.

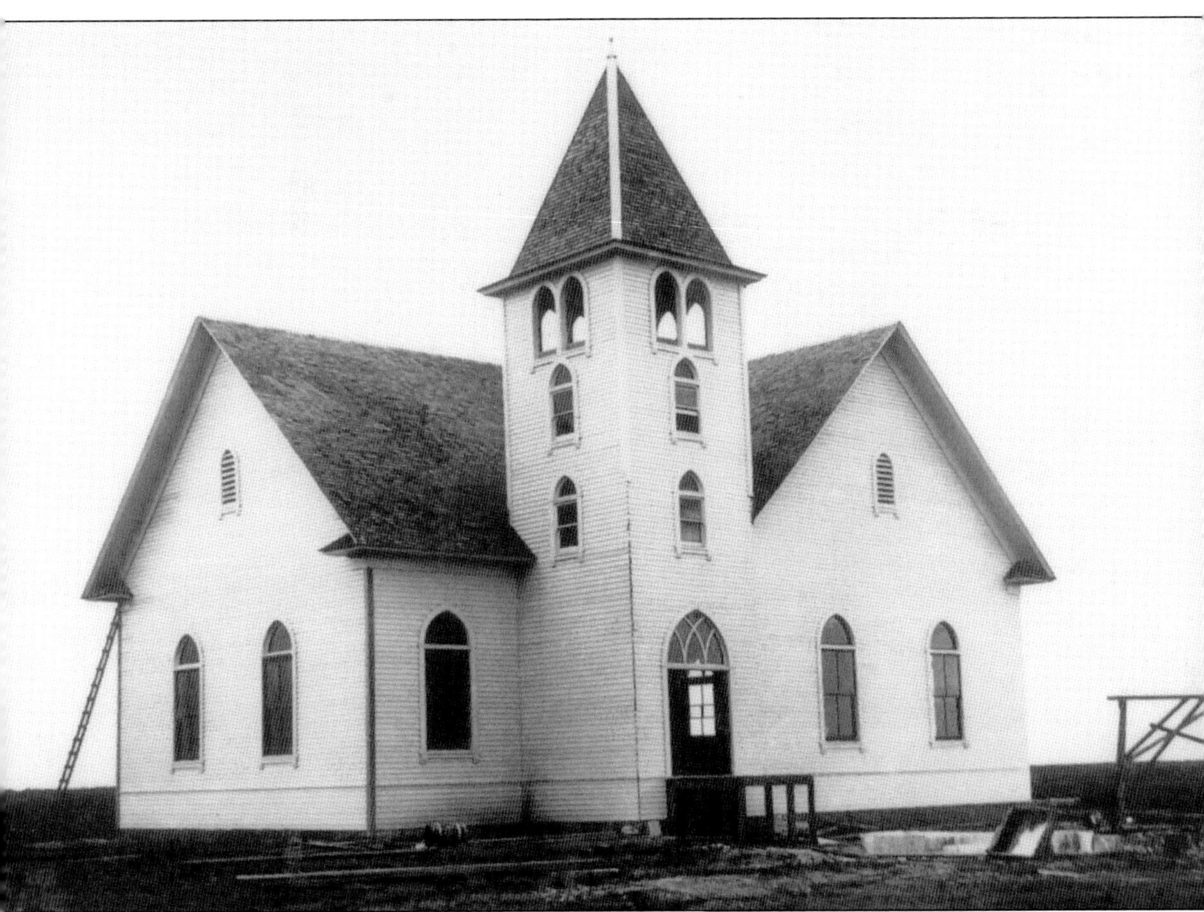

The Kerman United Methodist Church congregation was also formed in 1909. Their building in town was dedicated in May 1910. The Reverend W.H. Householder was the first pastor. For years, there was a Methodist church in town and another one in the country. The building at Madera and Shields Avenues was dedicated on June 11, 1961, as the Beulah United Methodist Church. The United Brethren Church and the rural Methodist church merged years ago. This congregation and the Methodist congregation in town merged at this site on May 19, 1994.

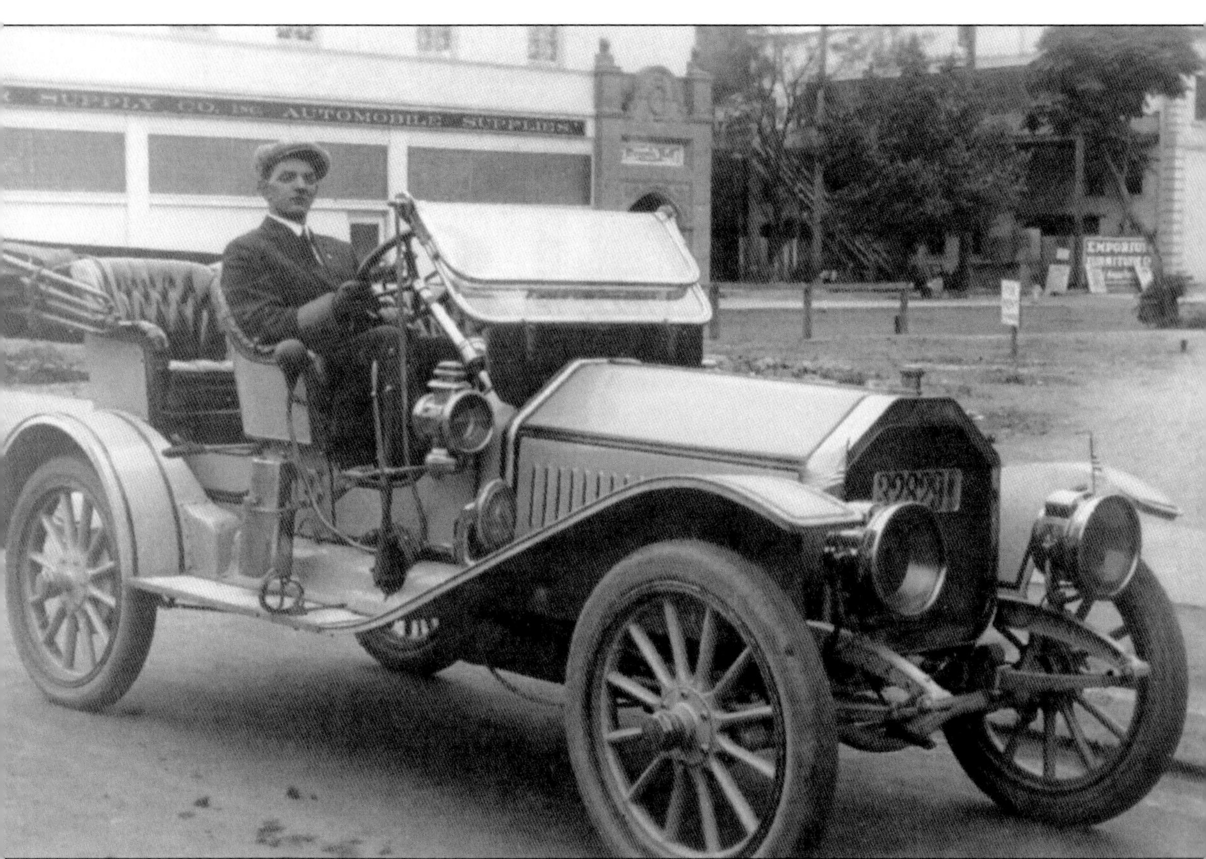

The tradition of Methodist circuit riders goes all the way back to John Wesley himself. Wesley preached as many as three sermons a day as he rode the circuit. Many churches in rural areas were too small to afford a full-time minister. Ministers rode the circuit on horseback to meet the needs of their far-flung flocks. Seen here is a 20th-century innovation. During the 1920s, Methodist minister Reverend Planetee road the circuit to serve the churches of Rolinda, Tranquillity, San Joaquin, and Kerman in his open roadster. Today, Kerman and Tranquillity have their own Methodist pastors.

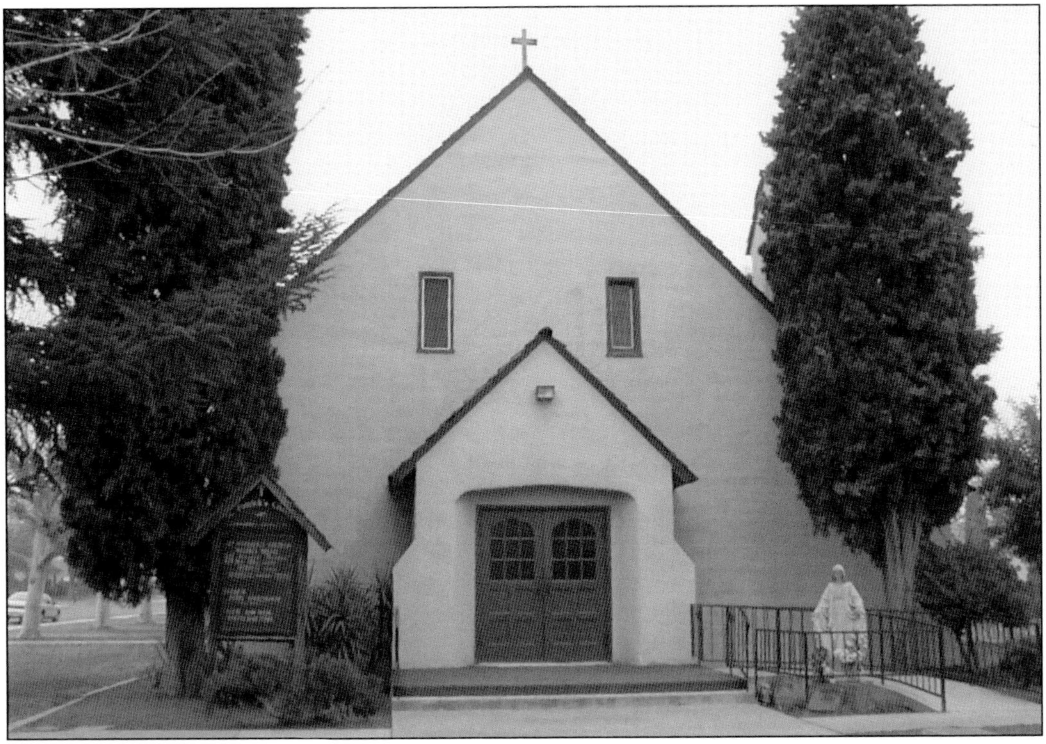

Other churches followed. The third church building in the community was St. Patrick's Catholic Church, dedicated on June 1, 1930. The original site was on the southwest corner of 6th and G Streets. The new St. Patrick's on Kearney Avenue was dedicated in 2002. Currently, there are some 3,000 members who call St. Patrick home. In the early years, St. Patrick's also ran a school. What is now the Enterprise High School of Kerman Unified began as the Catholic school.

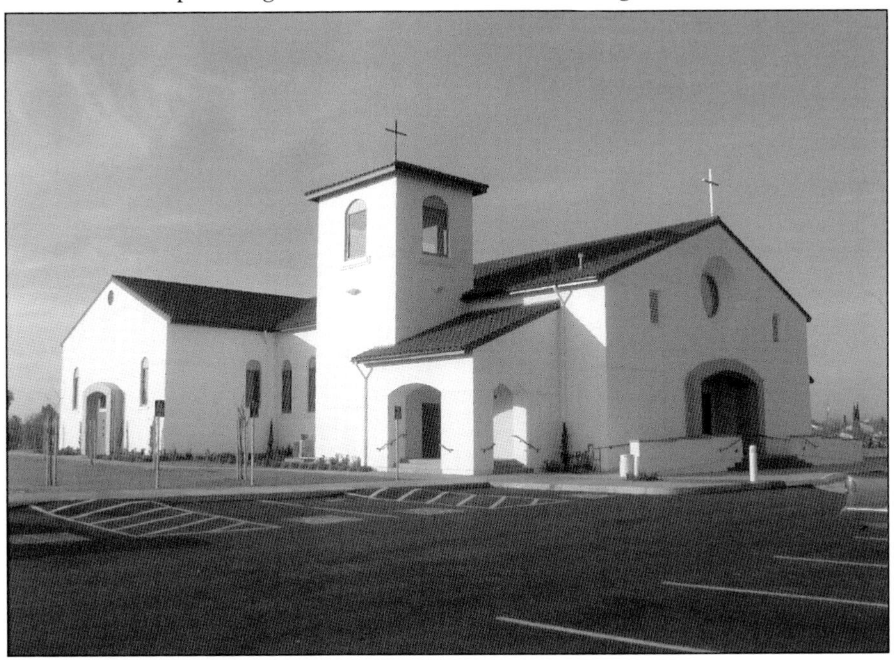

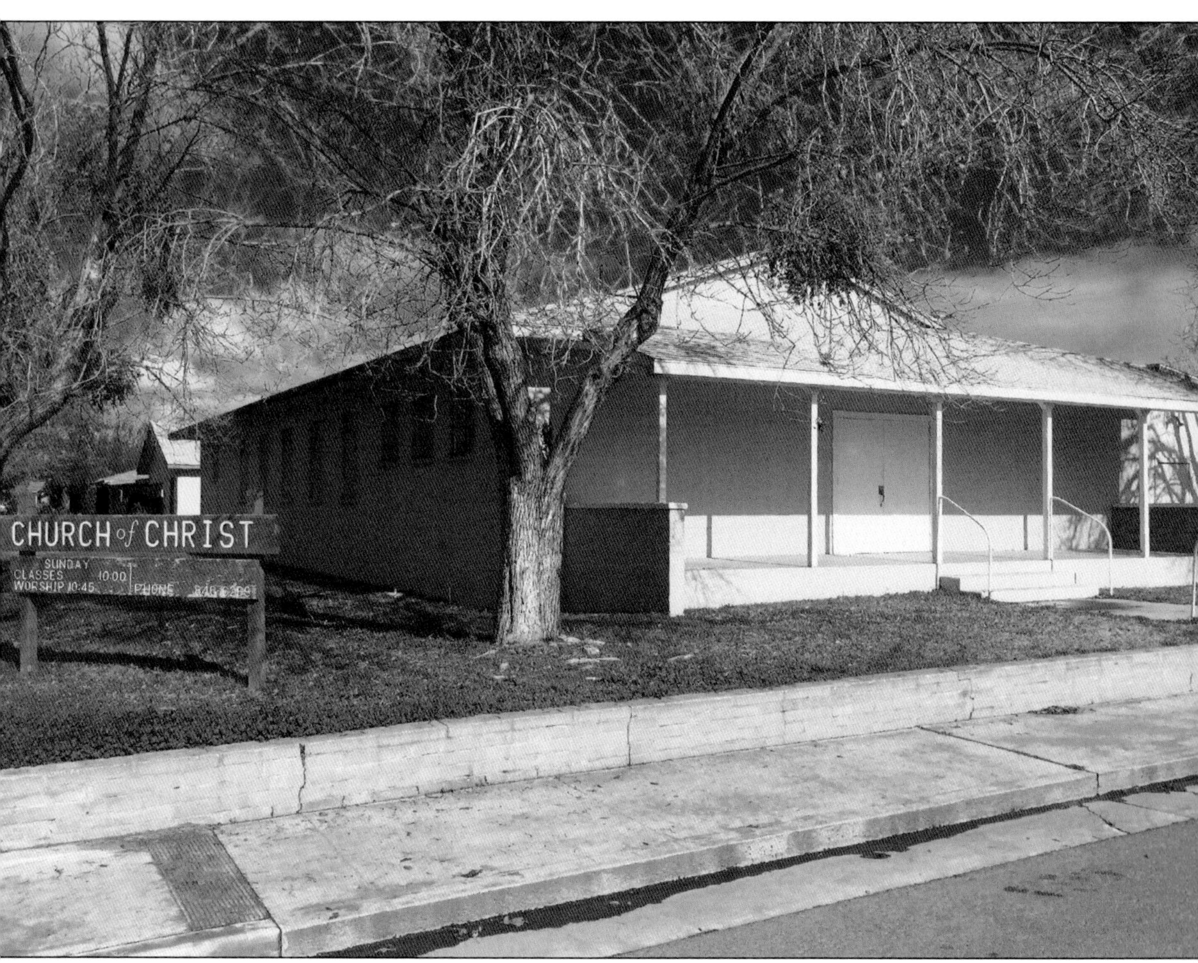

The Church of Christ was formed on March 10, 1940, with about 25 charter members. They met at the local Grange Hall until they constructed their own building on Eighth and D Streets in 1947. They quickly outgrew that building. In 1948, property on Sixth and G Streets was purchased. The current building, which seats over 200, opened in 1952. Over the years, the congregation has been involved in ministries in the community and mission efforts around the world.

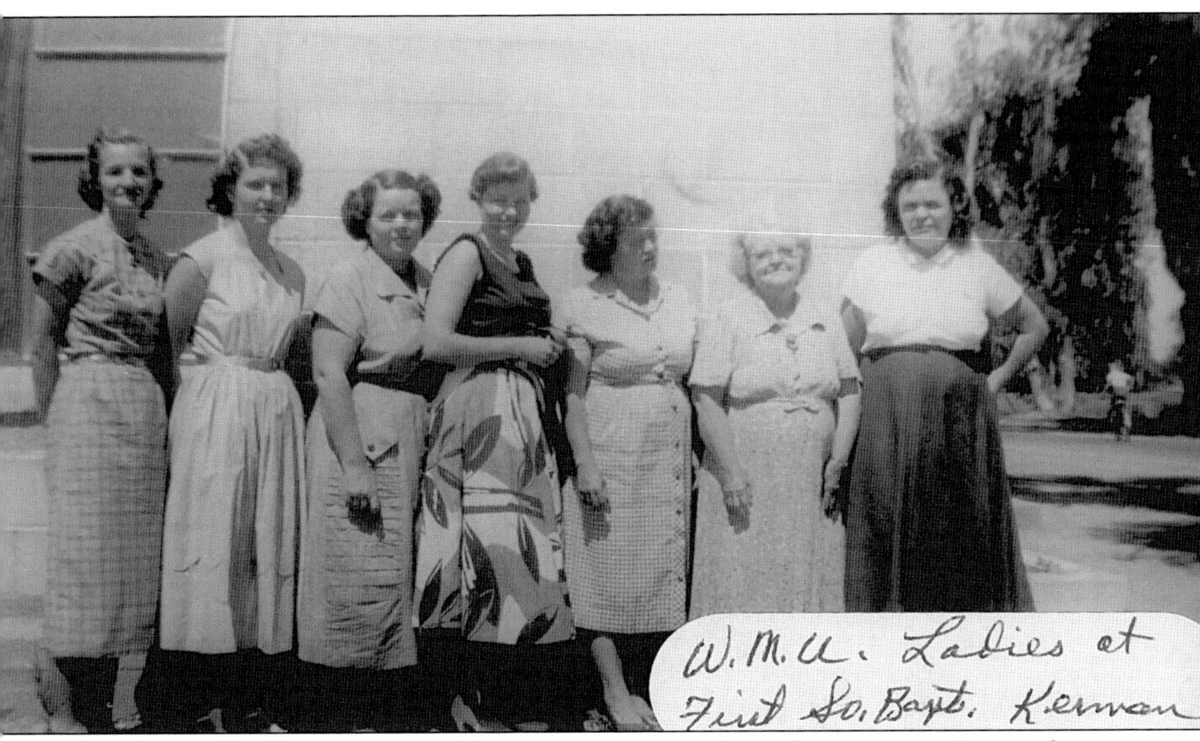

As seen in this picture of the Baptist Ladies Club, the Baptists have been active in Kerman for a long time. Both First Freewill Baptist and First Southern Baptist Churches erected new buildings in 1946.

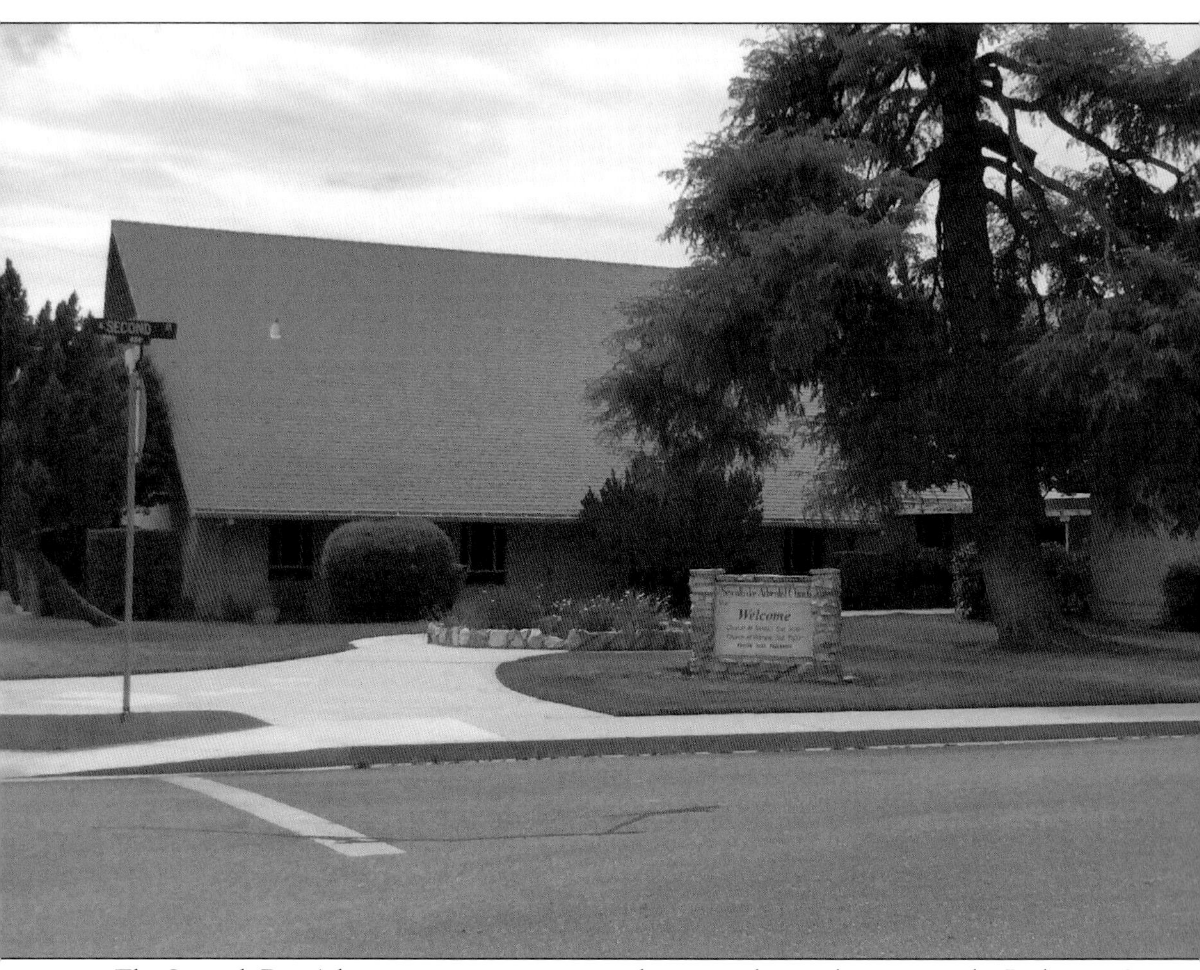

The Seventh Day Adventist congregation started meeting during the 1910s in the Biola area. In 1922, they were worshipping in a small church on Rolinda Avenue near the railroad tracks. As the congregation continued to grow, they started looking for a larger facility in the mid-1950s. Alver Georgeson, Clifford Faust, and Dr. Alvin Chaffin formed the committee to find a suitable location. Their current building was erected in 1963. In addition to worship services and Bible studies, the church holds health and spiritual seminars.

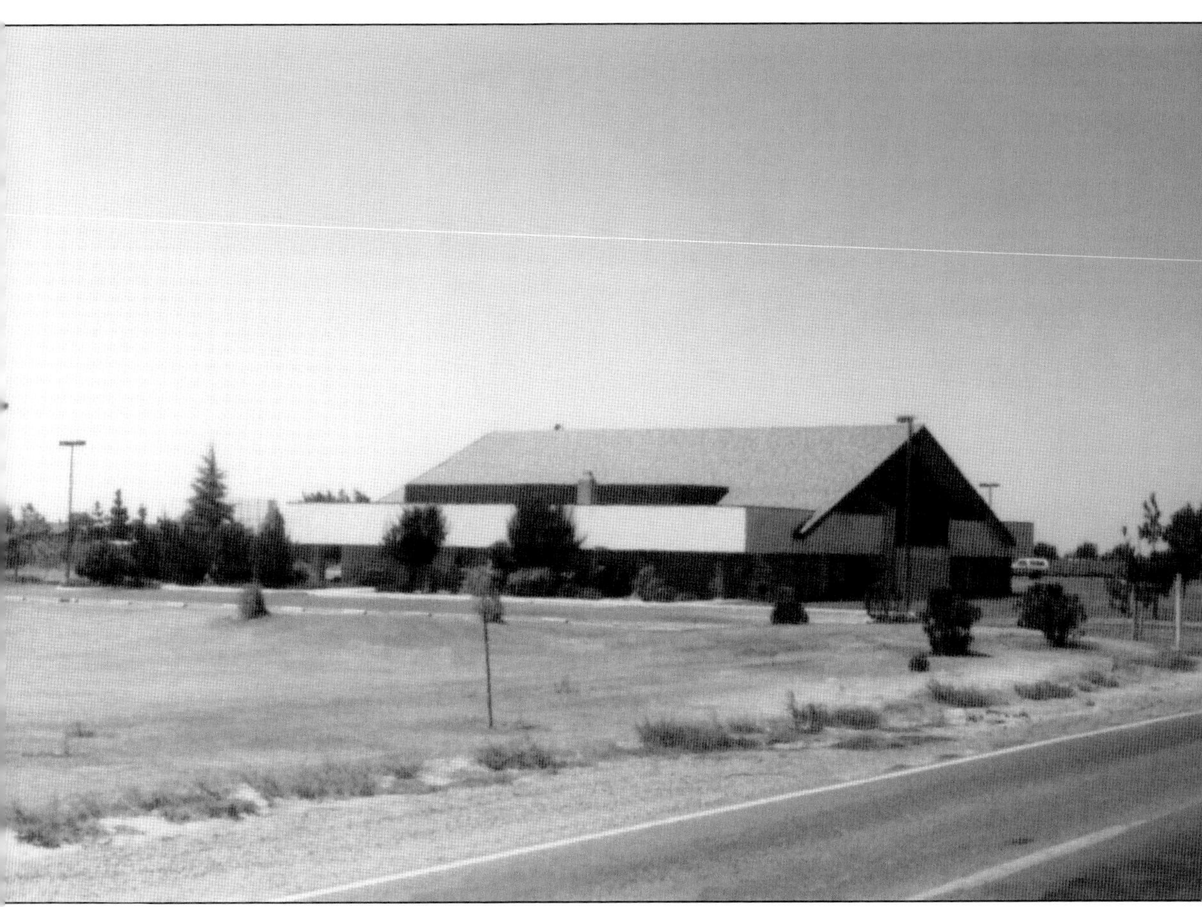

When the Kerman Covenant Church was formed in 1970, many Kerman families who had been commuting to Fresno for church were able to stay close to home for Sunday worship. The story of Kerman Covenant's founding is a little unusual. The families that formed the church came from four different denominations. The congregation formed as a result of the illness and death of Kerman farmer Jim Jerner. Jerner and his wife, Elaine, had attended First Covenant Church in Fresno. The congregation first met in the home of John and Helen Nord on Whitesbridge Avenue. When church members outgrew the Nords' home, they met at the Seventh Day Adventist church until their first building was completed in August 1971. Charter members agreed there would be no hairsplitting on doctrinal issues considering their varied backgrounds. The Covenant Church was and continues to be a home for those who hold to the essential affirmations of Christianity while agreeing to allow differences on nonessential elements of faith. The Kerman Christian School was established on the Covenant Church property in 1993.

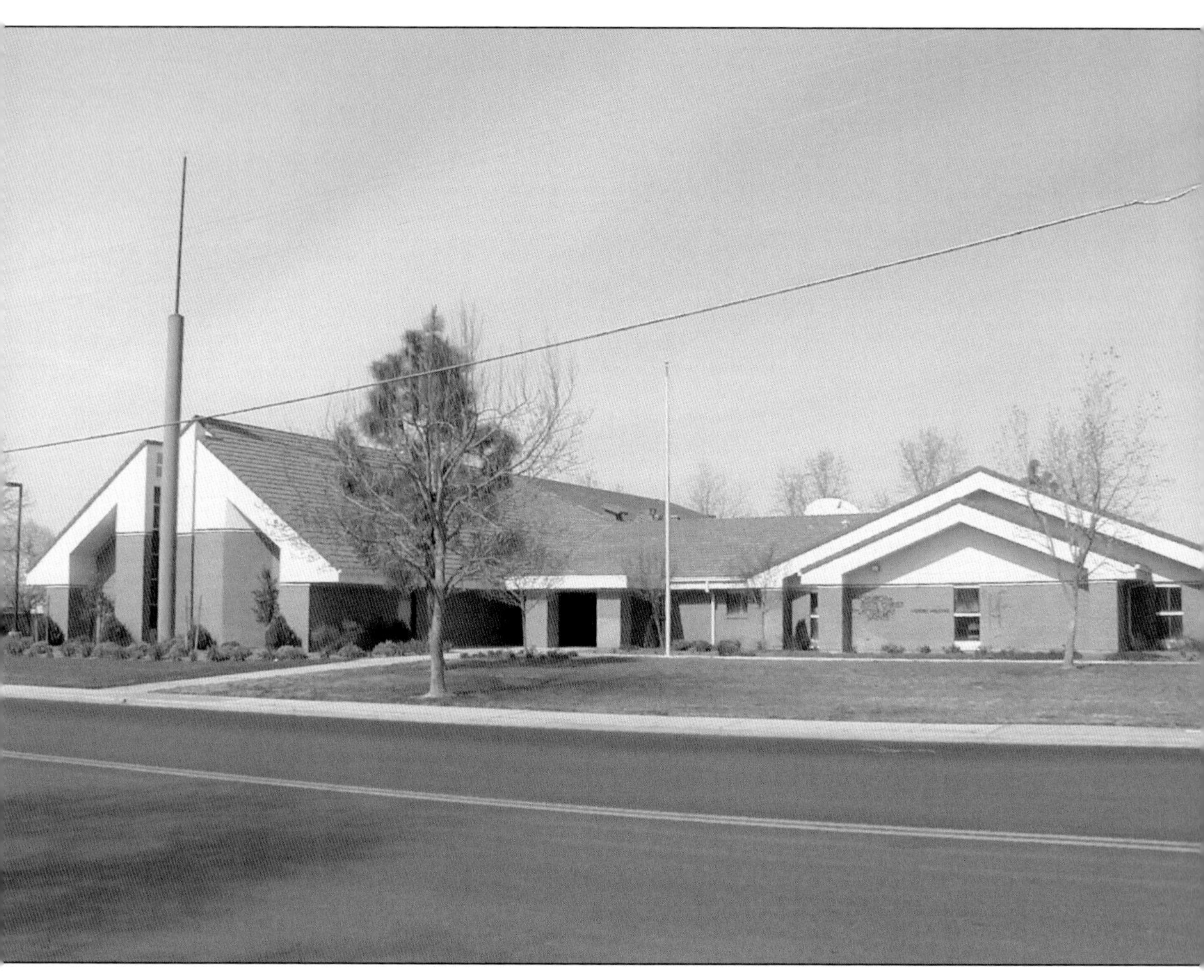

Like the members of the Kerman Covenant Church, local Mormons met in churches in Fresno for years. The congregation of the Church of Jesus Christ of Latter-Day Saints built their church in 1993.

Four

Schools

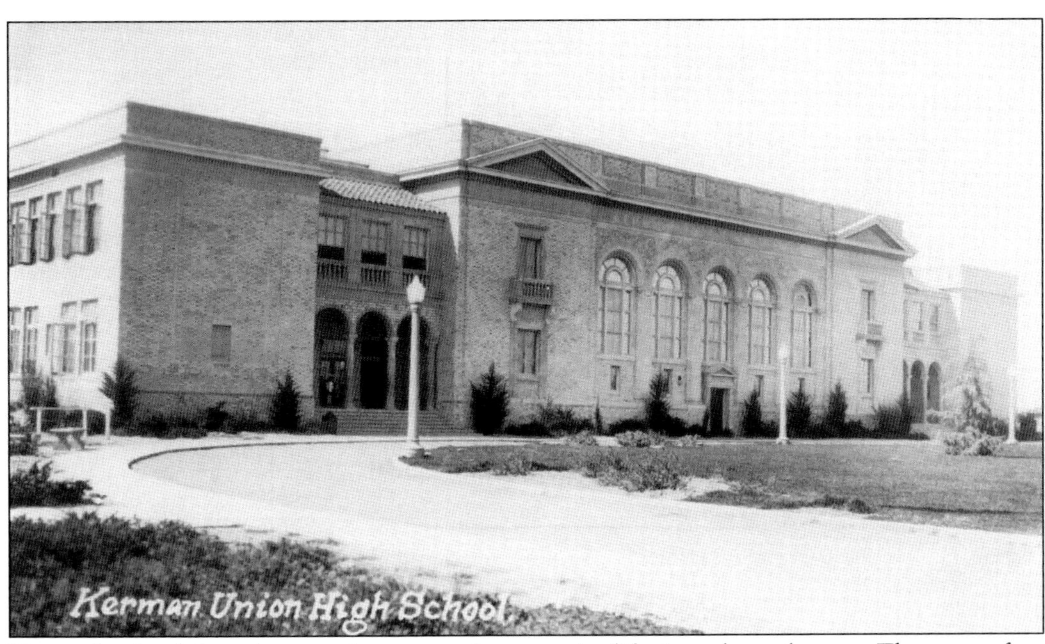

Kerman's schools have been at the center of community life since the early years. There were four elementary schools in the country outside the city limits. Sunset, Dakota, Vinland, and Empire Schools fed into the high school. Kerman Grammar School and Floyd District School also met in town. The first class of Kerman Union High School met in 1910 in the basement of Bethany Lutheran Church. That first class had 12 students.

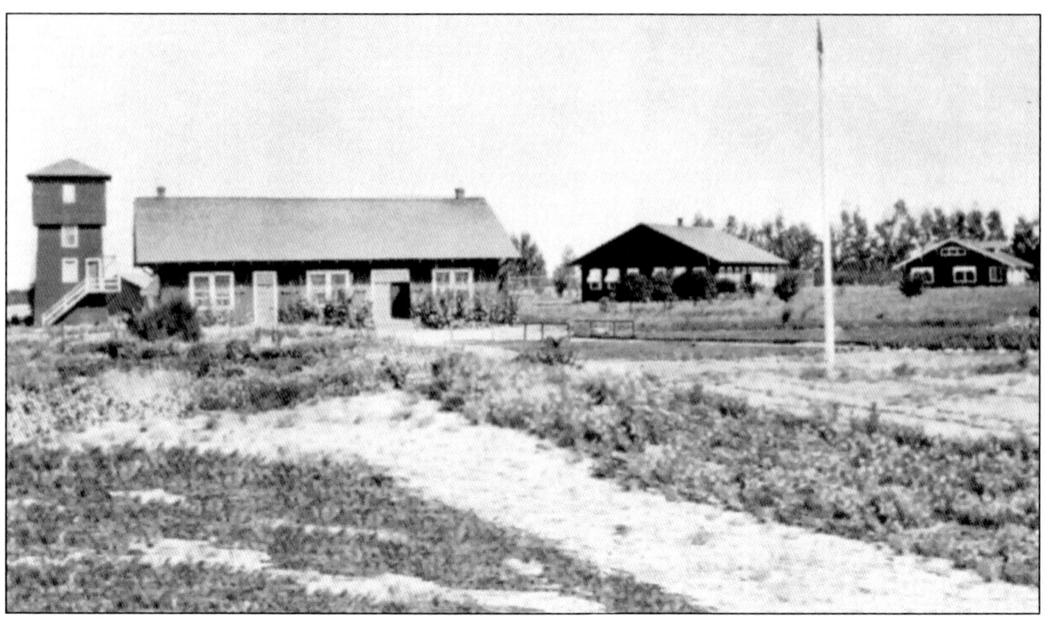

In 1913, land at Madera and Clinton Avenues was purchased and the first school buildings were constructed. Many have wondered over the years why the high school was built outside of town. As seen on the map below, the high school was located in the center of the country schools that fed into it. The first class graduated from Kerman Union High School in 1913.

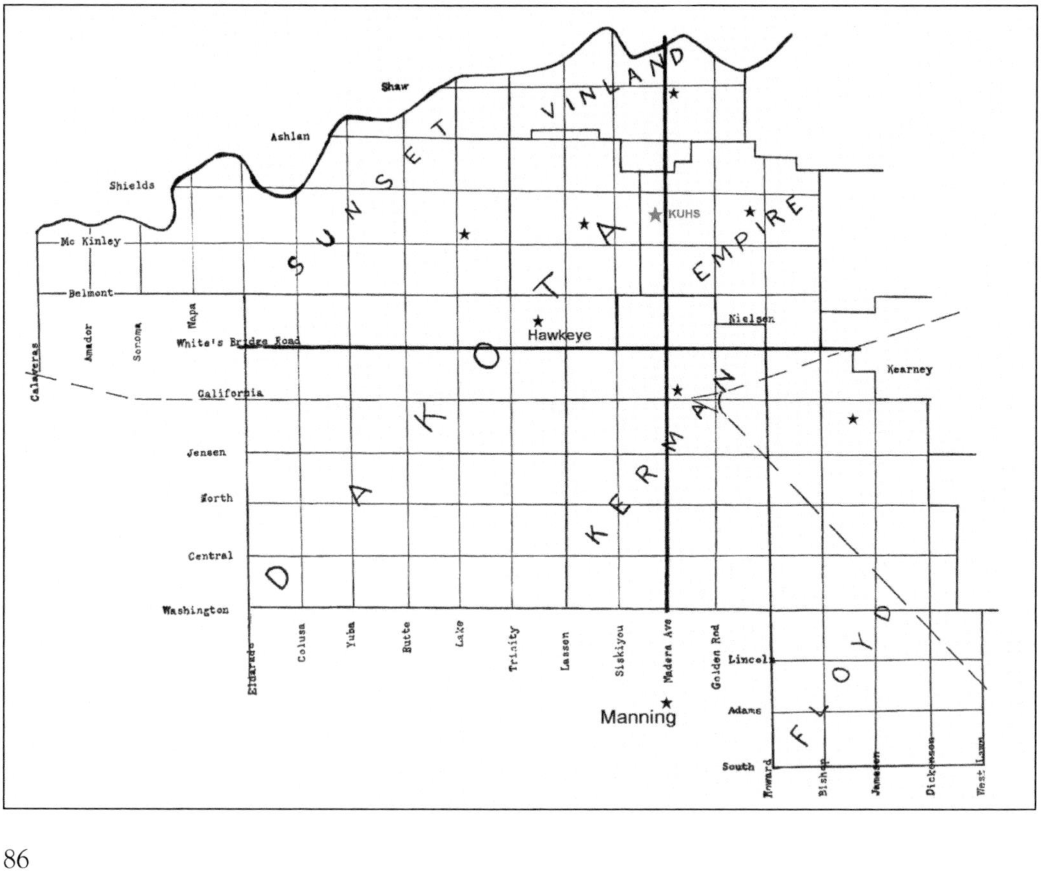

Shaw
Ashlan
Shields
Mc Kinley
Belmont
VINLAND
SUNSET
DAKOTA
EMPIRE
KERMAN
FLOYD
KUHS
Hawkeye
Nielsen
White's Bridge Road
Kearney
Calaveras
Amador
Sonoma
Napa
California
Jensen
North
Central
Washington
Eldorado
Colusa
Yuba
Butte
Lake
Trinity
Lassen
Siskiyou
Madera Ave
Golden Rod
Lincoln
Adams
South
Manning
Howard
Bishop
Jameson
Dickenson
West Lawn

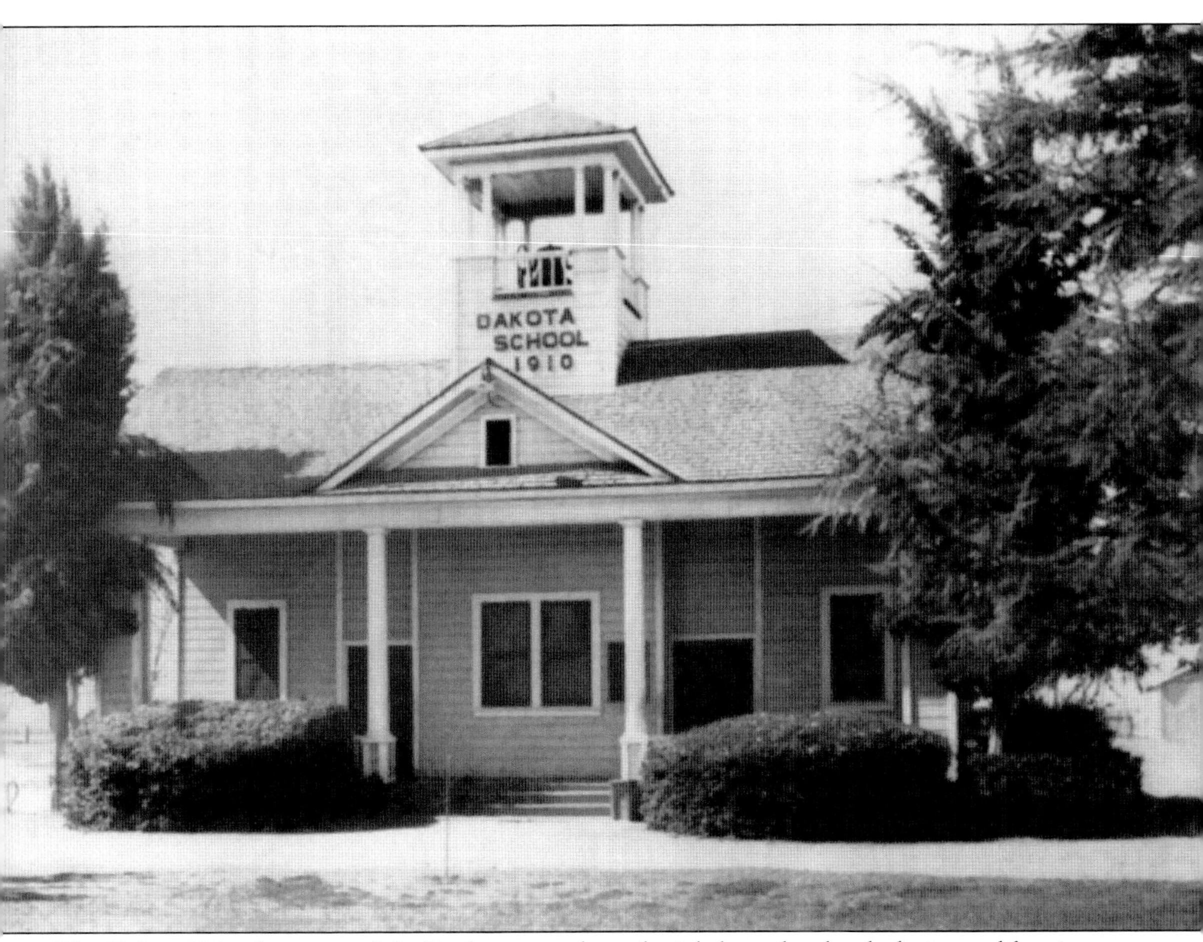

The Dakota School was one of the kindergarten-through-eighth-grade schools that served farming families in the Kerman area. Others included Sunset, Empire, and Vinland. Upon completion of eighth grade, students began attending Kerman High School.

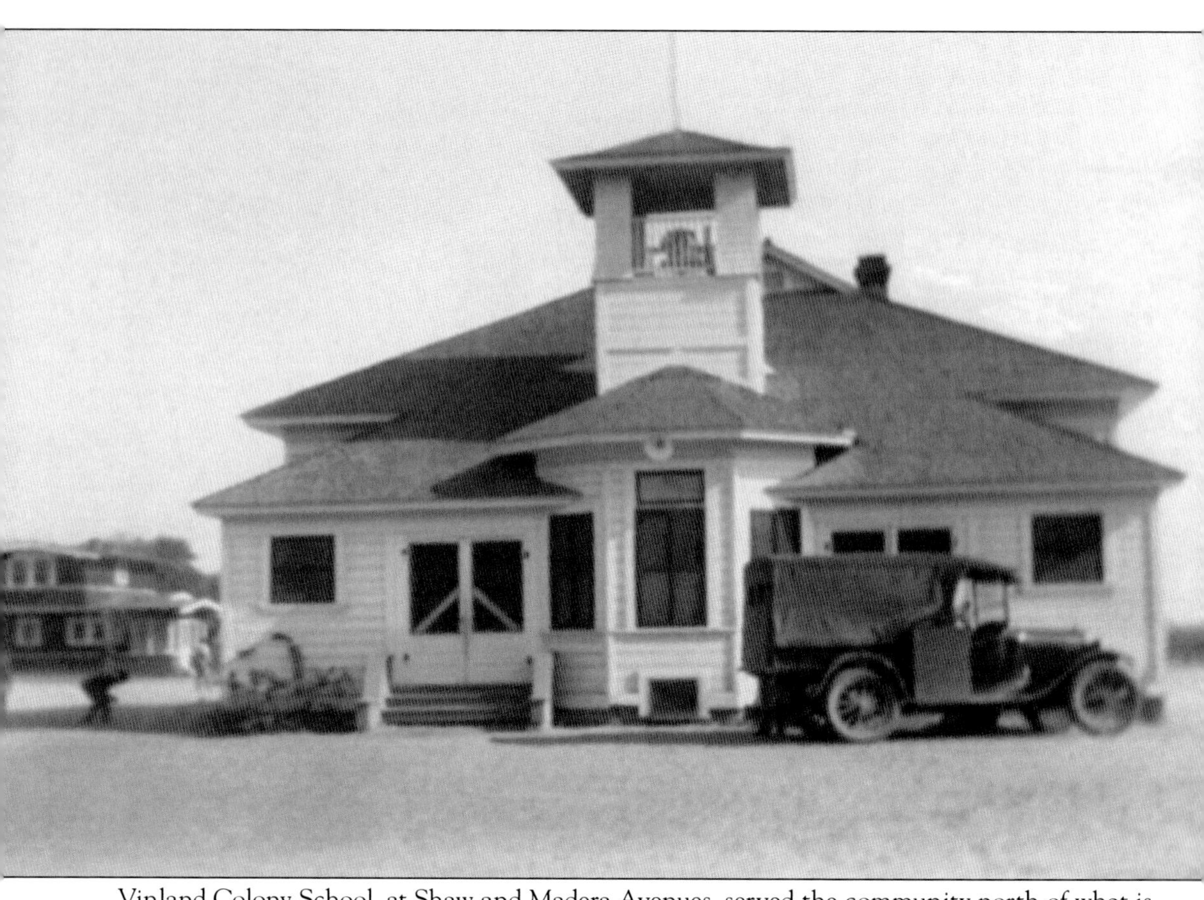

Vinland Colony School, at Shaw and Madera Avenues, served the community north of what is now downtown Kerman.

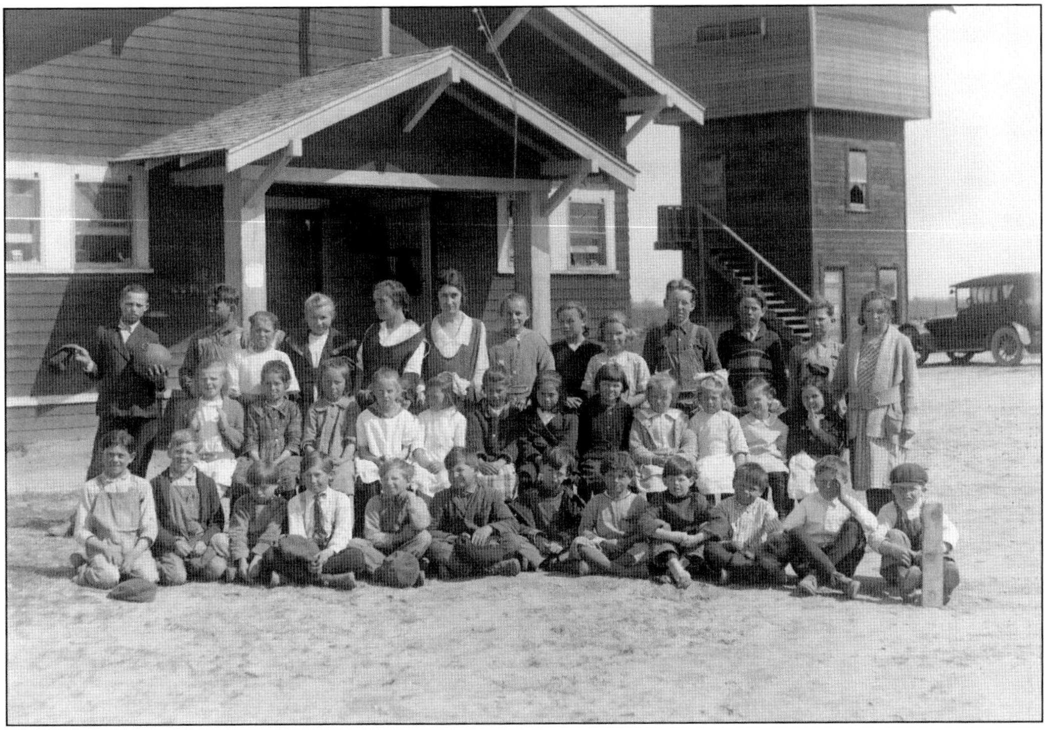

Students from Hawkeye Elementary School, situated near Whitesbridge and Lassen Avenues, also went to Kerman Union High School.

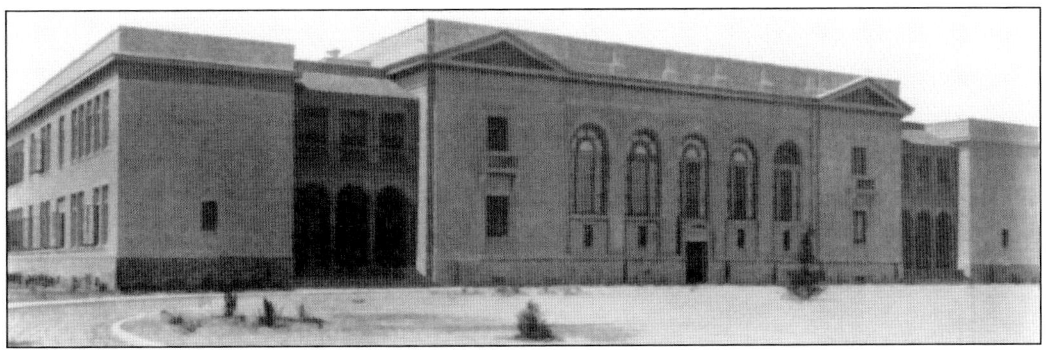

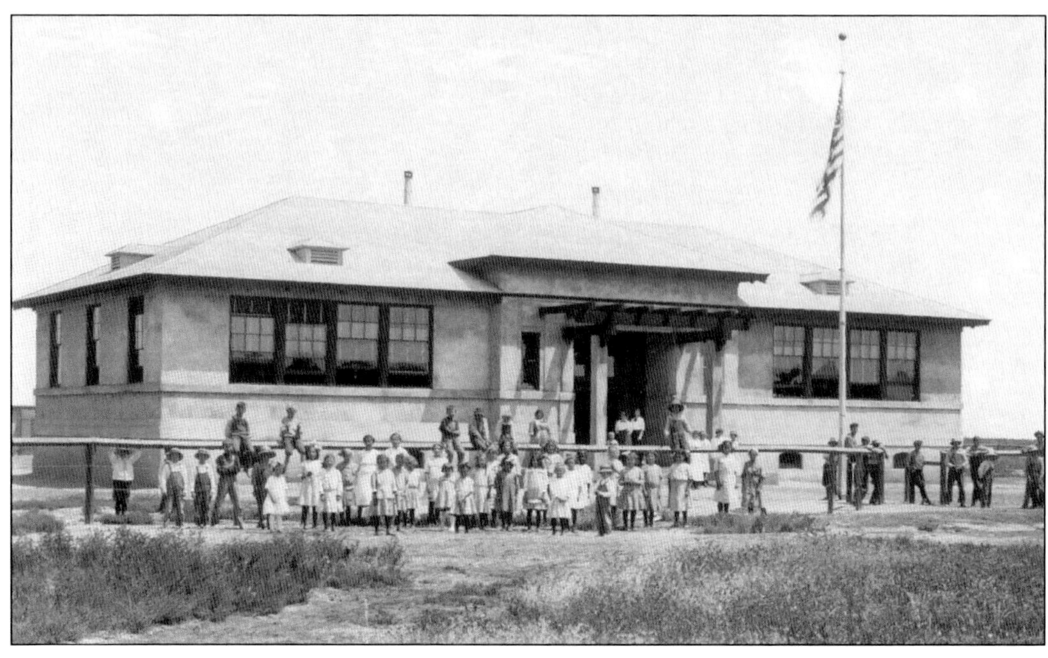

The Kerman Grammar School was built in 1909. Built of reinforced concrete, it has stood the test of time. Today, it serves the community as the Kerman Senior Center.

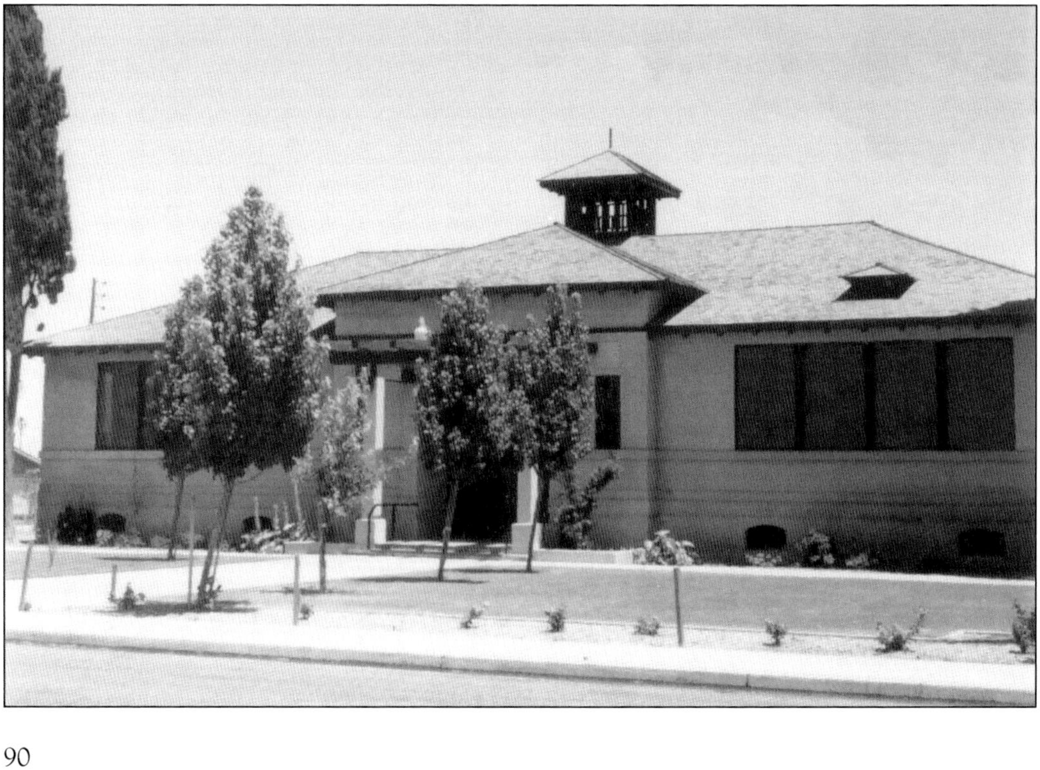

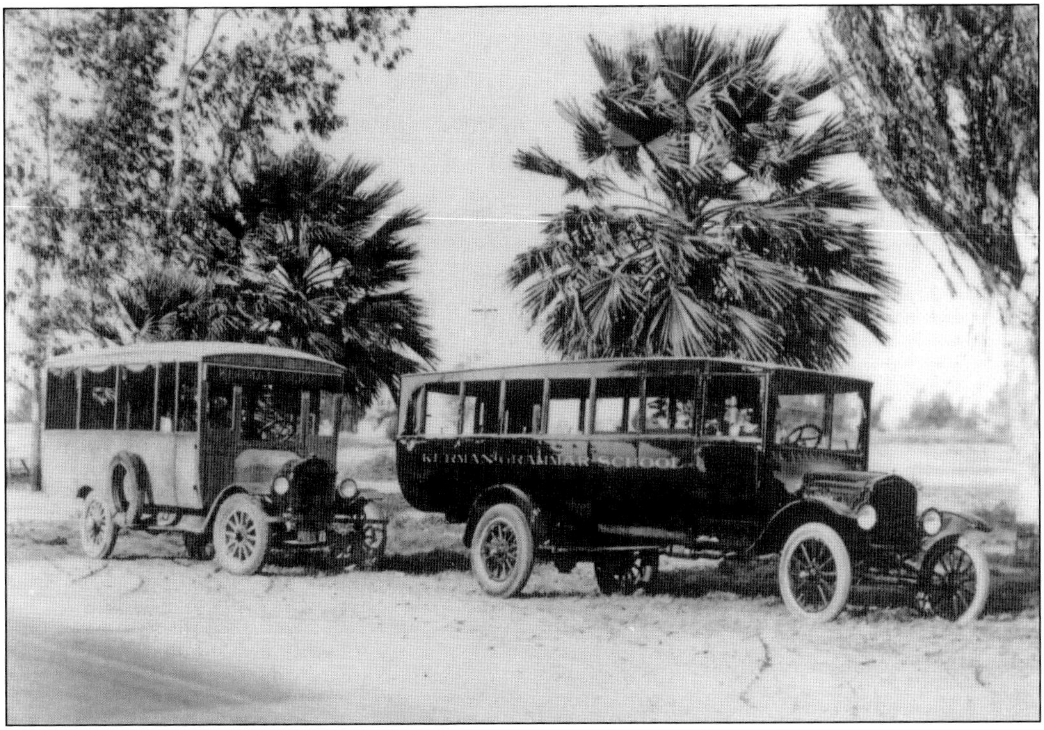

Of course, with farms spread out all over the countryside, very few students could get to school on foot. Seen here are some of the early school buses that were used to get students from home to school and back.

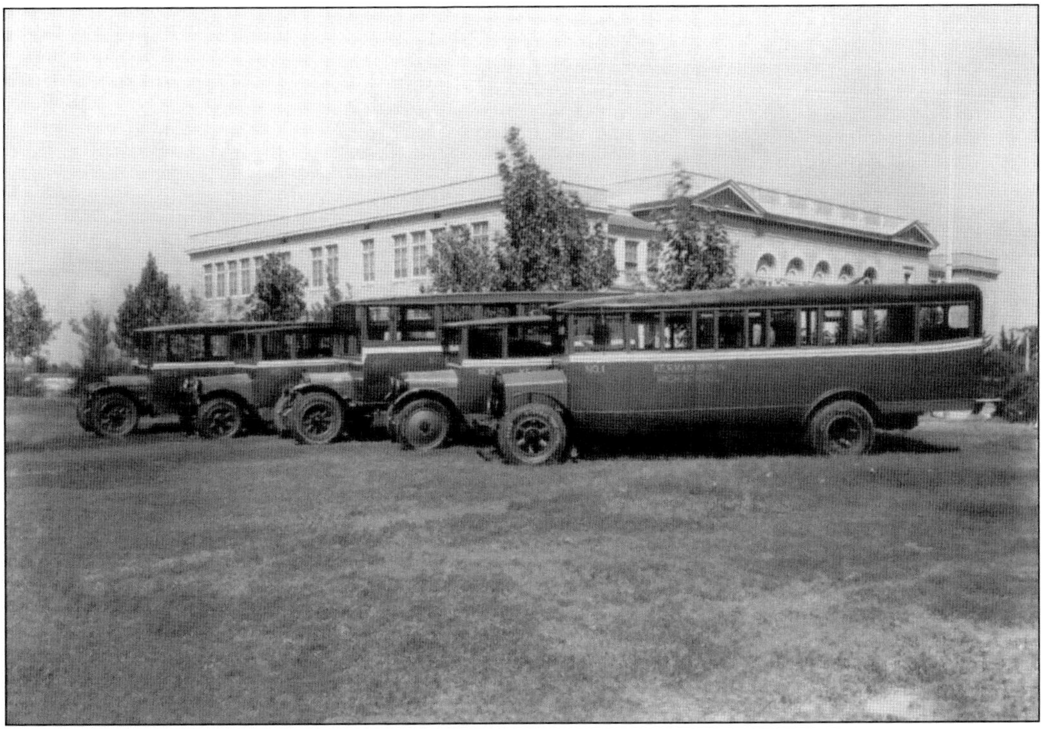

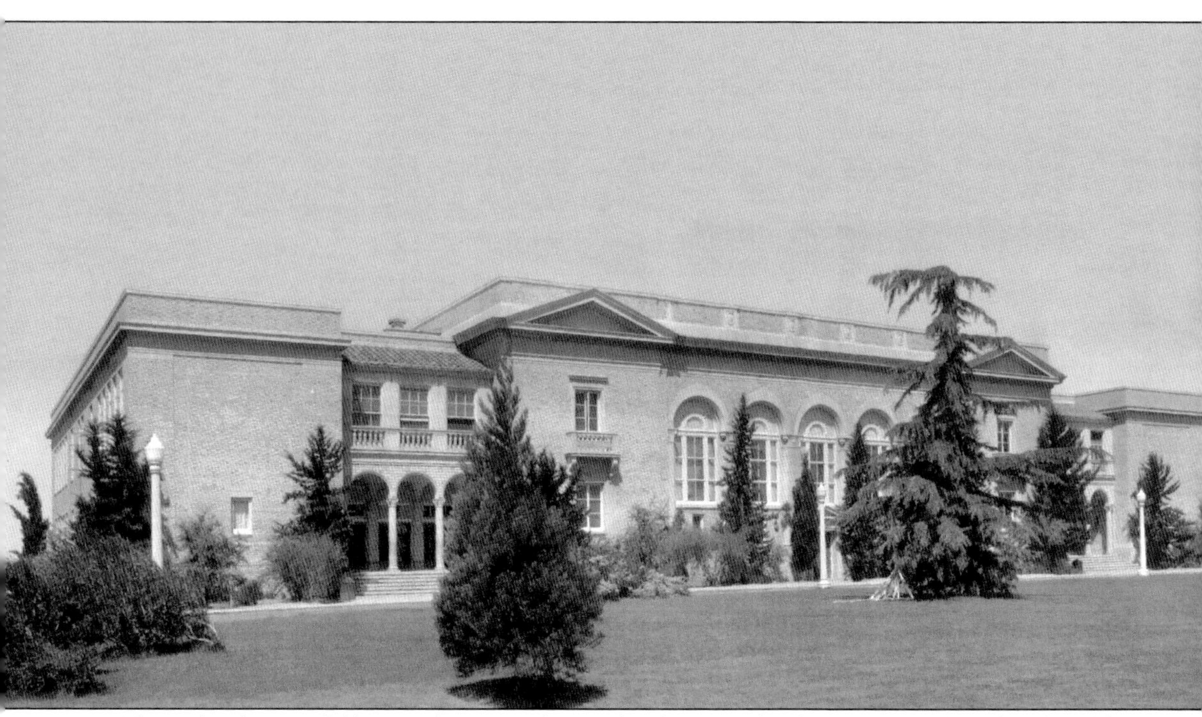

The only obvious difference between this early photograph of Kerman High School and how the school looks today is the growth of the trees around the building. The old high school was replaced by the current Kerman High School in 1967. Sadly, the historic old Kerman High School was destroyed by arsonists in 1998. Many of the bricks were saved and used in the new Kerman Telephone building on the south end of town.

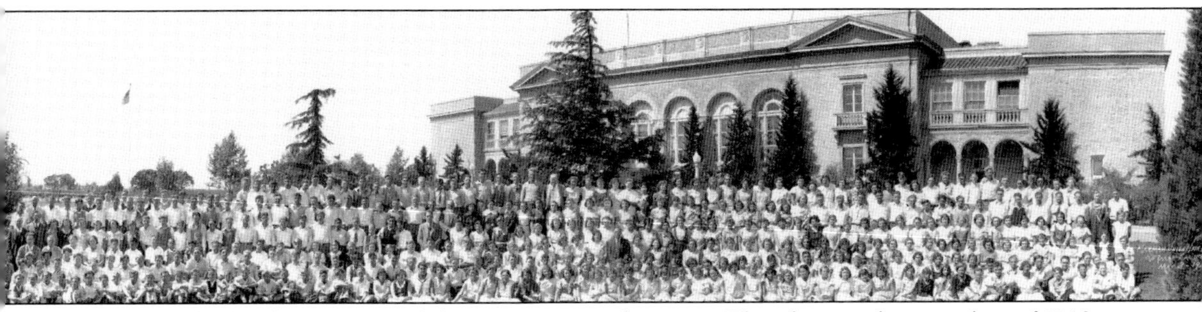

The student body of Kerman High has grown over the years. That first graduating class of 1913 was comprised of five students, and the centennial class of 2013 graduated 254 students.

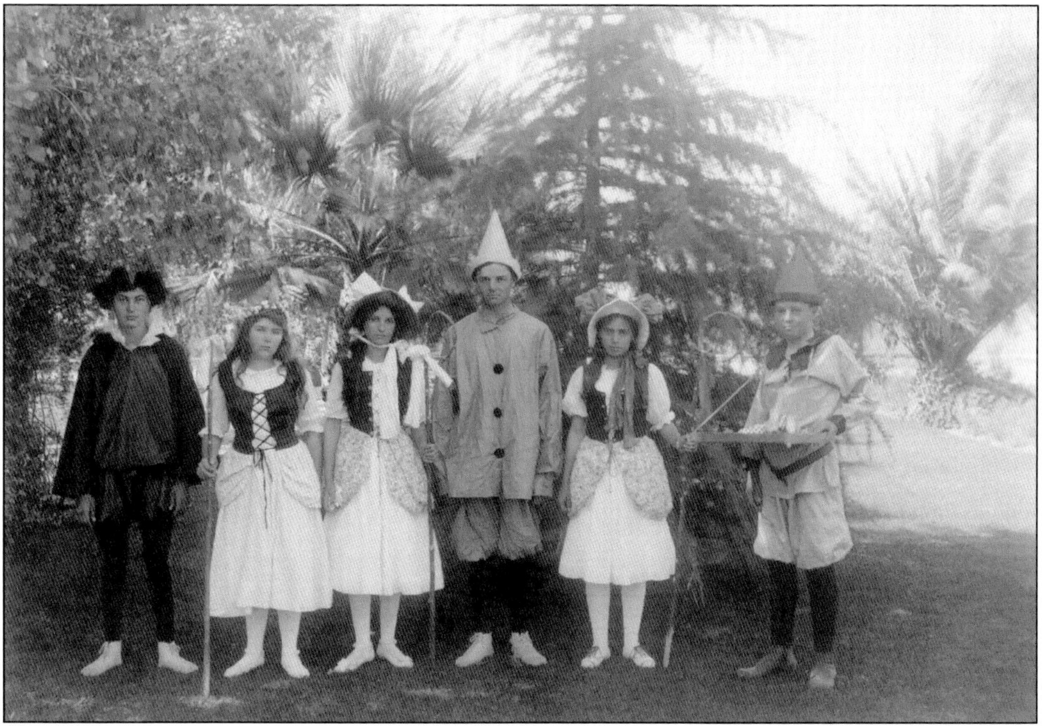

As with many rural communities, the high school was the center of community social life, especially before the days of television and the Internet. Above, students are dressed in costumes for a play. May Day celebrations were held for decades at the old Kerman High School. The highlight of the celebration was when teams from each elementary school competed to do the most elaborate May Pole wrapping. This event not only celebrated the coming of spring, but it also allowed elementary students to visit their future high school. Sadly, the May Day celebrations were discontinued in the 1960s.

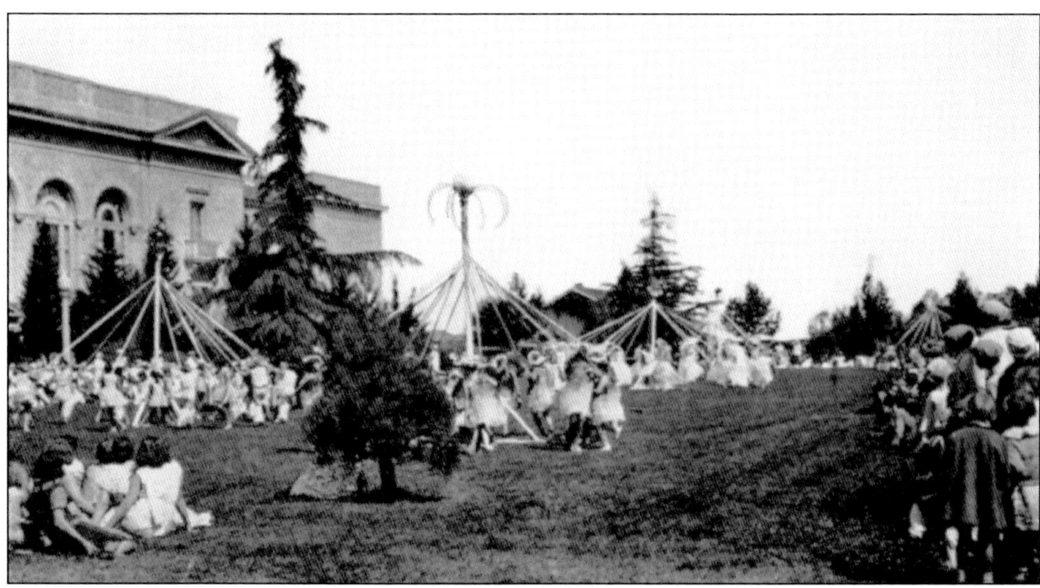

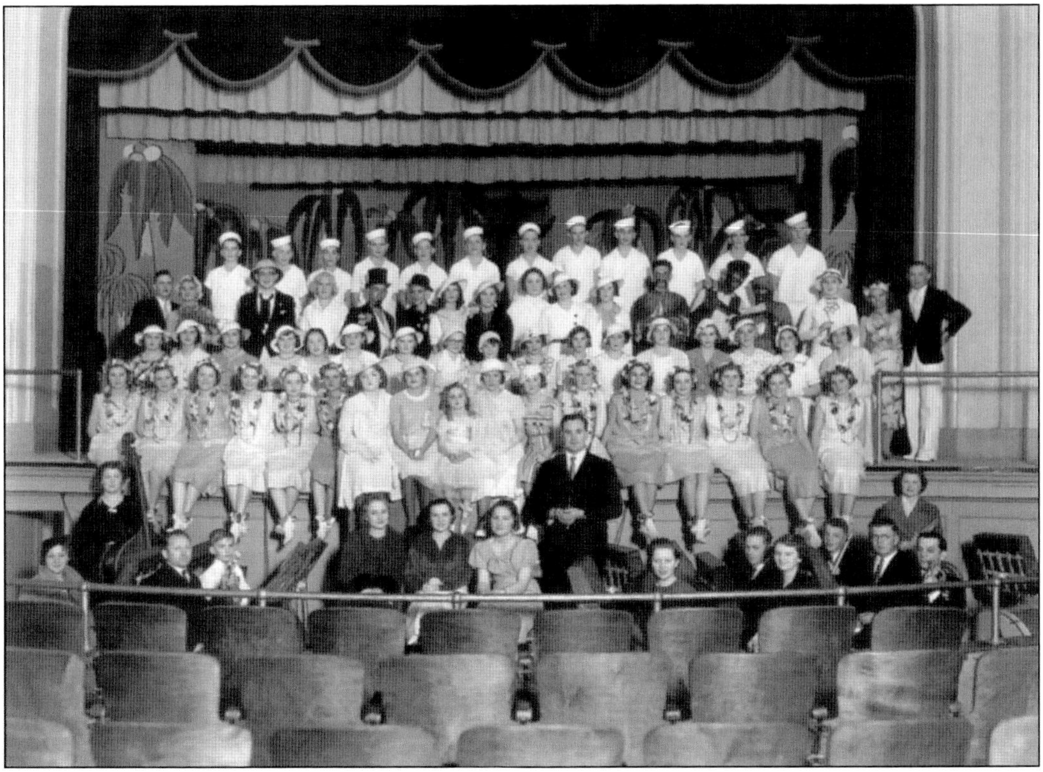

One of the architectural gems of the old high school building was its beautiful auditorium. It was a masterpiece of woodwork that provided an intimate setting for plays, concerts, and other gatherings over the years.

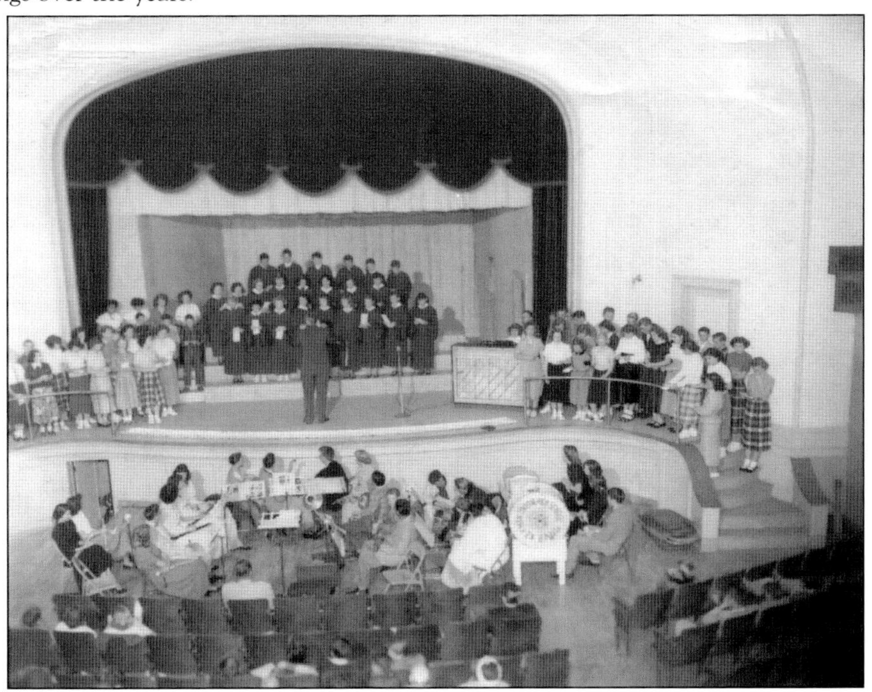

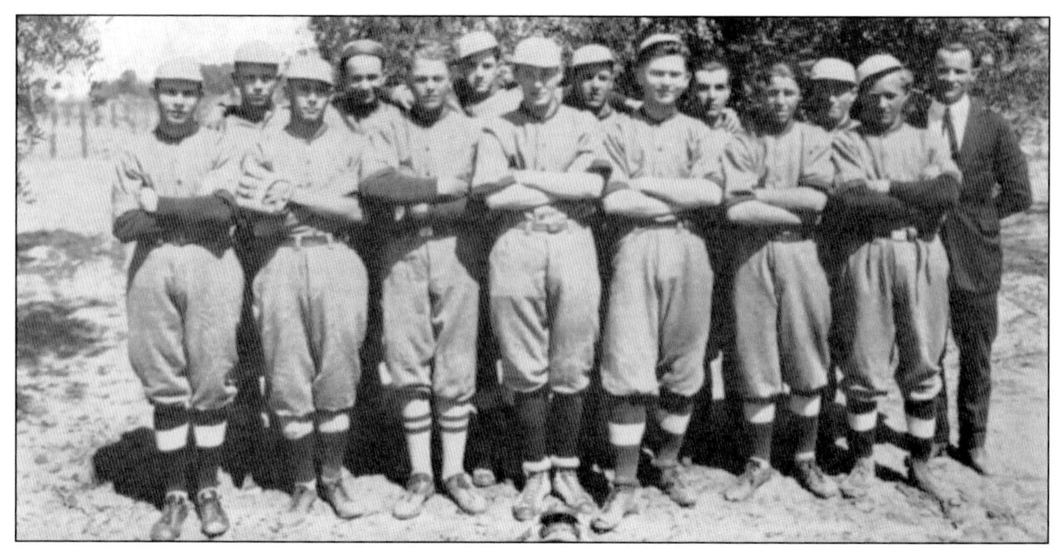

Sports have been popular in Kerman over the years. Featured here are the Kerman Union High School 1924 boys' and girls' baseball teams.

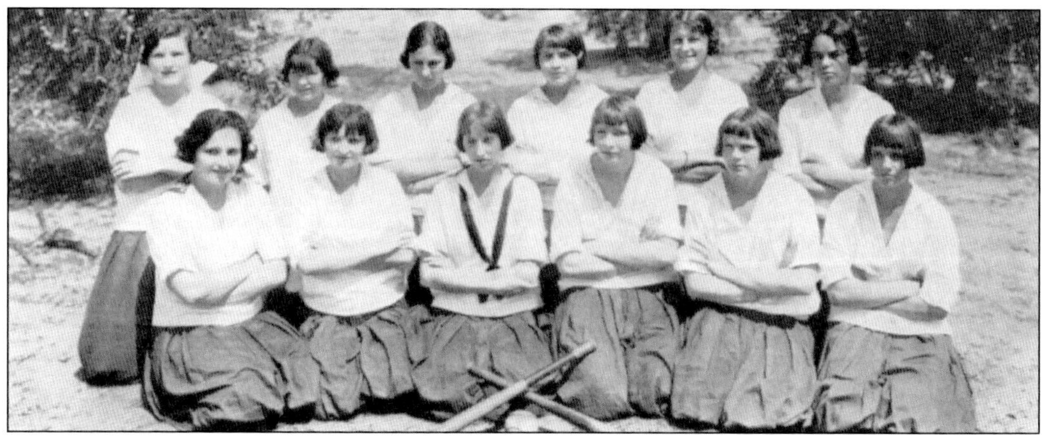

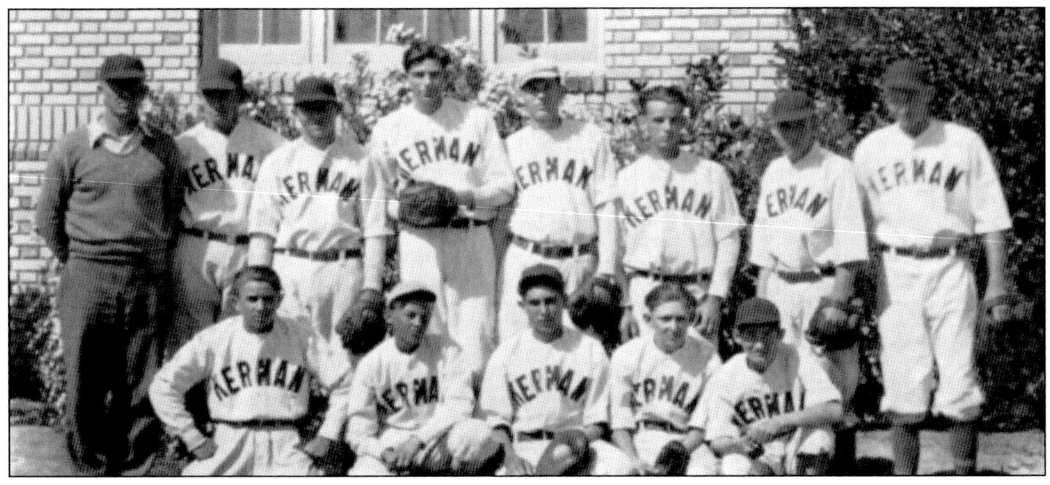

On this page, changes to the uniforms can be seen. There have been many championship teams in Kerman. Featured below are the 1964 Sierra League champions.

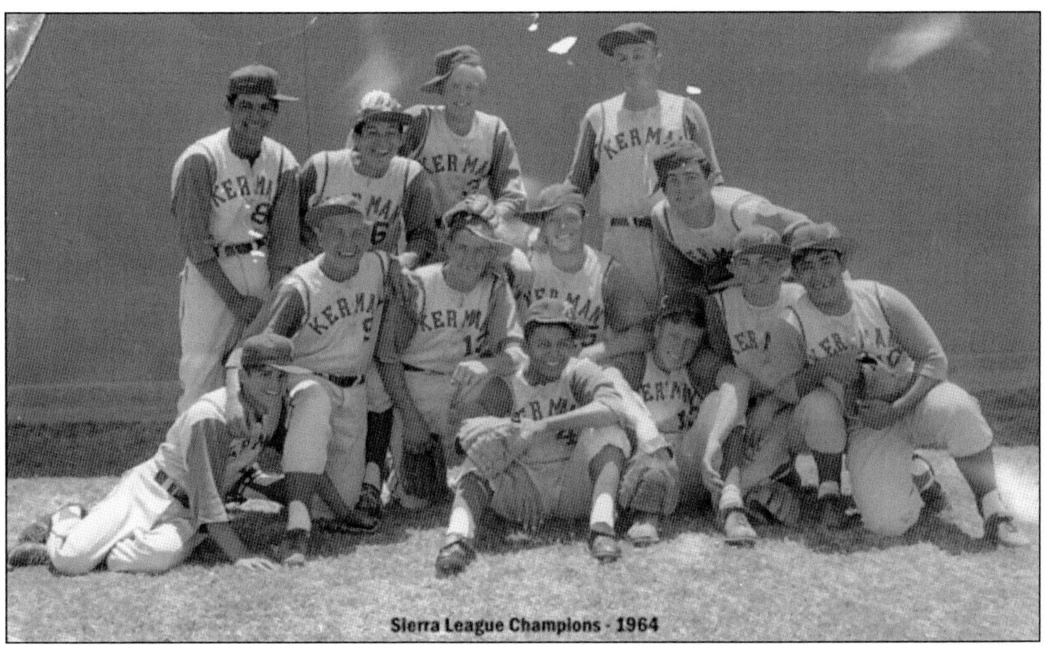

Sierra League Champions - 1964

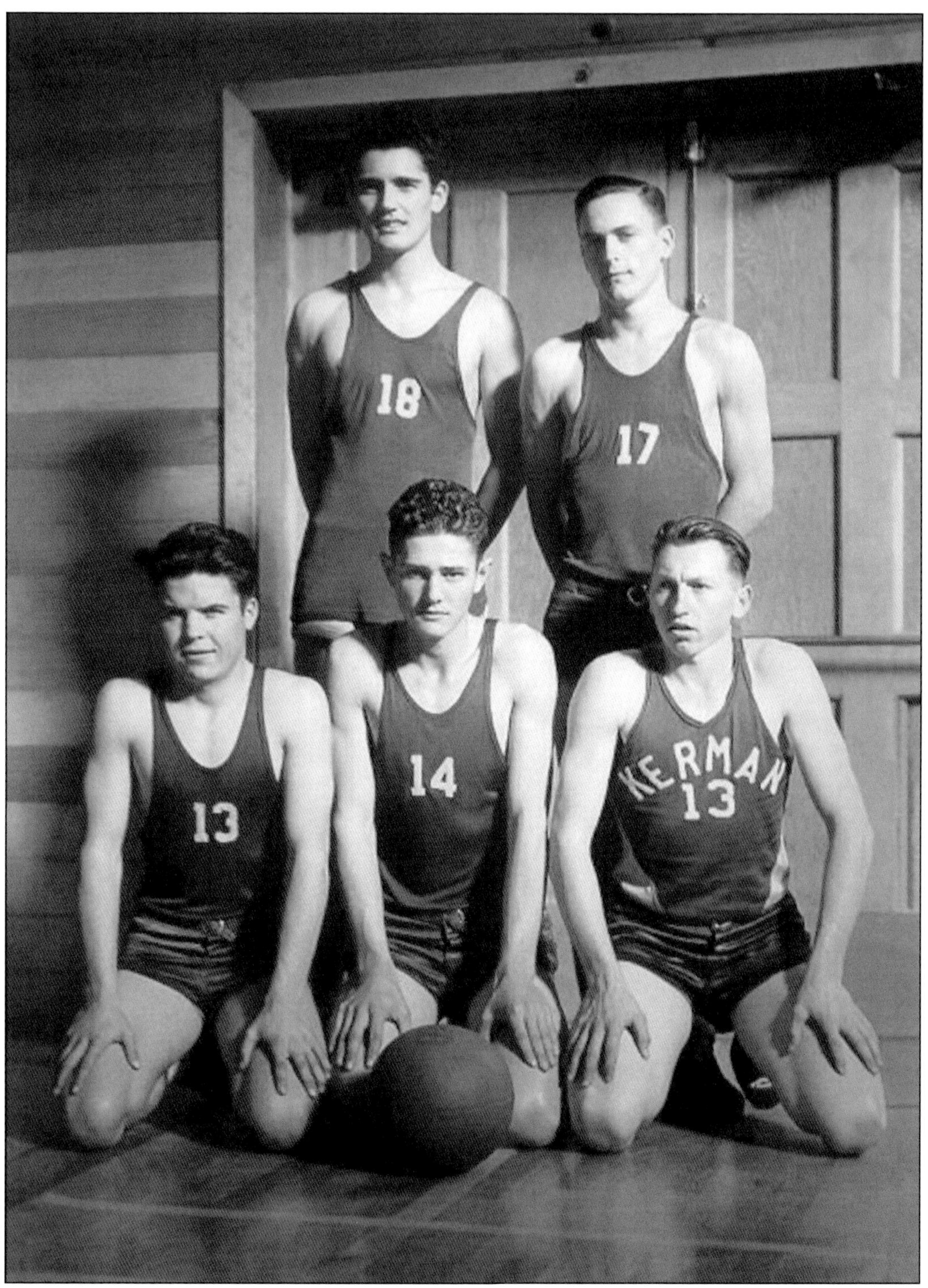

Of course, there were many other sports besides baseball, including basketball; one team is seen above. The gymnasium for the old high school was built in 1946.

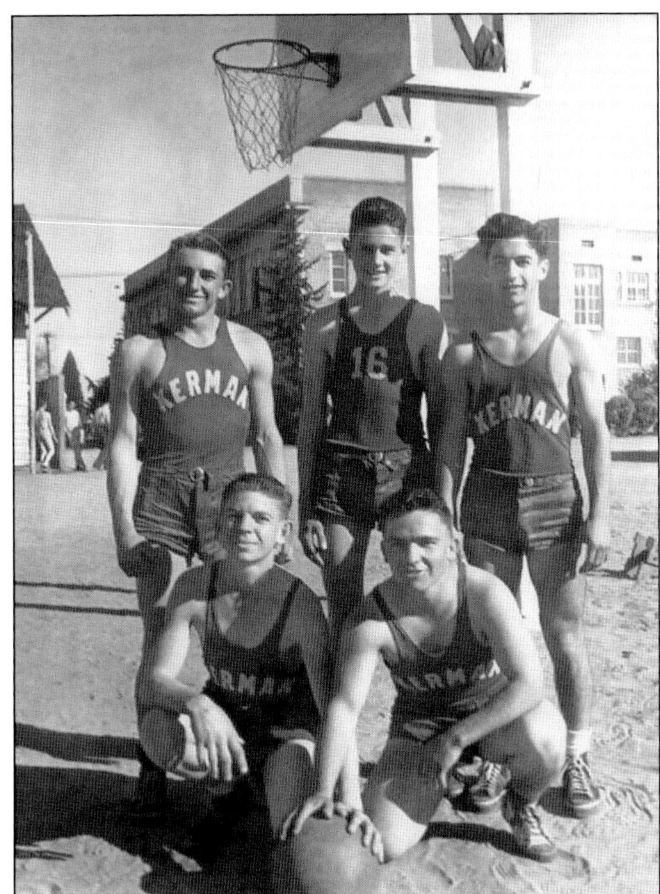

In the early years, it was not unusual for students to play more than one sport. Some young men played football in the fall, basketball during the winter, and baseball in the spring. The school was small enough that some athletes would play both offense and defense for the football team.

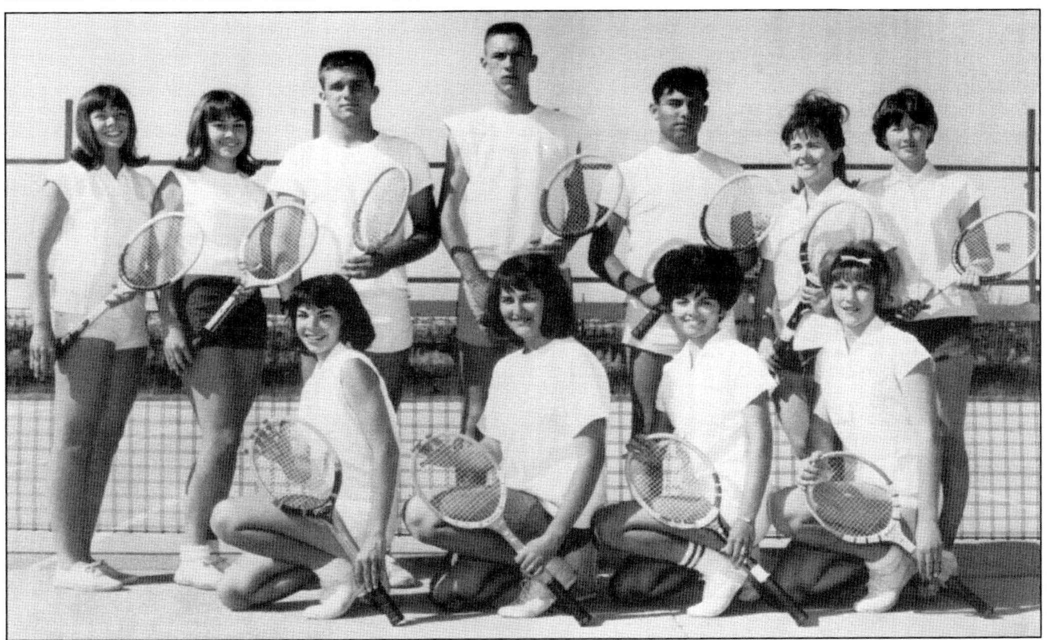

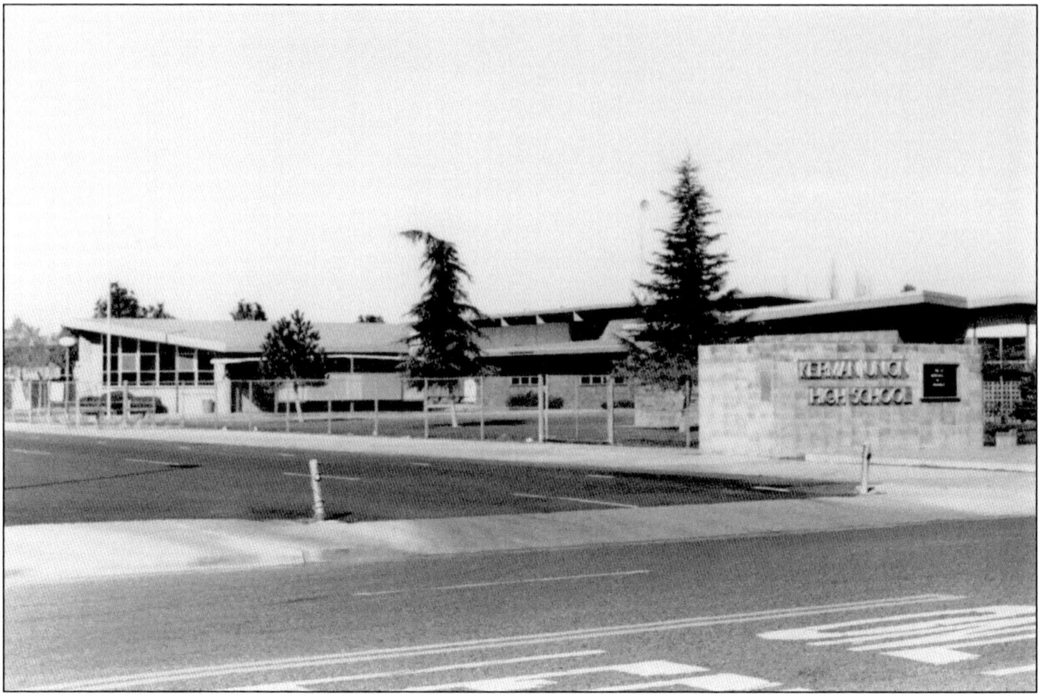

The new Kerman High School was built in 1967. This time, it was constructed closer to downtown Kerman. Since 1967, the town has grown around the high school, which is still a center for athletics, plays, and concerts. Visible below at right are Christmas trees, which were grown by agriculture students at the high school as a fundraiser up to the 1980s.

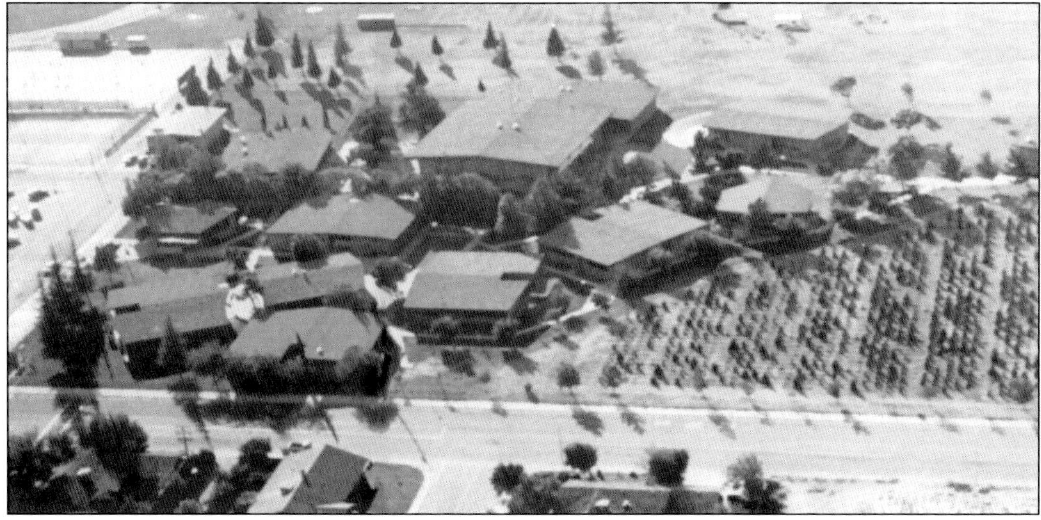

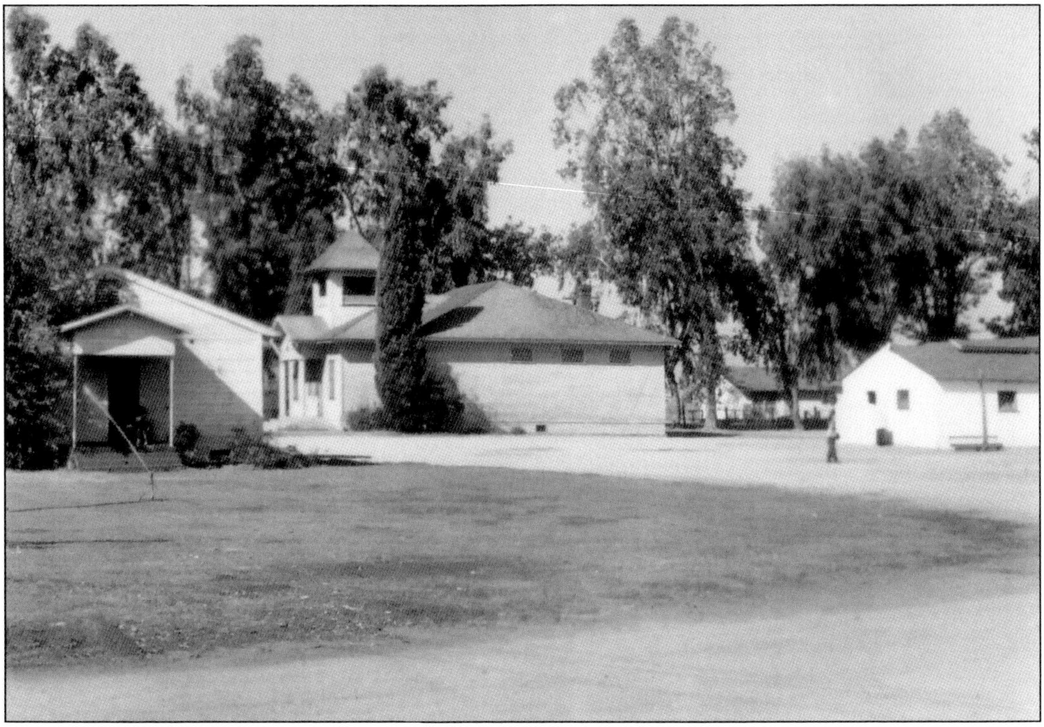

In 1956, Kerman Elementary and the Floyd District School were consolidated to form Kerman Floyd Elementary. Sun-Empire Elementary was formed by the consolidation of the Sunset, Empire, Hawkeye, and Vinland schools in 1955.

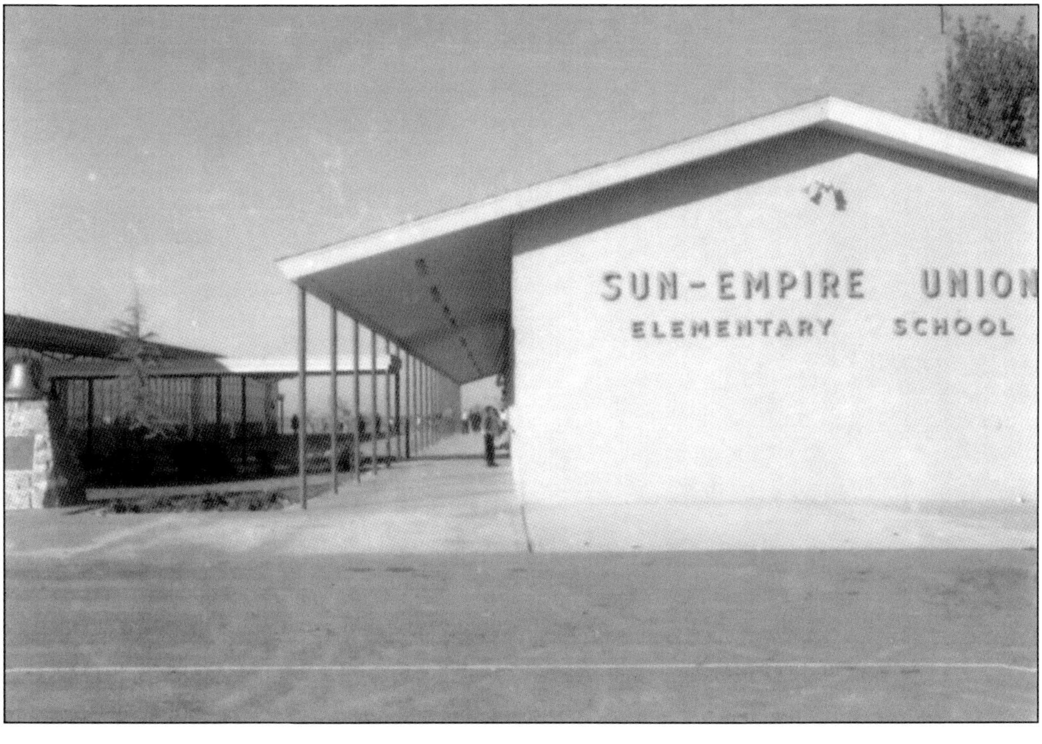

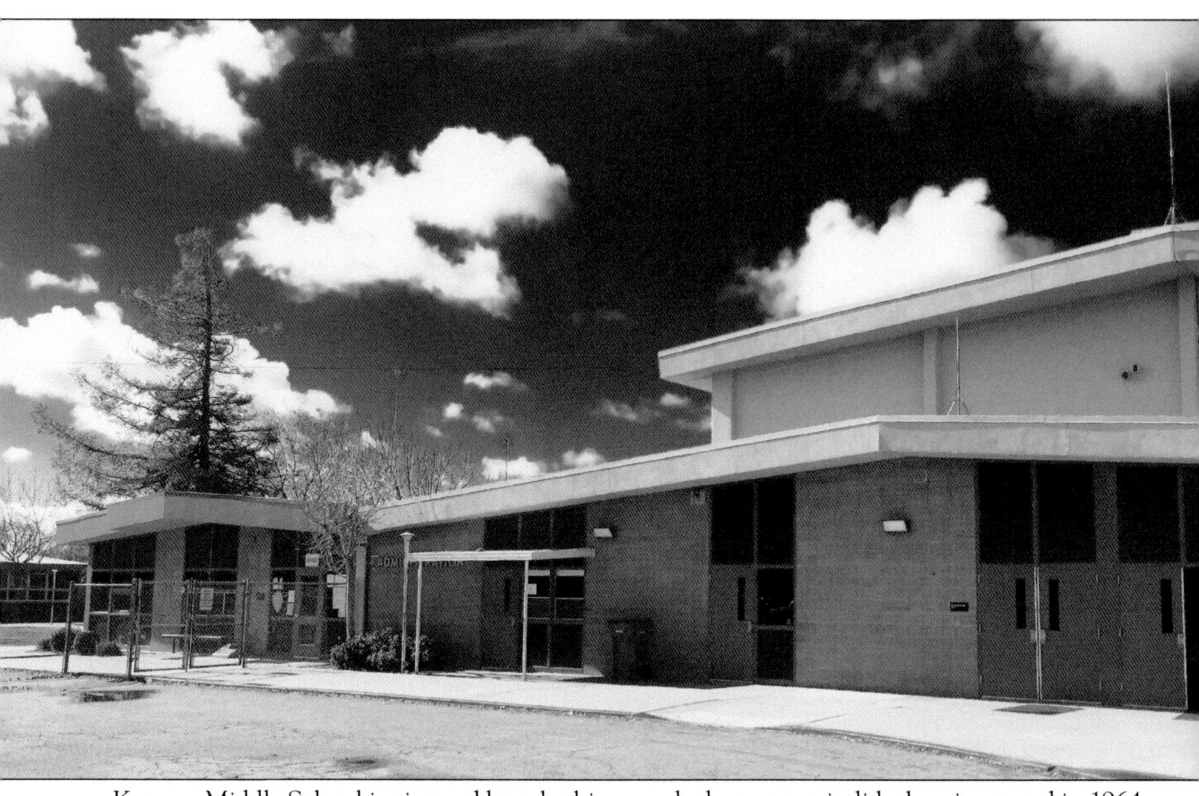

Kerman Middle School is pictured here looking much the same as it did when it opened in 1964. The trees have grown and there is fresh paint. Generations of Kerman students have gone through here on their way to high school.

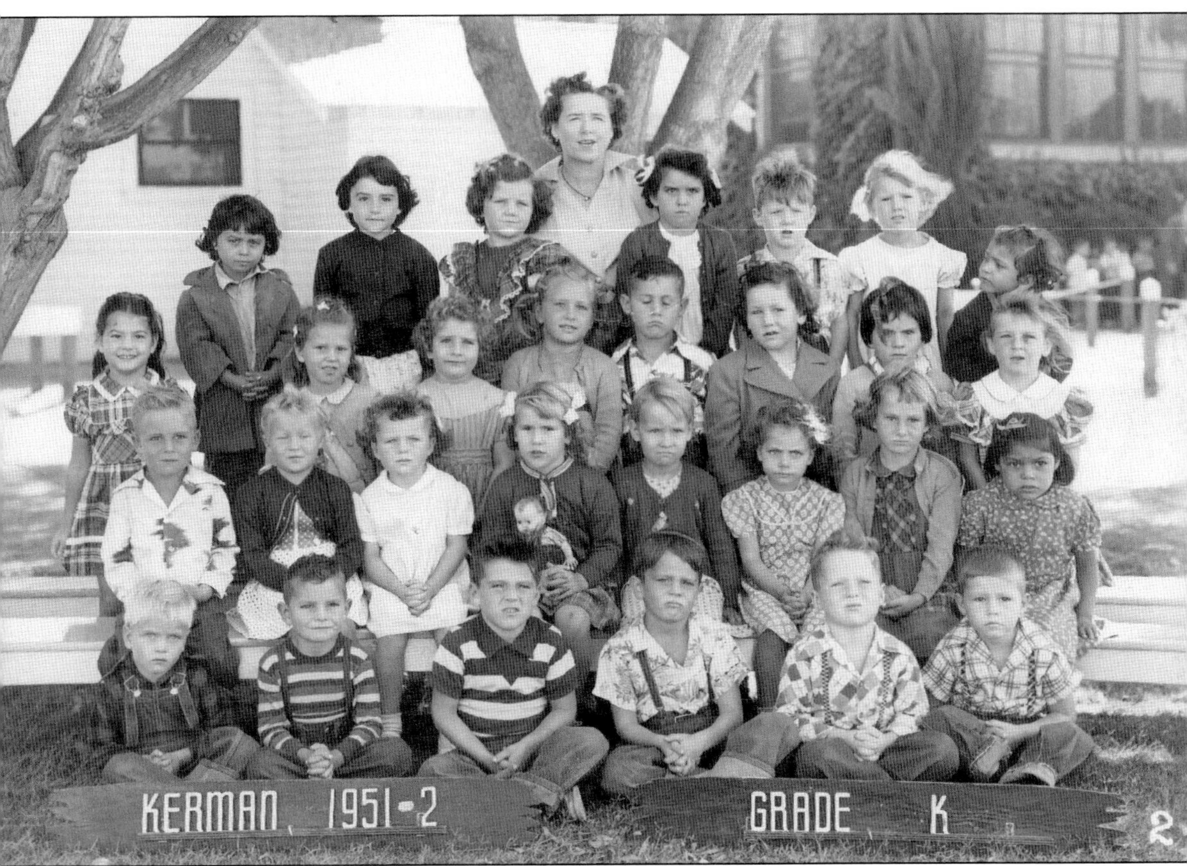

Early Kerman schools were rural. Each had a house on campus where the principal or a teacher lived. The schools had no air conditioning or cafeterias. Until the late 1940s, students had to bring their own lunches to school every day. Classroom discipline was strict.

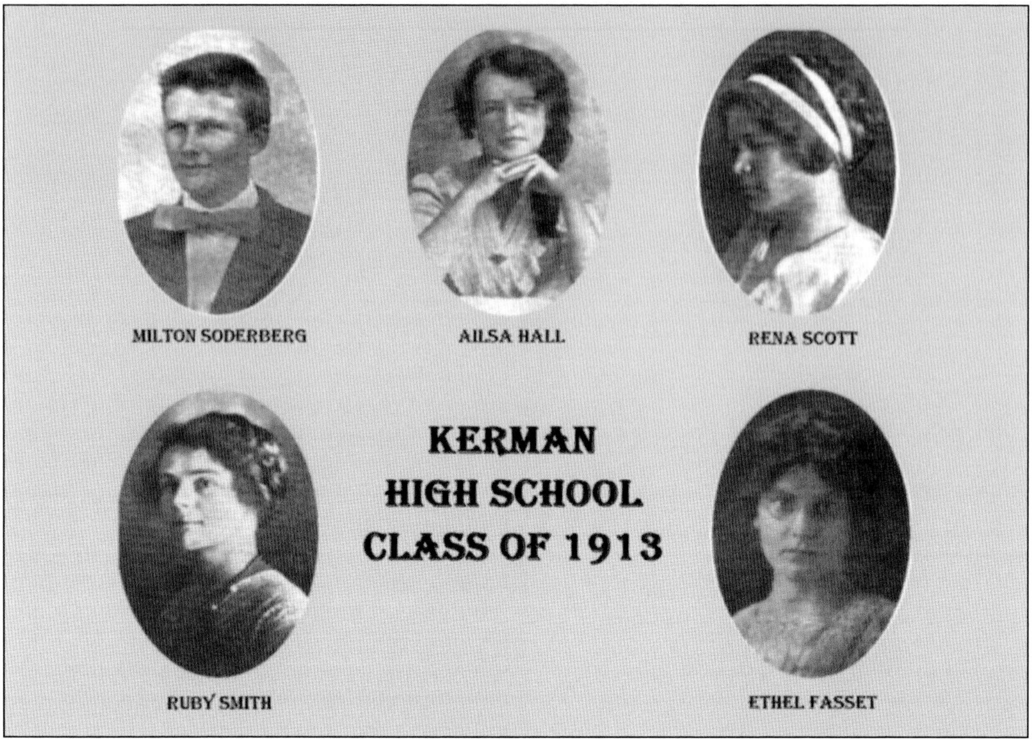

MILTON SODERBERG

AILSA HALL

RENA SCOTT

KERMAN
HIGH SCHOOL
CLASS OF 1913

RUBY SMITH

ETHEL FASSET

The first class of Kerman High School (above) graduated in 1913. The centennial class of 2013 is pictured below. In 1983, the people of Kerman voted to unify their schools into one district. New schools have been built as the community has grown. Liberty Elementary was erected as an intermediary school in 2002. Goldenrod Elementary was opened in 2012. New schools are being planned for future growth. (Below, courtesy of Pam Millspaugh.)

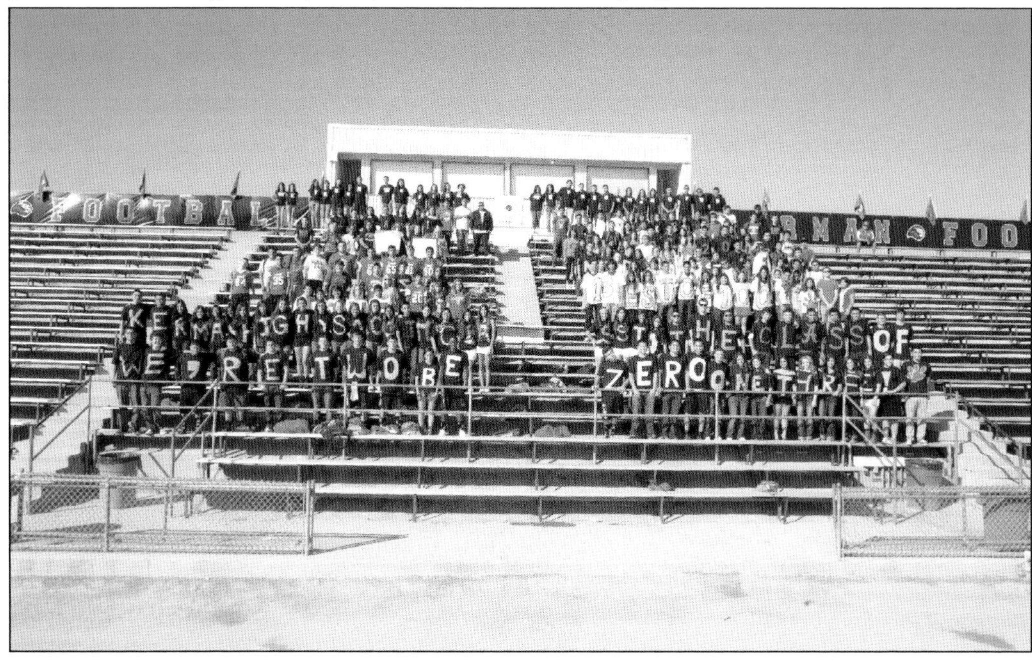

Five

Local Government

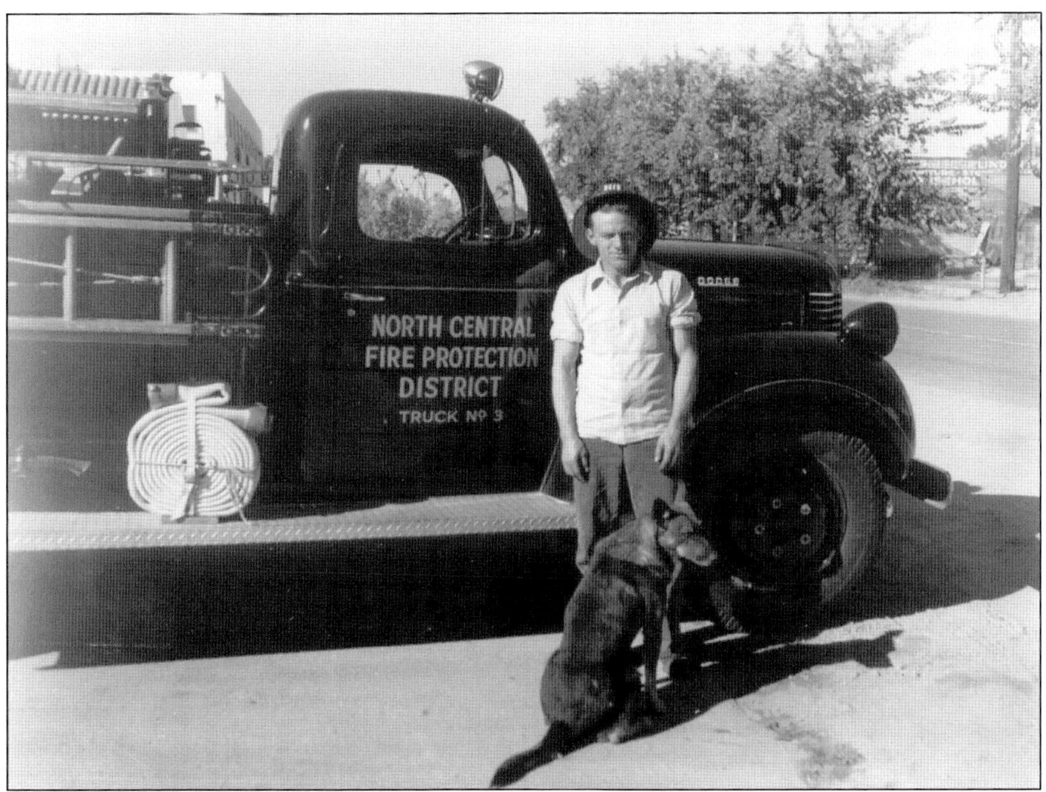

Kerman has been blessed with generations of excellent community leaders and civil servants. While there have been the usual ups and downs at city council meetings over the years, there has always been hometown pride in our local police officers and firefighters.

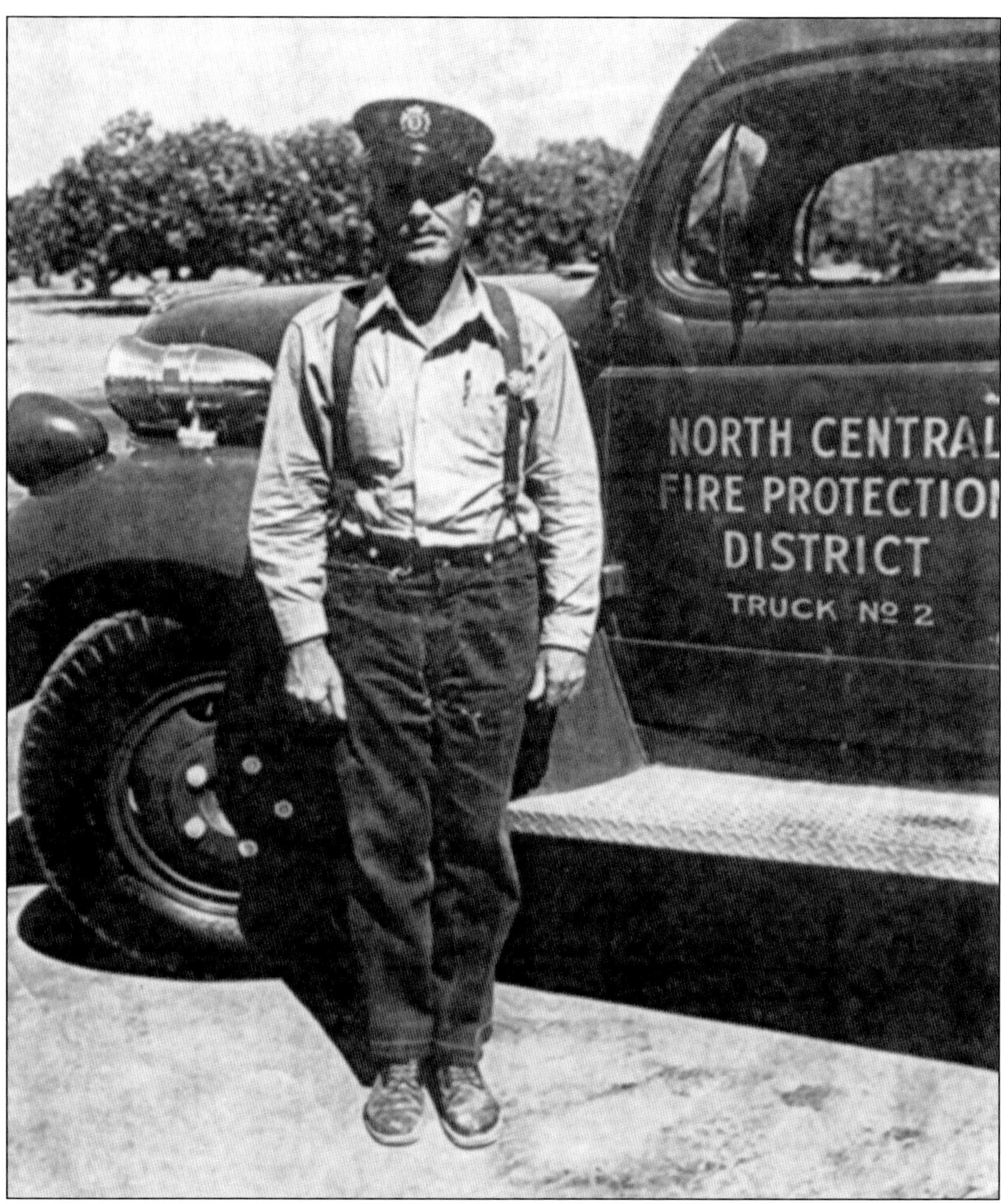

The earliest local firefighters were volunteers, as in many communities. Before long, Kerman was part of the North Central Fire Protection District, which included the homes and farms outside of Kerman towards Fresno.

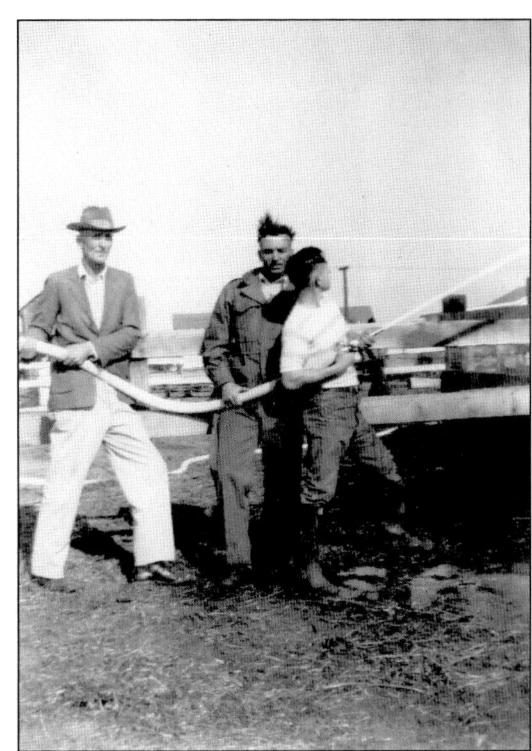

Like many small towns, the roots of today's professional fire department go back to volunteer community members. In these photographs, local residents learn how to handle high-pressure fire hoses.

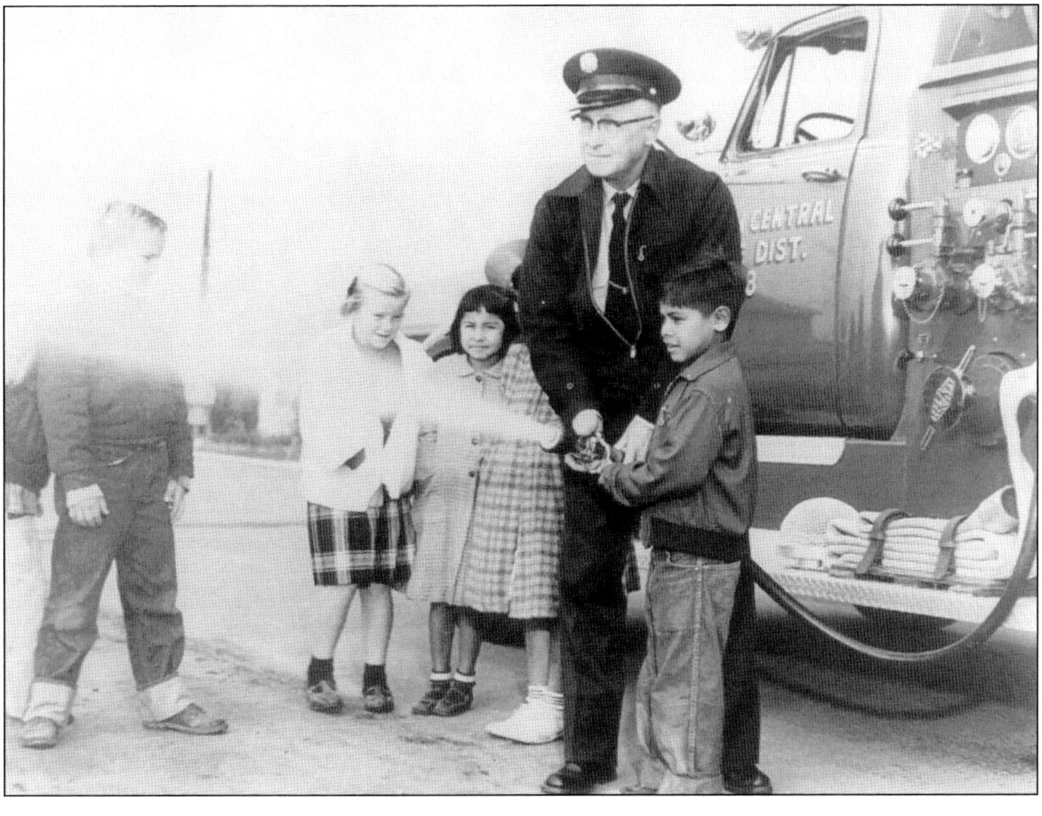

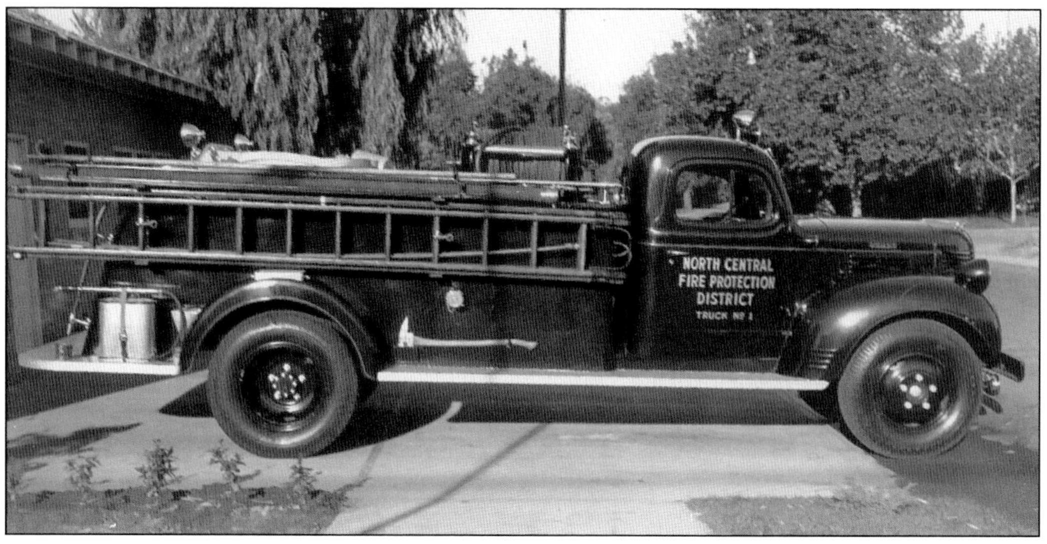

It was a proud day when Kerman's first fire truck rolled into town. The new truck and the tanker that followed greatly improved fire protection for the town and the surrounding farms.

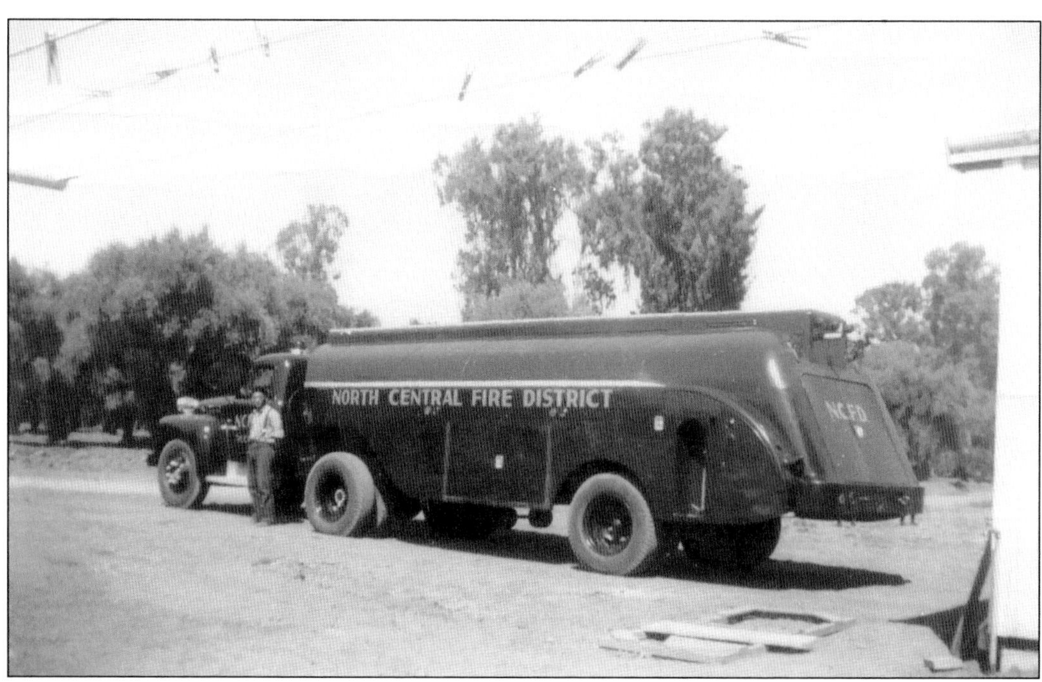

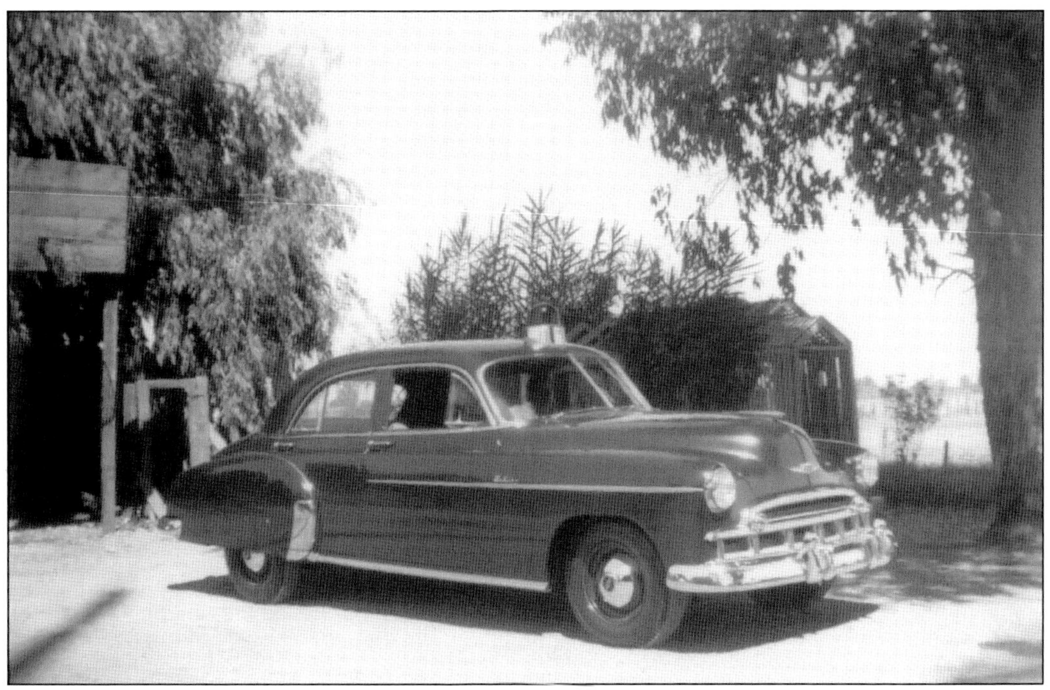

Pictured here is the car of Kerman's first fire chief, I.H. Cordy, who held the job from 1946 to 1965.

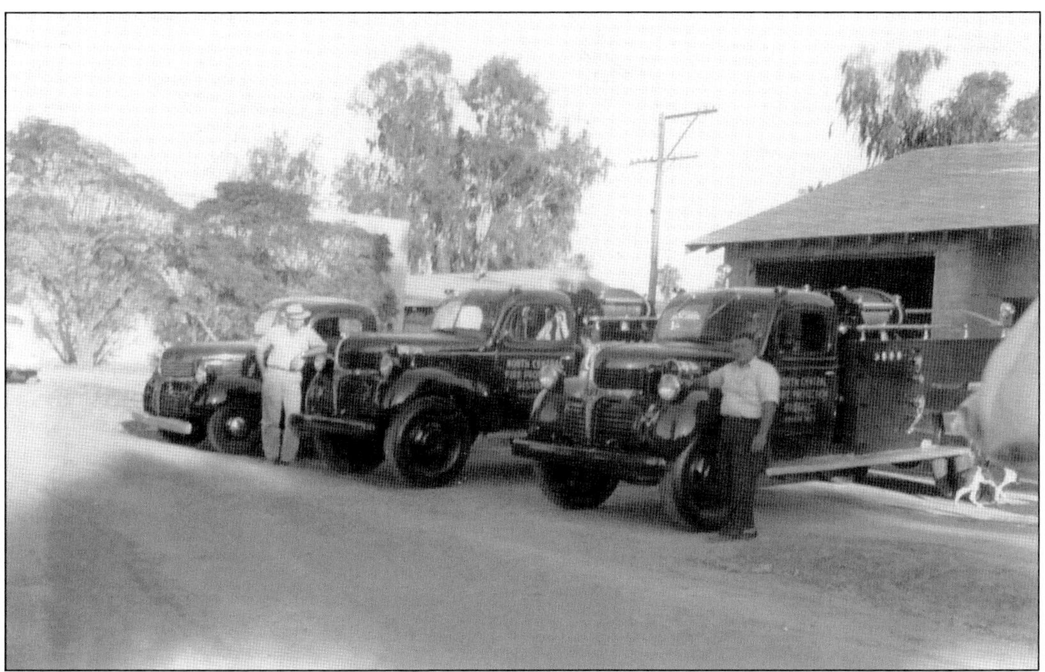

Gradually, the North Central Fire District built up a fleet of modern firefighting equipment to help protect the community.

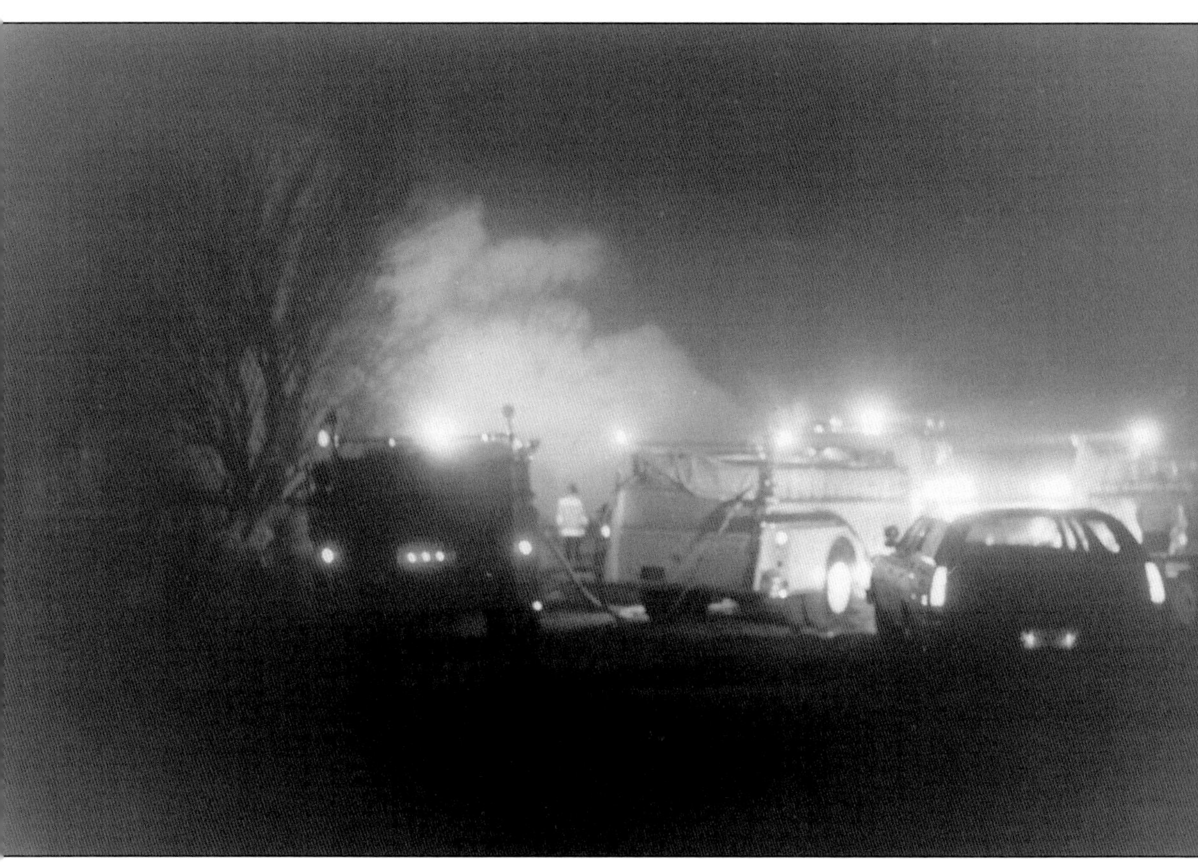

Men of the North Central Fire District are seen here fighting a nighttime tire fire. The North Central Fire Protection District was formed in 1947 after a large fire in Biola was allowed to burn for three days because there were not enough resources in nearby Fresno to cover the fire.

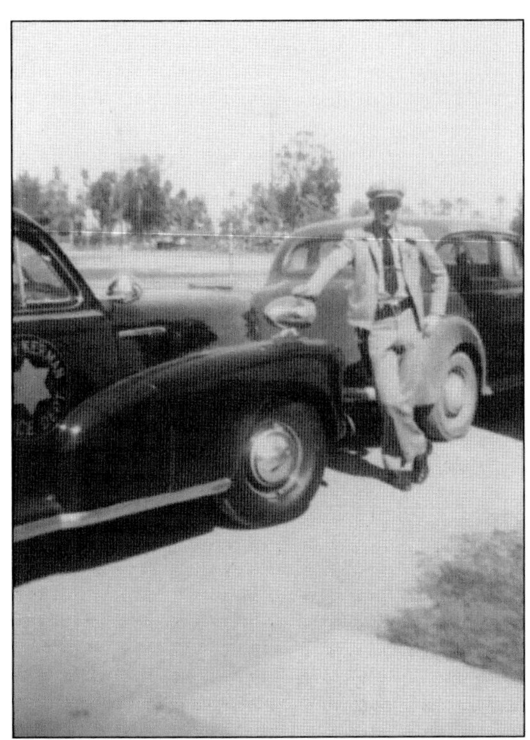

At right, one of Kerman's finest stands ready to protect the community. Below, officers investigate a car wreck.

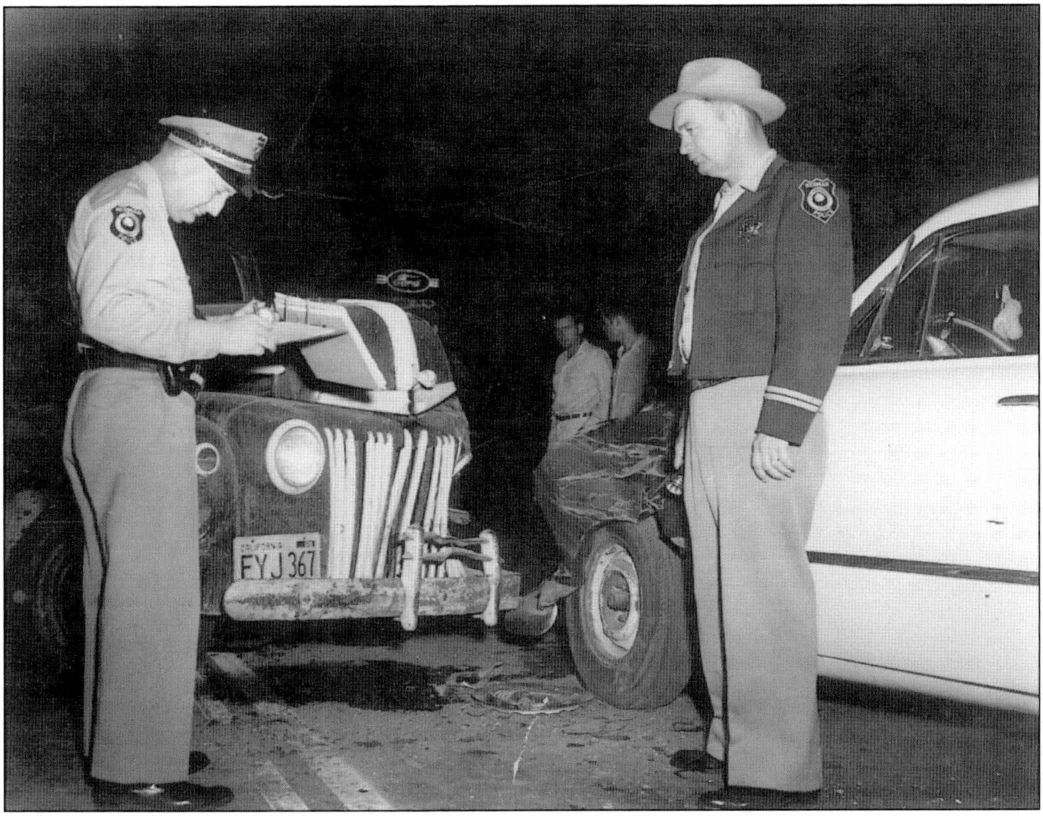

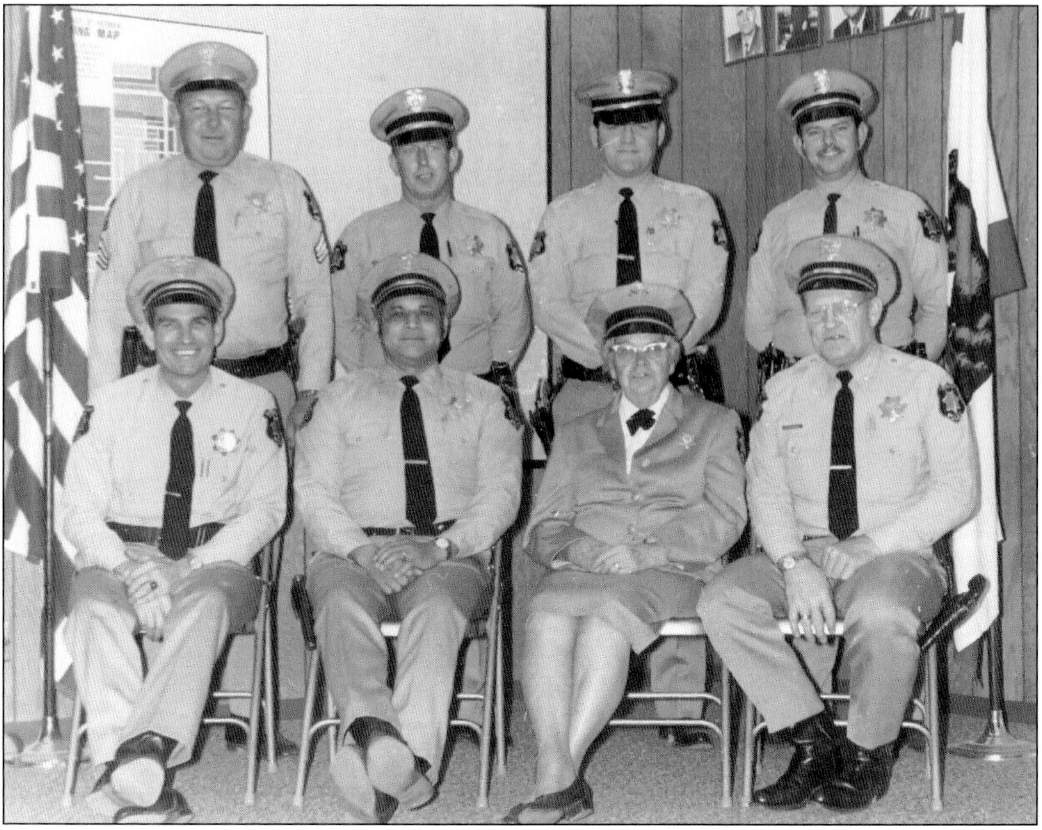

Roy Logan was Kerman's first police chief. He held the job from 1946 to 1948.

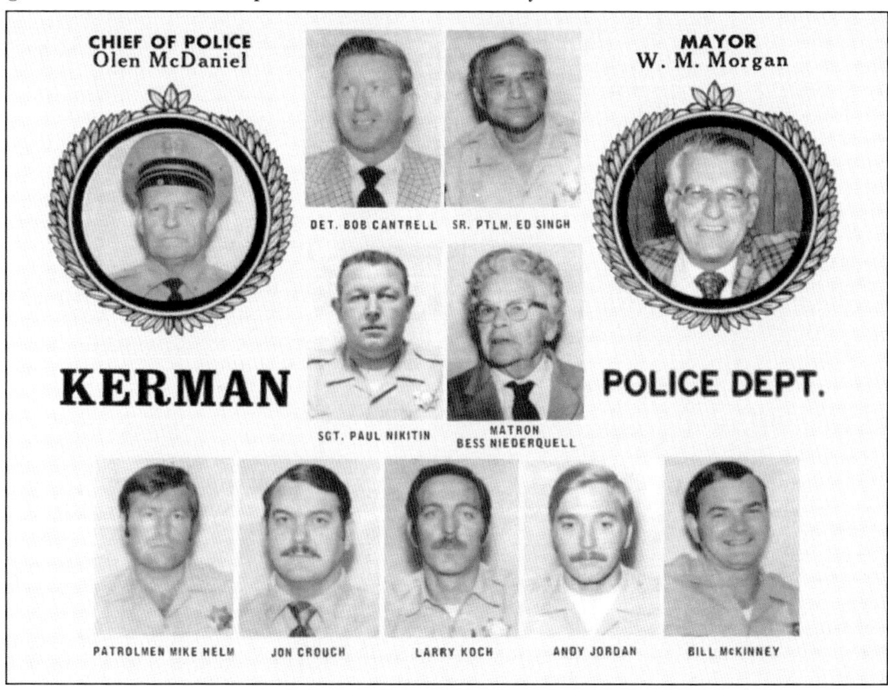

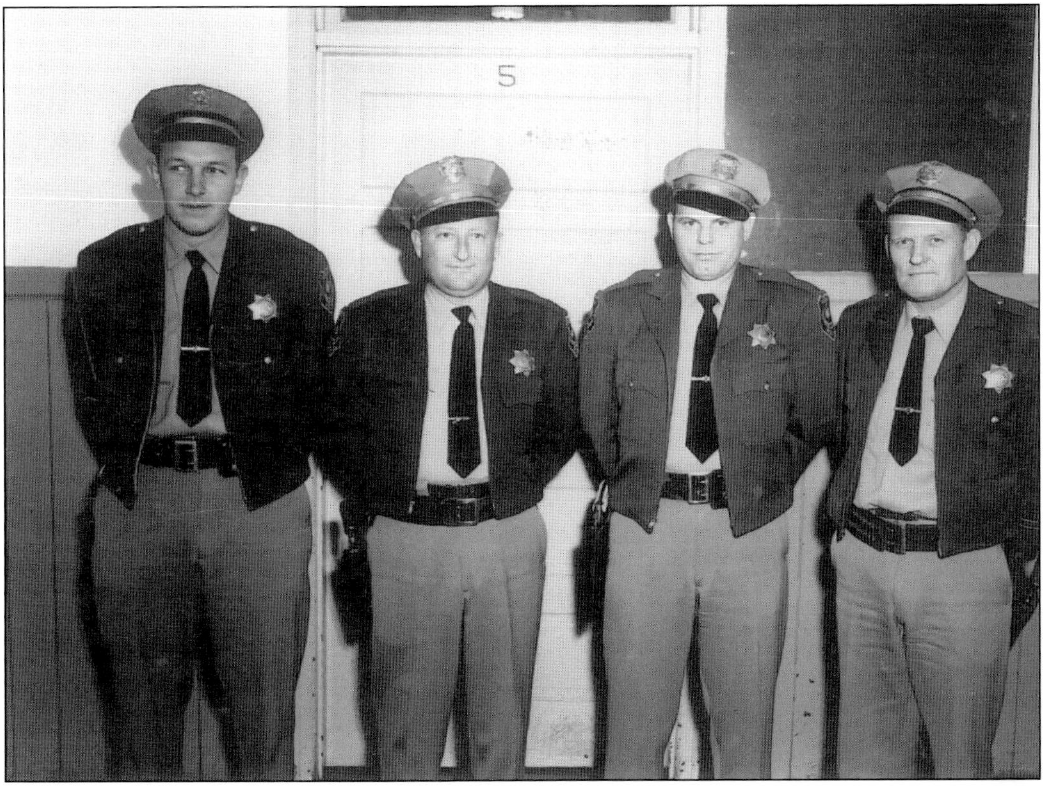

Above, Chief Roy McElroy is pictured with three police offers, while another officer is seen at right.

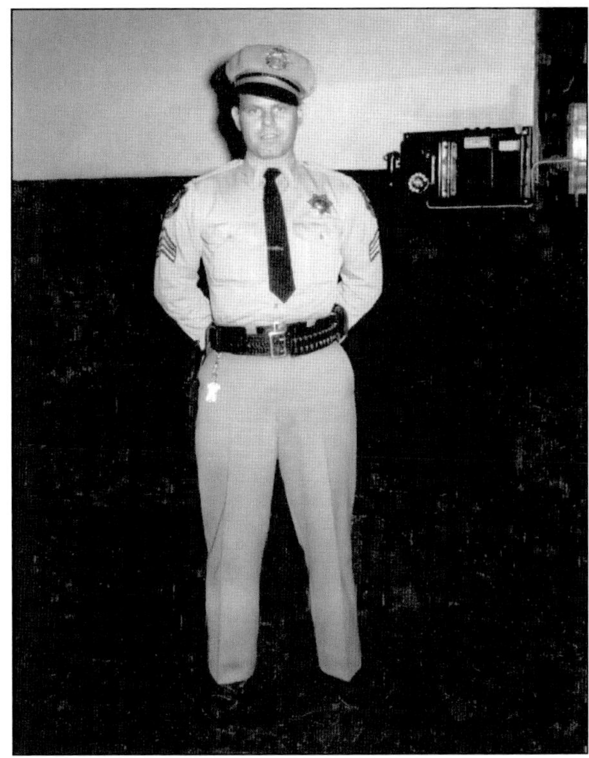

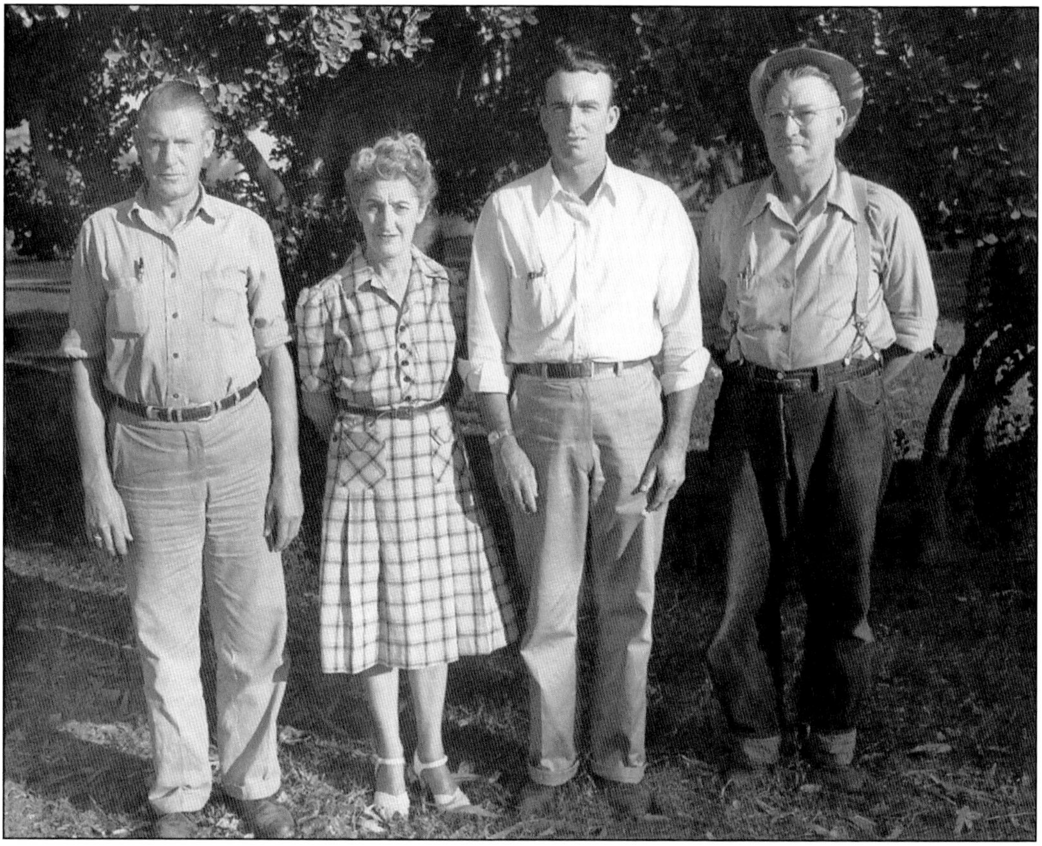

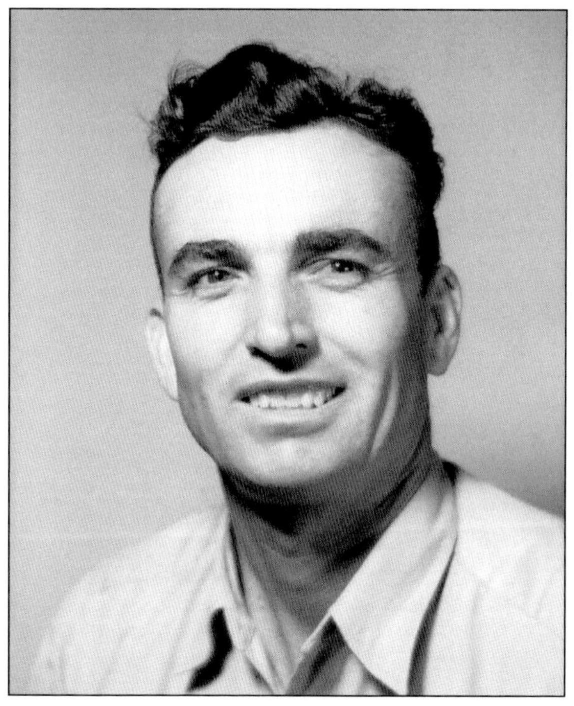

Equality has long been important in Kerman. When the city incorporated in 1946, the first city council (above) included Ila Moore (second from left), a local fourth grade teacher. The first mayor was Ben Middleton (left), who held the job for 10 years. Middleton was a devoted community servant active in the town's affairs for decades.

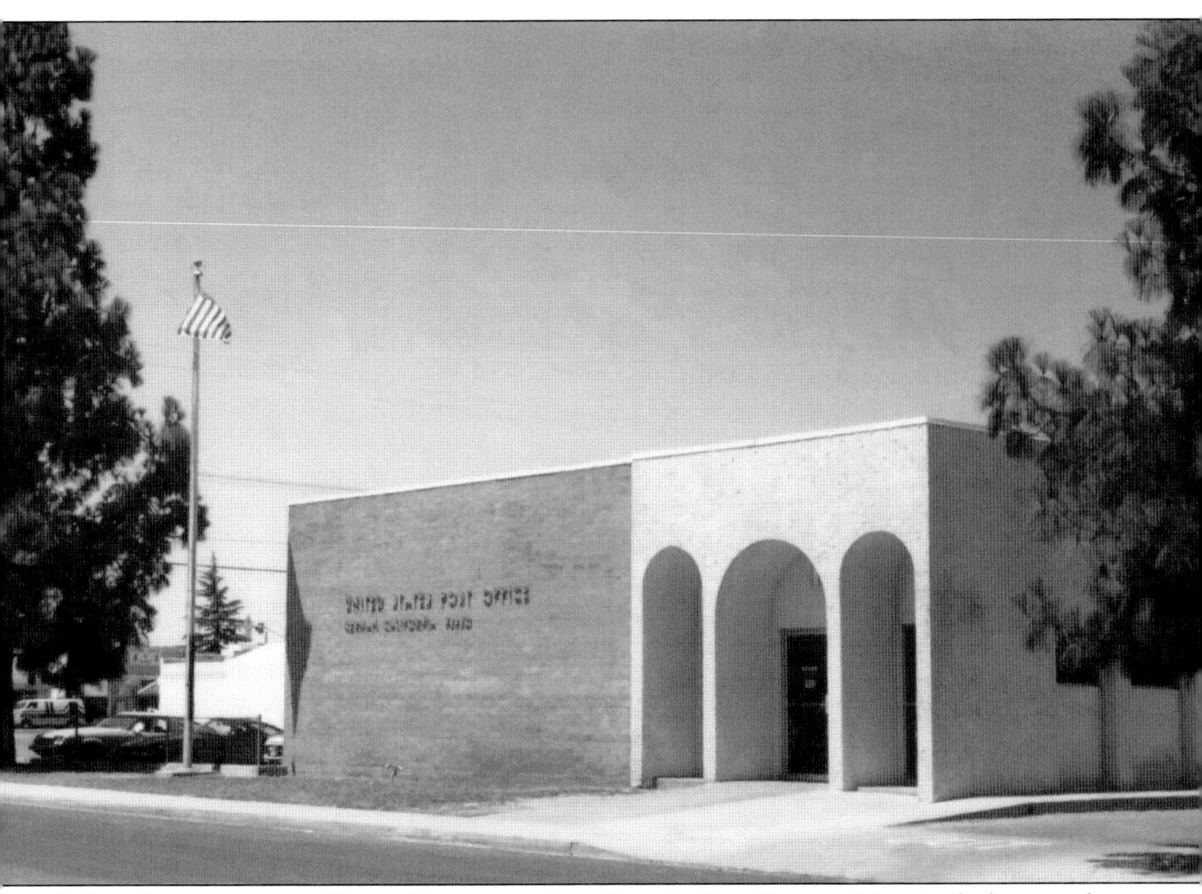

Before there was a post office in Kerman, mail was brought from Kearney Mansion by horse and buggy. The post office in Kerman has moved around over the years. The first location was at the train station. The post office moved up along Plaza Park; later, it moved up on Madera Avenue. The current post office was built in 1965.

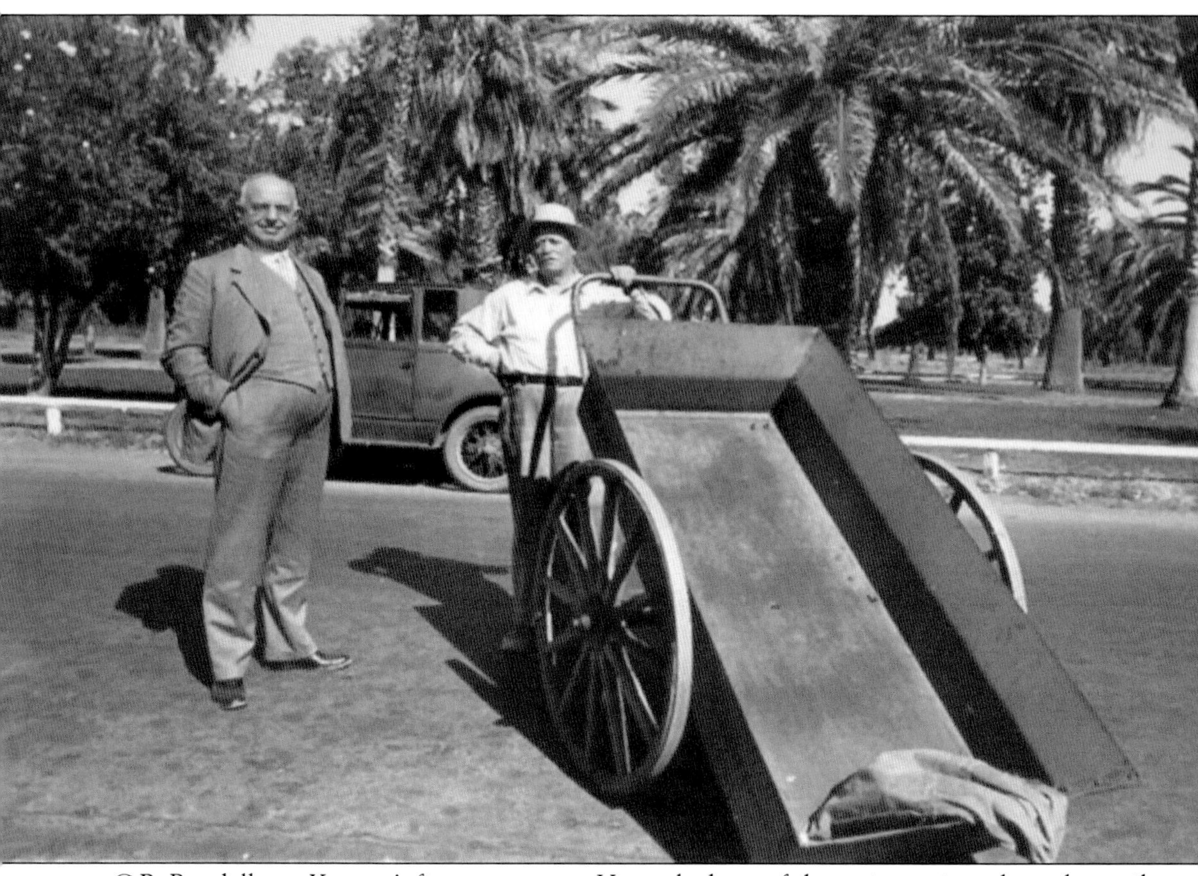

C.B. Randall was Kerman's first postmaster. He worked out of the train station where the mail was delivered. When the post office moved up to Plaza Park, the mail was hauled in a cart from the train station to the post office by Carl Steigt.

Six

Fun in the Sun

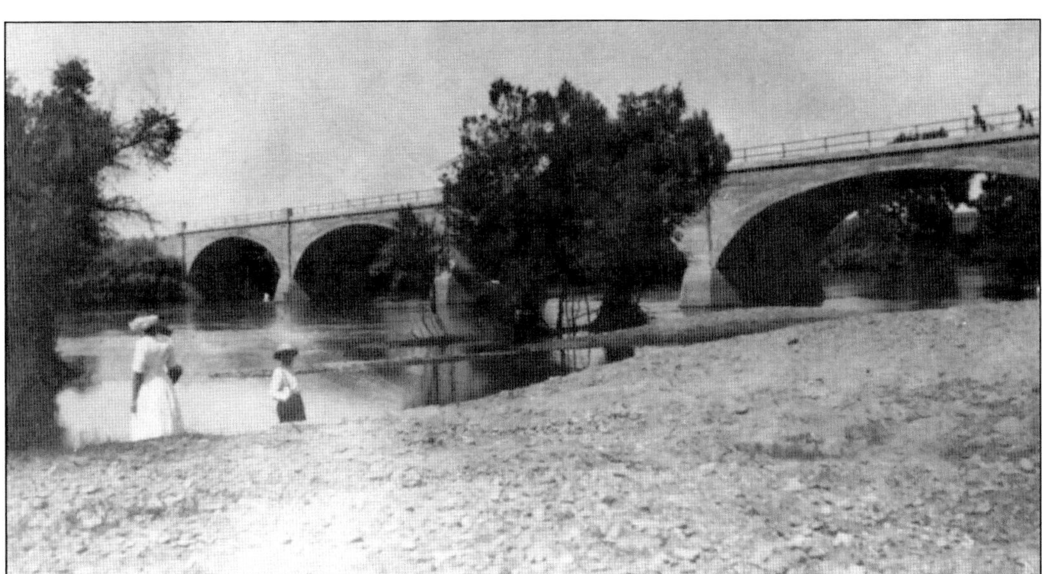

Then and now, beating the valley's summer heat often involved water, either by fishing or swimming. There are a lot of long days in farming, but the folks of Kerman have long known how to have a good time.

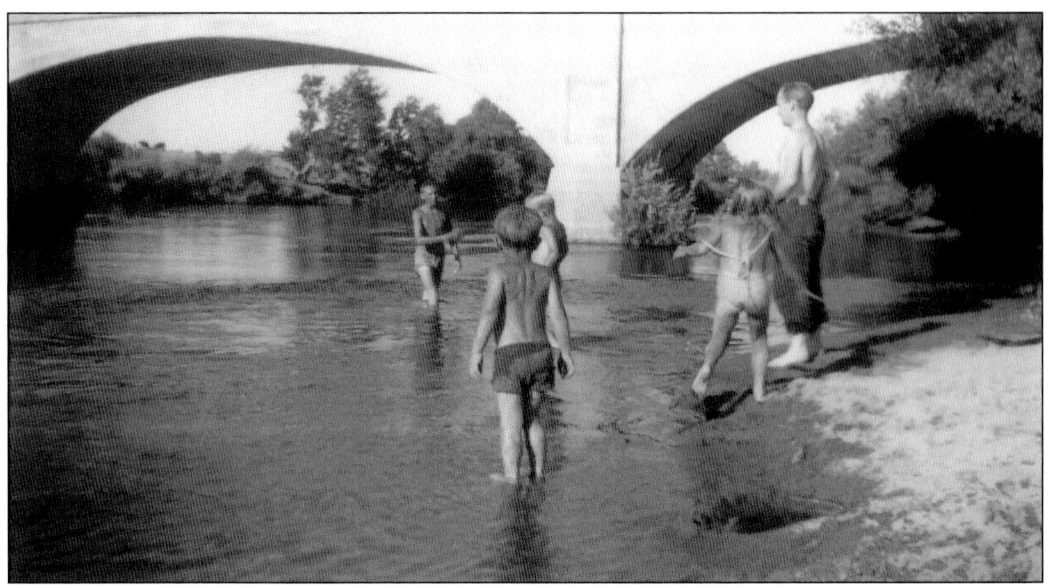

Pictured here are children playing near Skaggs Bridge in icy water from the high Sierras. The area near the bridge north of town has long been a favorite place for people to cool off from the summer heat.

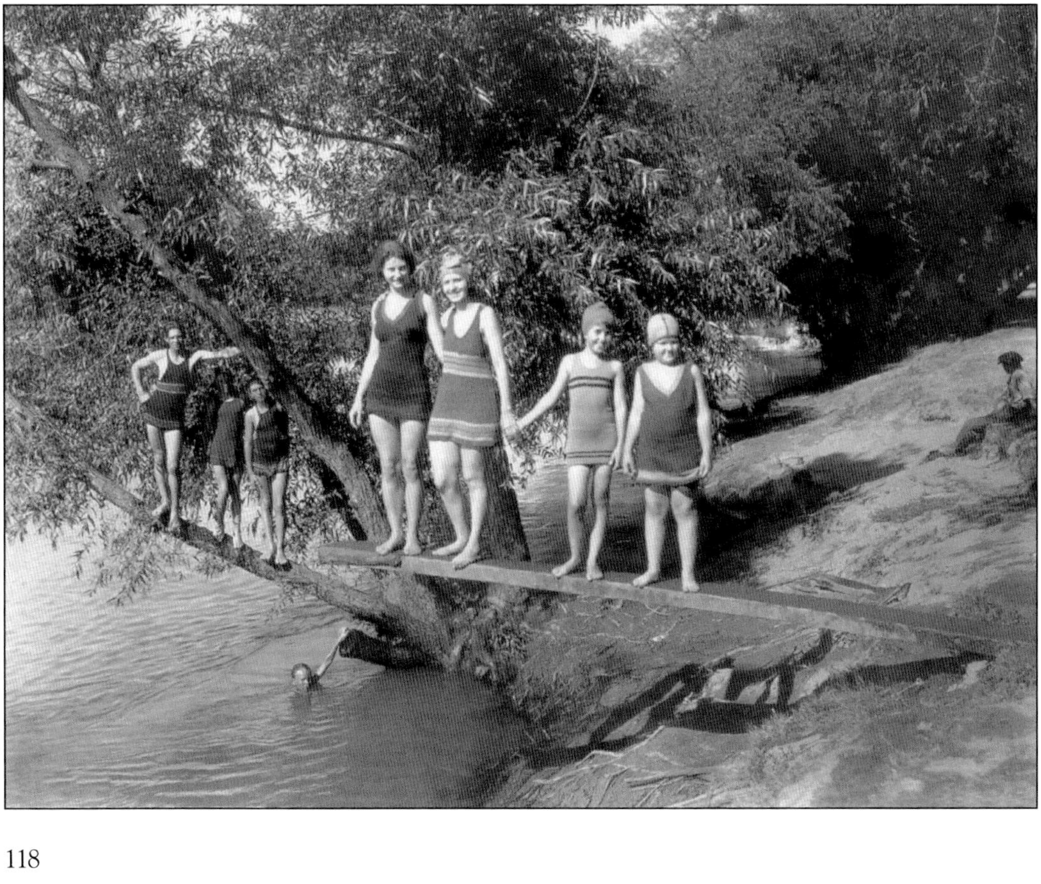

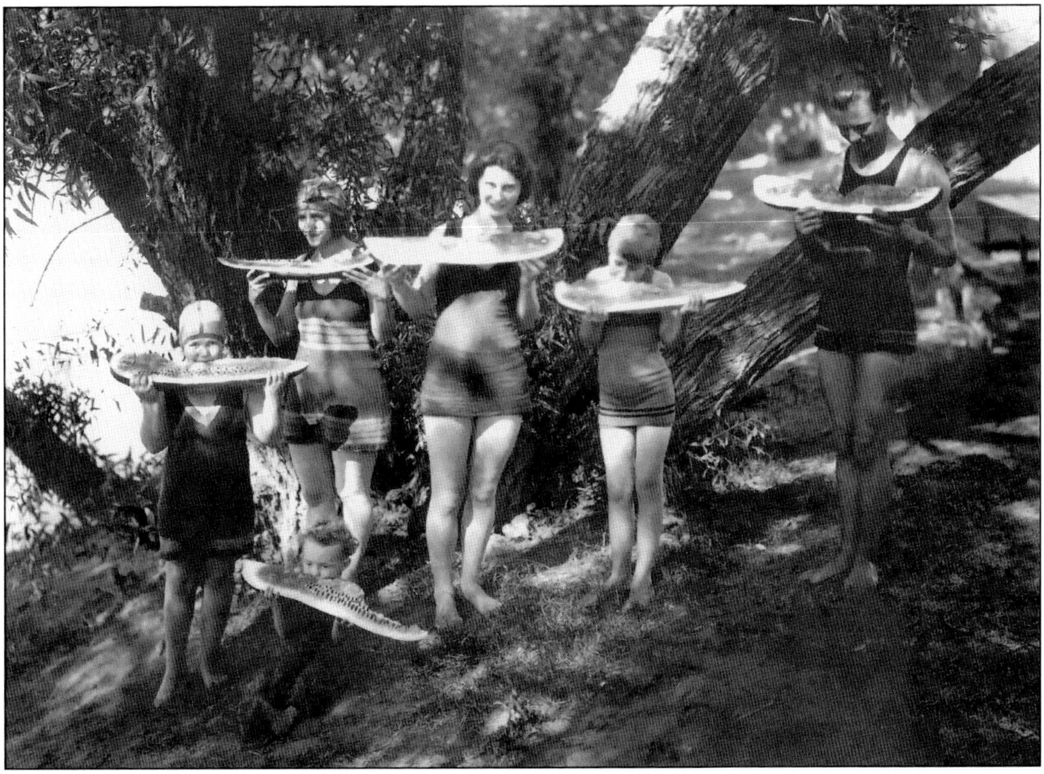

The watermelon queen is pictured above on the San Joaquin River. Below, locals enjoy some time on the water.

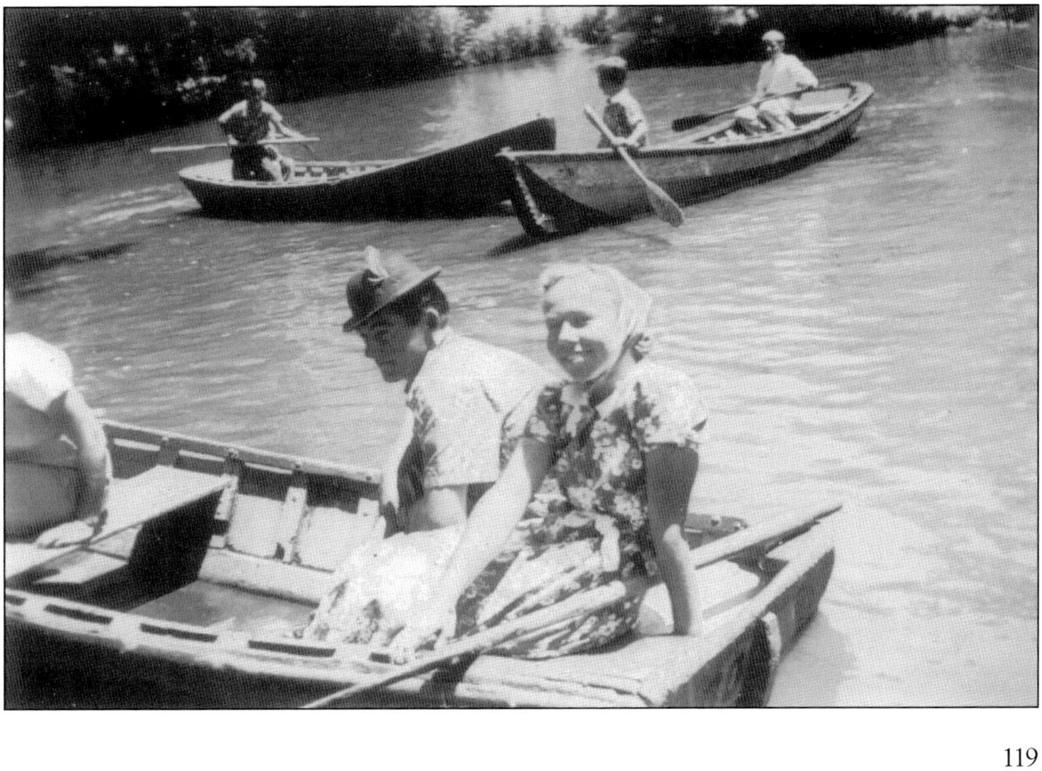

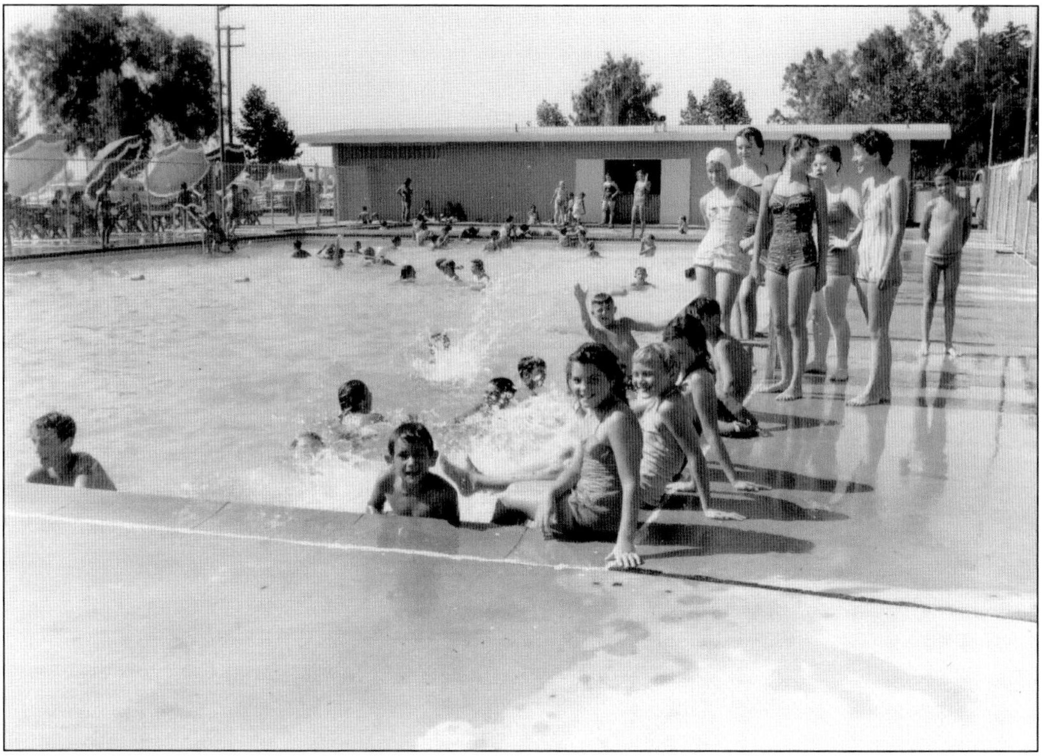

Locals are seen here at the Kerman Pool under the watch of Kerman lifeguards.

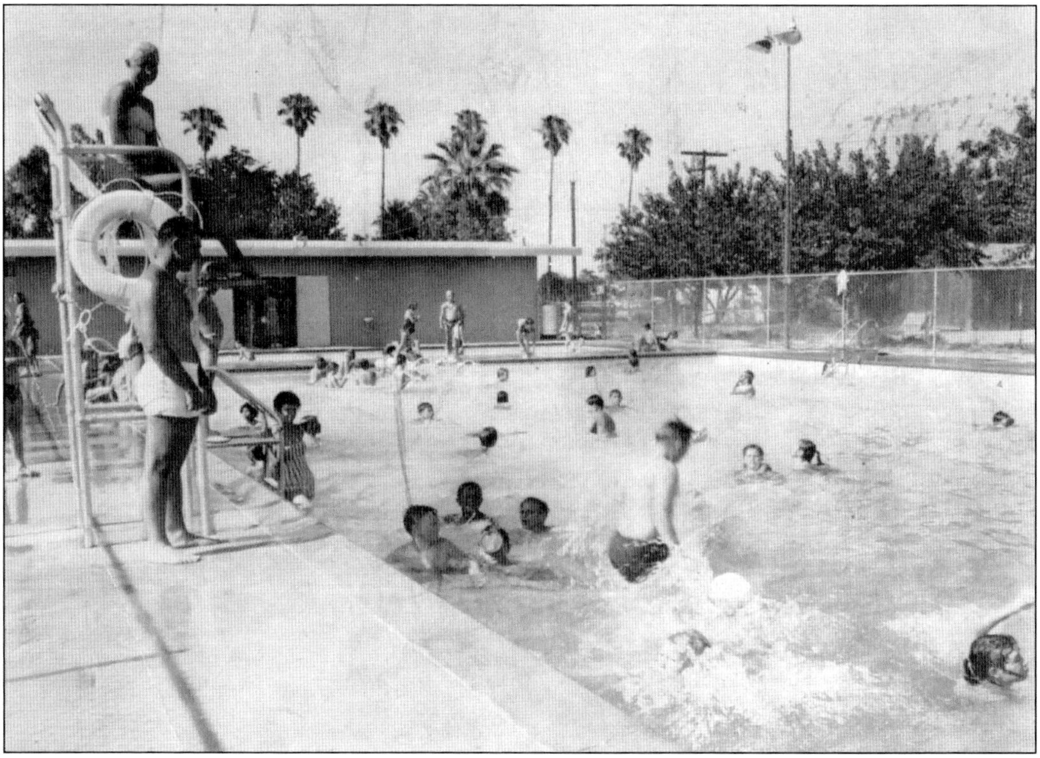

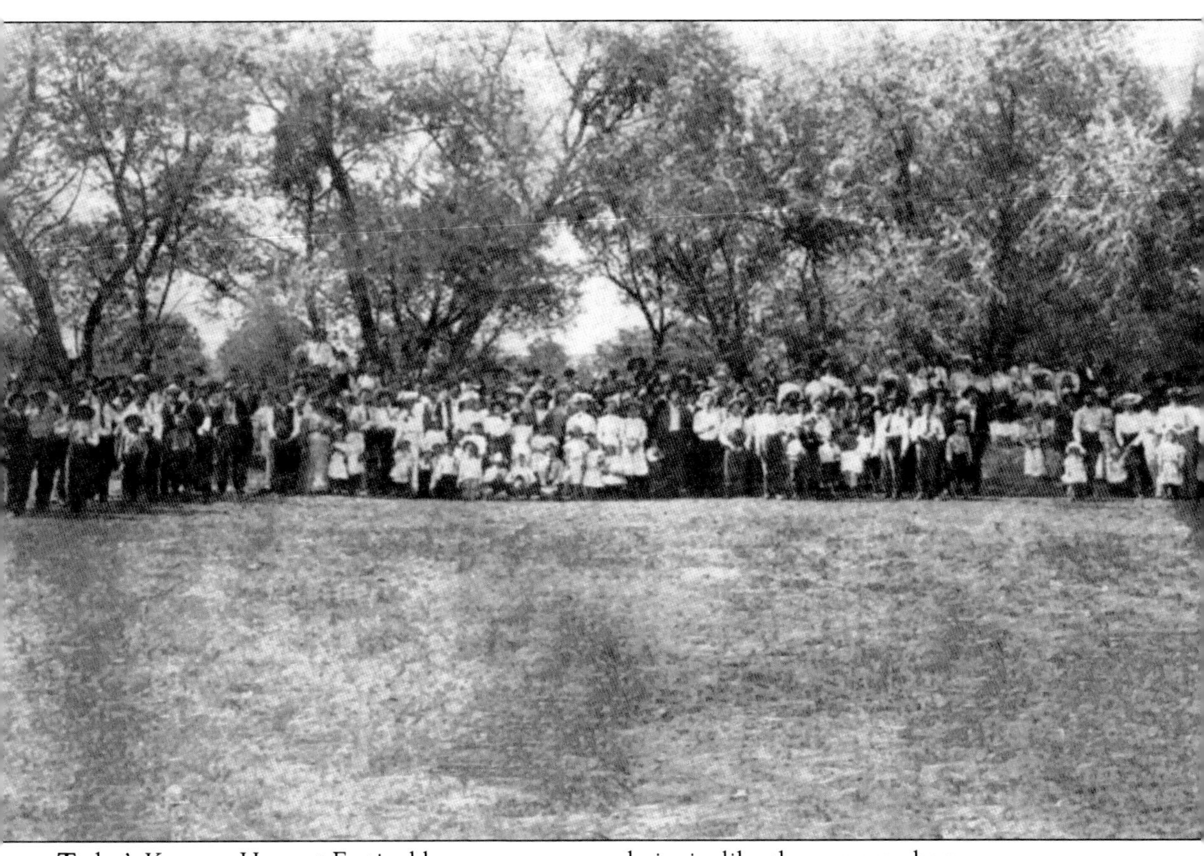

Today's Kerman Harvest Festival began as an annual picnic, like the one seen here.

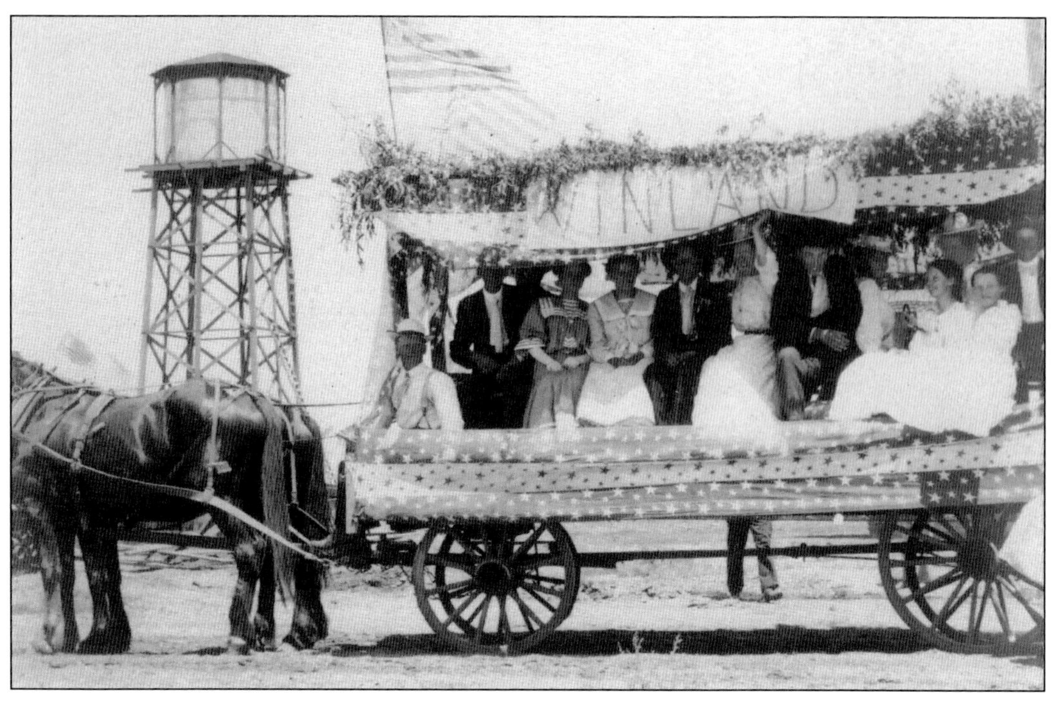

The annual Harvest Festival Parade has a long history. The first parade in Kerman was in 1906, the year the town was formed.

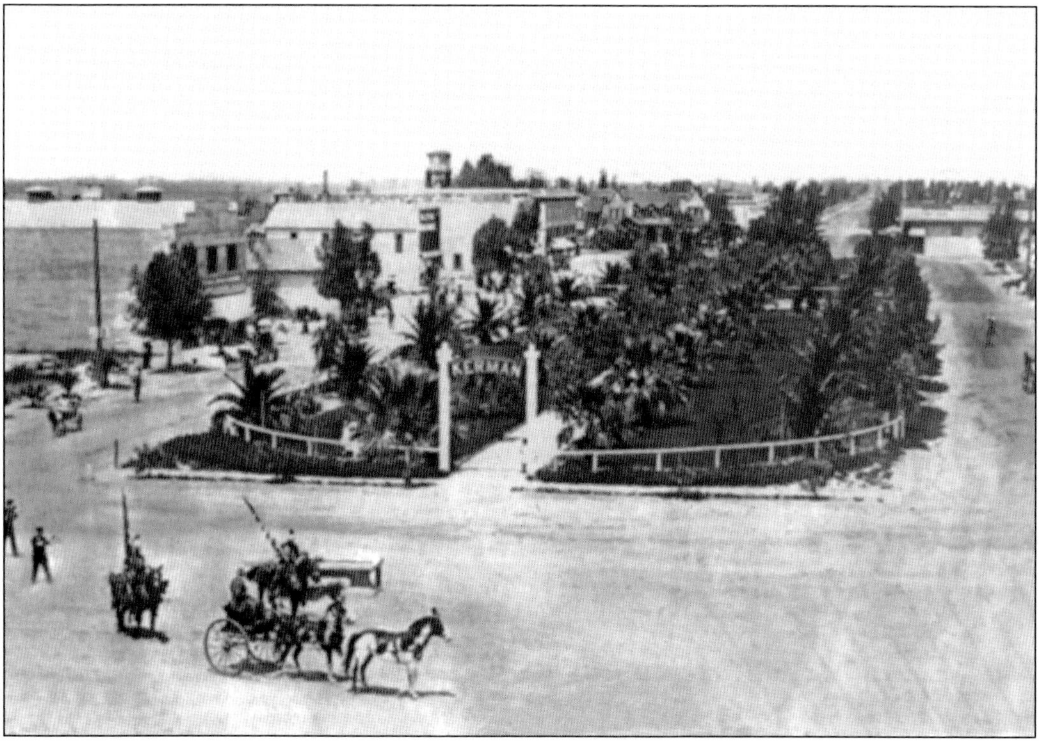

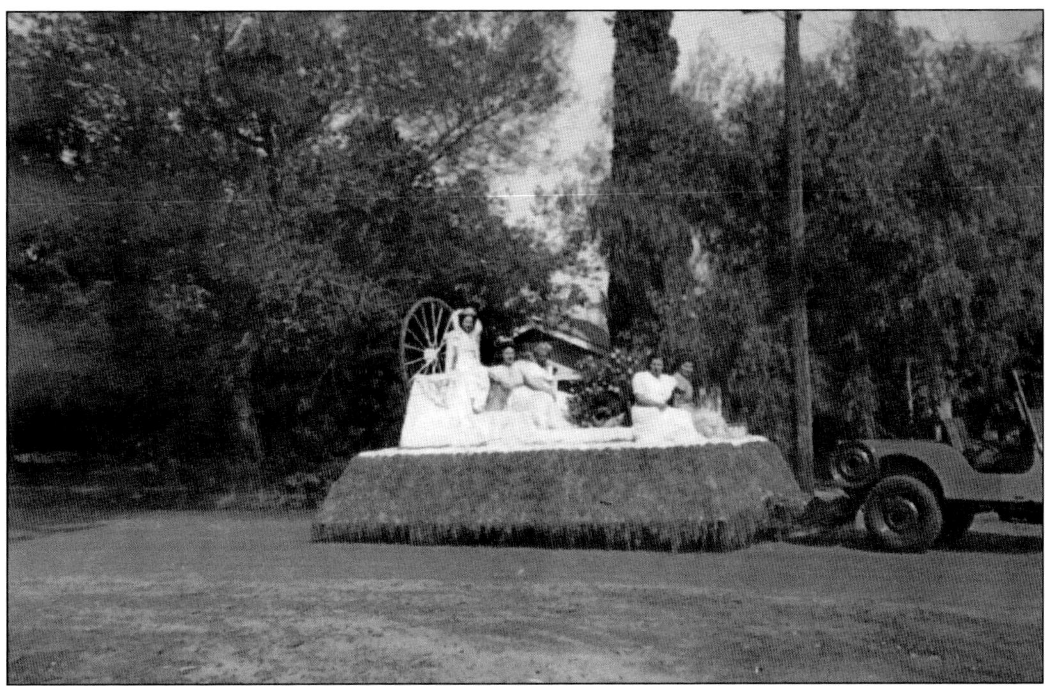

The 1945 photograph above shows one of Kerman's early Harvest Festival queens. This was the year World War II ended. Note the Army Jeep pulling the float. By 1954, the Kerman Women's Club had a highly decorated entry, as seen below.

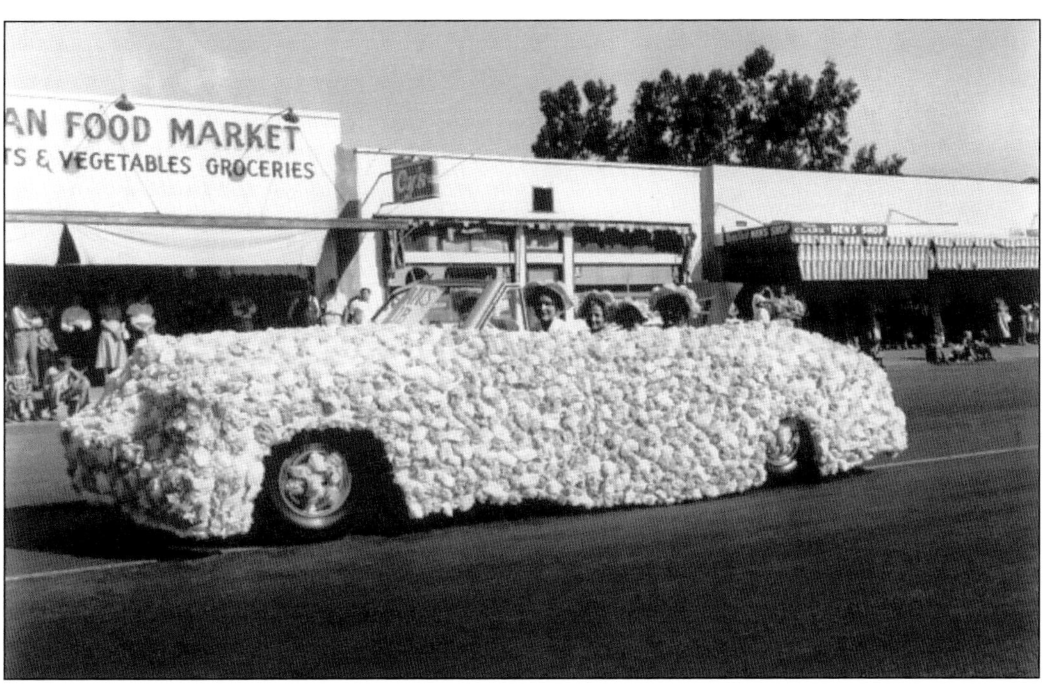

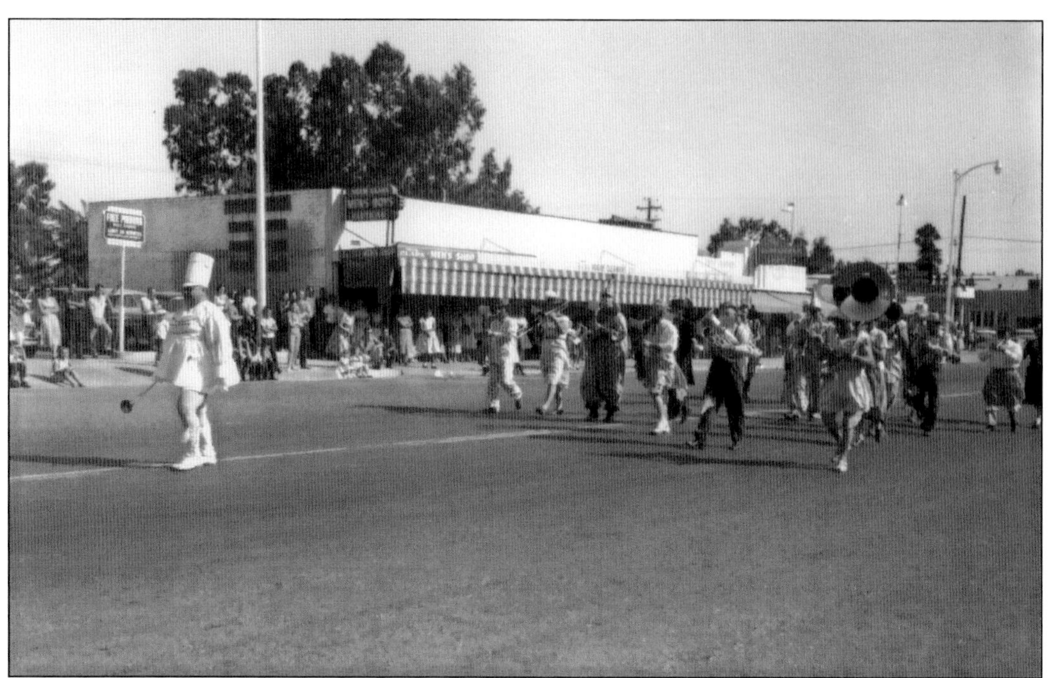

Founded in 1950, the Kerman Community Band has been known for good music and high spirits over the years. Their costumes are legendary. The band features everything from clowns and hobos to "matronly" housewives.

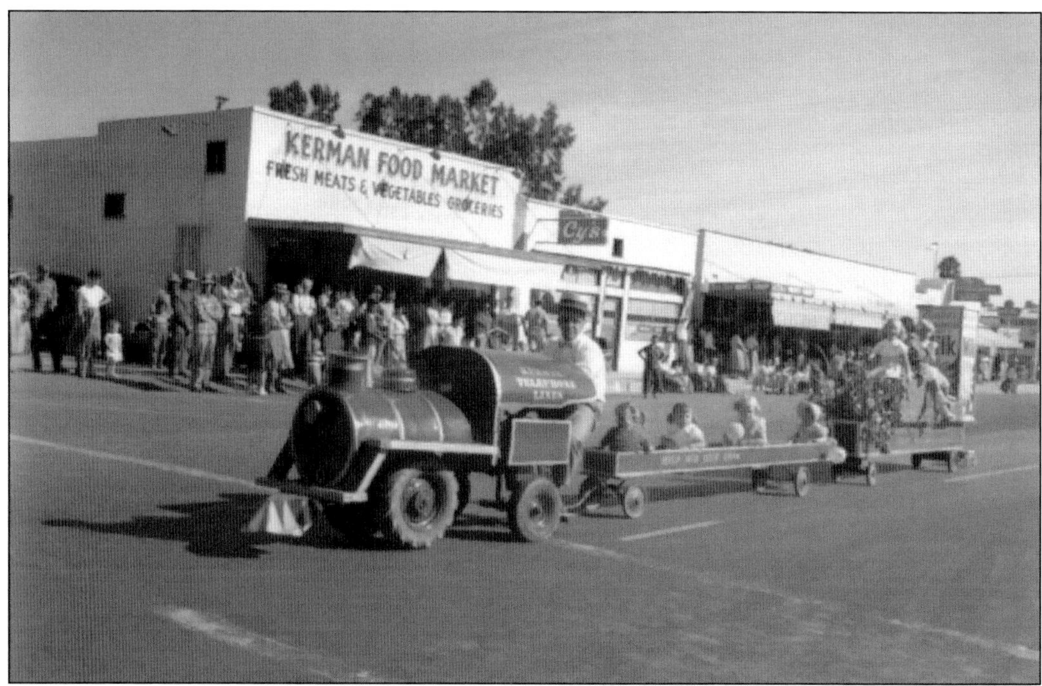

The Harvest Festival Parade has a large variety of participants; seen here is Kerman Telephone founder Bill Sebastian with children on a miniature train. School bands, sports teams, and local elected officials also fill the parade.

Seven

Veteran's Park

Over the years, many young men and women have left Kerman to serve their country. Too many never came home. In 2003, the name of Plaza Park, Kerman's historic center, was changed to Plaza Veterans Park to honor those men and women who have left home to defend it. In a small town, locals personally know those who leave to serve in the military. They worry about them while they are gone and grieve for them if they are lost. Over the last hundred years, the palm trees of the park have grown tall. The flags of each branch of the service are flown in the center of the park. There are monuments to honor those who have served. Some are personal, like the monument to Kerman's World War II flying ace, Ray Wetmore. Wetmore flew a P-51 Mustang, "Daddy's Girl," in Europe. There, he earned two Distinguished Service Crosses, two Silver Stars for bravery, and six Distinguished Flying Crosses as a combat pilot.

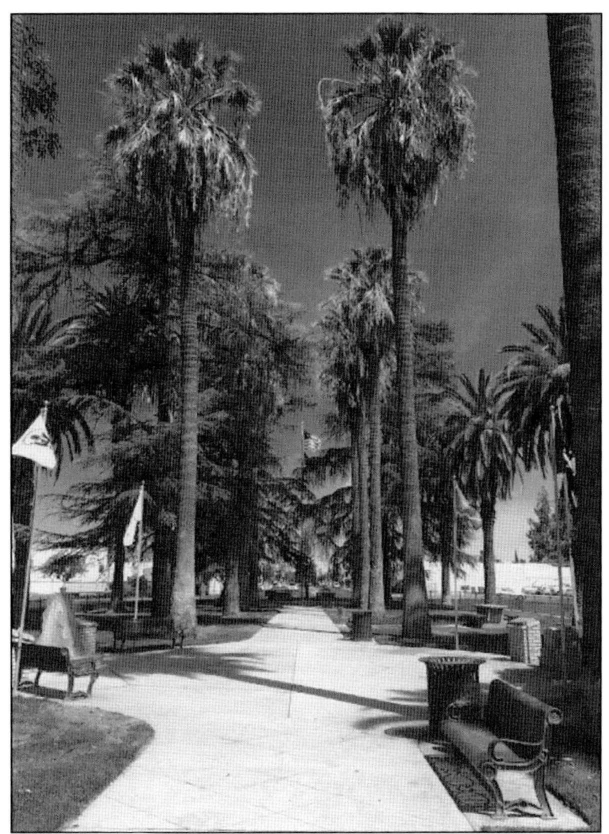

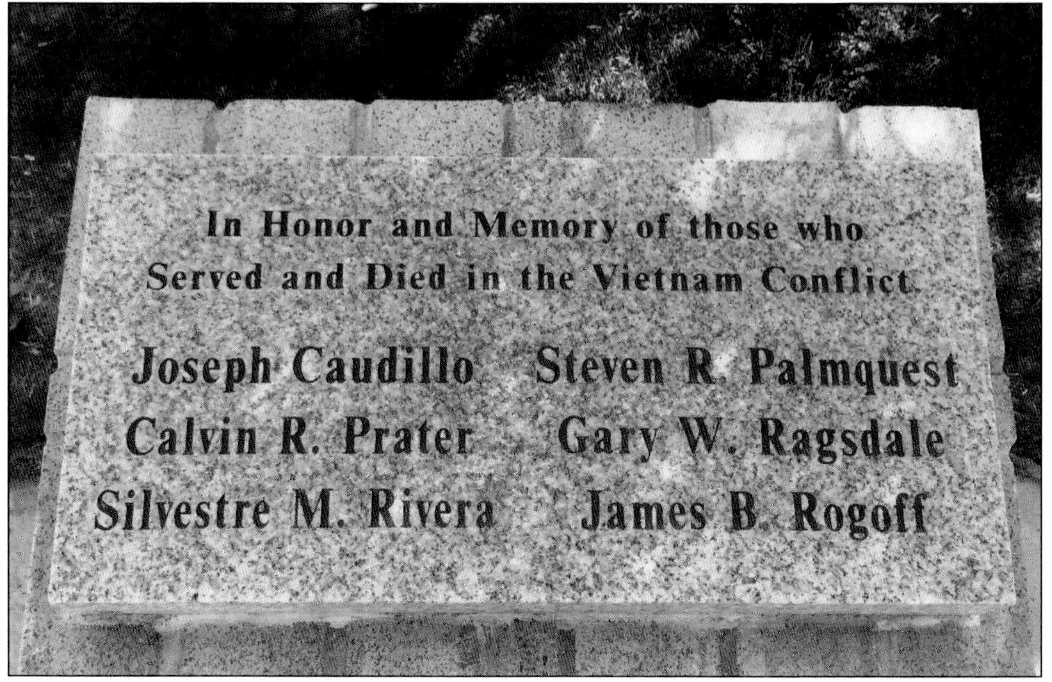

HONORING THOSE WHO SERVED. This VFW monument says a lot about the country's veterans, and it also reflects the sense of community in Kerman.

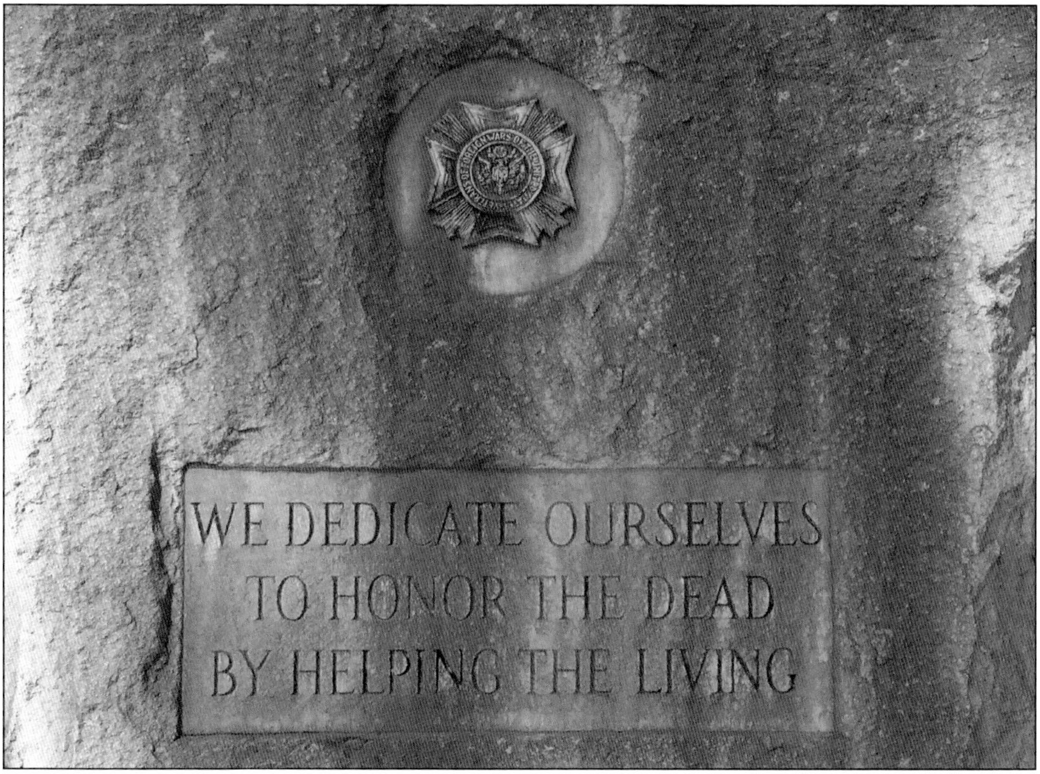

Bibliography

Patterson, Richard M. *Historical Atlas of the Outlaw West.* Johnson Books, 1984.

Rehart, Catherine Morison. *The Valley's Legends and Legacies.* Fresno, CA: Word Dancer Press, 1996.

———. *The Valley's Legends & Legacies III.* Fresno, CA: Word Dancer Press, 1999.

Roosevelt, Theodore. *An Autobiography.* New York, NY: De Capo Press, 1985.

Smith, Wallace. *Garden of the Sun: A History of the San Joaquin Valley, 1772–1939.* 2nd ed. Fresno, CA: Linden Press, 2004.

White, Olen. *Kerman: The First 100 Years 1906–2006.* Kerman, CA: Self-published, 2006.

Discover Thousands of Local History Books Featuring Millions of Vintage Images

Arcadia Publishing, the leading local history publisher in the United States, is committed to making history accessible and meaningful through publishing books that celebrate and preserve the heritage of America's people and places.

Find more books like this at
www.arcadiapublishing.com

Search for your hometown history, your old stomping grounds, and even your favorite sports team.

Consistent with our mission to preserve history on a local level, this book was printed in South Carolina on American-made paper and manufactured entirely in the United States. Products carrying the accredited Forest Stewardship Council (FSC) label are printed on 100 percent FSC-certified paper.

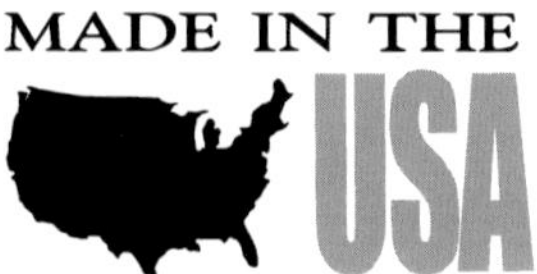